For Court, Manor and Church

Education in Medieval Europe

j·r·vibber

The Shoemaker and His Apprentice

 THE BURGESS
HISTORY OF WESTERN EDUCATION SERIES

For Court, Manor, and Church
Education in Medieval Europe

Readings edited and introduced by
Donna R. Barnes, Ed.D.
Hofstra University

Burgess Publishing Company
426 South Sixth Street • Minneapolis, Minnesota 55415

DEDICATION
To the memory of Ella D. Priestley

Copyright ©1971 by Burgess Publishing Company
Printed in the United States of America
Library of Congress Catalog Card Number 72-182076
SBN 8087-0264-5

1 2 3 4 5 6 7 8 9 0

Preface

With this volume, the Burgess History of Western Education Series continues by presenting readings on educational practice during the medieval period, roughly A.D. 450-1500. The purpose is to provide a sampling of the diversity of educational arrangements used to teach people requisite societal roles. Selections chosen portray instruction institutionalized in convents, monasteries, cathedral schools and universities; instruction provided under contracted tutelage either for knighthood or membership in a craft gild; and informal agricultural instruction provided by peasant families.

This volume is consonant with others in the series focusing on fertile moments in the history of western education, such as Ancient Greece, the Renaissance, and the Enlightenment. The central theme permeating this series is that unique historical conditions gave rise to a range of educational ideas and practices which not only were integral to the times under consideration but which have also endured.

The volumes in the series are for use by university students in courses in the History of Education and the History of Educational Thought; instructors may utilize the works either as books of readings or as supplements to texts. Students in Social or Cultural Foundations of Education, Philosophy of Education, as well as Social and Intellectual History could employ the volumes as supplementary studies.

ACKNOWLEDGMENTS

The editor wishes to gratefully acknowledge the cooperation of those scholars and publishers who have consented to the inclusion in this edited book of readings of materials from works for which they hold copyrights.

Gratitude must also be expressed to Mr. Stephen Weitzman and Mrs. Caryl Carnow, former graduate assistants in Foundations of Education at Hofstra University, who assisted in the preparation of the bibliography; to Mrs. Polly Vibber and Miss Sara Sowers, who helped in typing draft versions of the manuscript; to Mrs. Mavis Normington of the Bugbee Memorial Library in Danielson, Connecticut, Mr. Frank Darmstaedter of the Jewish Theological Seminary Library in New York City, and Miss Bonnie Young of The Cloisters, Metropolitan Museum of Art, for their insights and assistance in locating sources of materials for the present volume; and to Mrs. Judy R. Vibber for the linedrawing of the shoemaker and his apprentice.

Finally, the encouragement of Professor J. J. Chambliss, of Rutgers University, Professor John Hardin Best, of Georgia State University, and Mr. Alex Fraser and Miss Dora Stein of Burgess Publishing Company is deeply appreciated.

August 1971   Donna R. Barnes

Contents

Introduction

"EDUCATION during the Middle Ages" is typically taken to mean a discussion of the grammar schools and universities of the twelfth and thirteenth centuries, with nodding reference to the fact that Christian monasteries are credited with having preserved classical learning when the barbarian invasions into the Roman empire threatened to destroy not only buildings and roads but also books and ideas.

While formal educational institutions (such as schools and monasteries) are important, it must be noted that "education" did not "die" during the period of time between the Fall of Rome and the Discovery of America—nor was "education" confined to such formal institutions of learning. Every child born into medieval society, be he aristocrat or peasant, male or female, Christian, Jew, Moslem, or "barbarian," was *educated,* that is, initiated into the beliefs, fears, hopes, fantasies, activities, songs, tales, rhythms, and life styles expected of him by the elders of his society. The perpetuation of any cultural group depends not only on the biological reproduction and

1

physiological survival of its members, but equally upon the cultural transmission of its "identity" to the young, who must learn to fill the roles ultimately vacated by their elders upon death. Any history of medieval education which limits itself to formal institutions of instruction thereby leaves out altogether a vital area, namely the way in which most people came by their education. Schooling was important for the few (and will not be overlooked in this volume); but education was a necessity for all.

Clearly, it would not be possible to reconstruct the education of every child who lived during the time we are considering (450-1500); nor do we do justice to the concept of education if we limit it exclusively to the young; however, it seems only prudent to begin this edited series of readings by explicitly stating the author's view that education is a social process in which the human being learns how to cope with the demands of his social milieu and his physical environment. As those demands change, so, too, does the necessity arise for the individual to learn anew; as one means of coping proves inadequate or dissatisfying (for any number of reasons), there is again the need to learn. In a fairly stable society, the individual can be reasonably comfortable with the "learning" he has acquired in the process of reaching adulthood; in a society fraught with change (social, economic, political, technological, religious, or intellectual), the individual finds greater need for "new learning." The medieval period is one marked by moments of relative stability and moments of intense dynamism and change; moreover, there is not one society to be examined, but a number of societies. This present volume represents, then, not only a selection of readings, but also a selection of "educational moments." It is hoped that the reader will find the selection sufficiently diverse and sufficiently representative to provide a "taste" of the ways in which humans learned to cope with living during the centuries which later historians have come to label as "medieval."

Medieval education is like a broad river whose banks are marked by important continuities as well as dramatic changes. Its origins can be traced to a number of streams—the classical heritage of the Graeco-Roman era, the ancient religious tradition of the Jews, the ferment which accompanied the establishment of the Christian Church, the Arabic (and later the Islamic) culture, as well as the deep-rooted traditions of those Northern European tribes known variously as Goths, Vandals, Huns, Norsemen, Vikings, or Barbarians. Each in its own way, sometimes as a mere trickle, at others in a rushing flood, brought important contributions to the tide of medieval education.

In a search for both continuities and shifts in education brought about by the mingling of these various streams and by changes in patterns of living, this study will focus on the following dimensions of medieval education: (1) the agricultural education of the peasant classes; (2) chivalric education for the nobility and their retainers in the arts of warfare and weaponry, in horsemanship, in competitive sport, and in the etiquette of courtly love; (3) the religious and intellectual education offered within the cloistered monastery; (4) apprenticeship training in diverse crafts which sprang up with the division of labor, creation of gilds, and emergence of a city-based middle class of merchants and craftsmen; (5) the development of schools and universities and the subsequent extension of higher education not only to the clergy, but to members of the laity as well; (6) medical training for doctors and barber-surgeons; (7) the education of women in their occupational roles as well as in their responsibilities for the management of home and husband and/or for the service of God; and (8) rabbinic studies amongst the Jews.

PART I

Agricultural Education for Peasant Classes

WORKING and living off the land was the major economic enterprise of the medieval period; yet those individual peasants who performed the agricultural tasks remain largely unknown to contemporary readers, forming what Lynn White has appropriately termed "the silent majority." [1] Records of manor courts and estate accounts provide some indication of task responsibilities and the system of land use and taxation. "Piers the Plowman" and Chaucer have provided some poetic accounts of agricultural workers; further, Alexander Neckham's *De Nominibus Utensilium* [2] and the *Itinerarium Cambriae* [3] of Giraldus also offer descriptions of the imple-

[1] Lynn White discusses the influence of technological change upon this segment of the population in *Medieval Technology and Social Change*.

[2] Urban Tigner Holmes provides a translation of a portion of Alexander's inventory of equipment and household effects in peasants' homes in his study, *Daily Living in the Twelfth Century*.

[3] Giraldus Cambrensis, also known as Gerald of Wales (c. 1146-c.1220), was a cleric who travelled extensively through Ireland, Wales and England as well as to Paris and Rome both as a scholar and as an administrative functionary. He described his travels in detail in several accounts including the *Journey Through Wales (Itinerarium Cambriae)*, the *Topography*

ments employed in peasant life as well as the housing available. Contemporary records do not individualize the life of the peasantry, however: The most readable account of peasant life is the imaginative reconstruction of the life of Bodo, the peasant, and his wife, Ermentrude, written in this century by the British historian of medieval economic institutions, Eileen Power.[4]

What did the peasant child need to learn? Every child born into a peasant family had to learn from his parents, whether they were serfs or freemen, how to function within a more or less complex hierarchically structured farm environment by understanding which feudal or manorial workers and overlords were entitled to expect from him the performance of labor and the payment of taxes (usually in kind) as well as subjugation to authority. Furthermore, he had to learn how to work the land; when to plant; how to plow; when and where to spread manure; how to recognize when grain was ripe for harvest; how to yoke oxen; how to milk cattle; how to remove eggs from the nest without cracking them or getting pecked by disgruntled hens; how to mend thicket fences; how to daub walls and thatch a roof; and how to brew beer. Finally, peasant children learned from their parents those ancient charms to ward off harm to themselves and their crops and animals; and they learned from their parish priests when to attend mass and how to mumble a *pater noster.*

Boys learned to behave as their fathers did; girls were taught by their mothers what women's responsibilities involved. Typically, peasant children received this education in a very unself-conscious way. Following at his father's heels and watching and imitating his father's movements, a child learned how to guide a plow along with

---

of Ireland *(Topographia Hibernica)* and *The Description of Wales (Descripto Cambriae).* Urban Tigner Holmes, *Daily Living in the Twelfth Century,* pp. 122-123, points out that Gerald gave a series of public lectures on his travels in Ireland while he was a visiting scholar at Oxford. According to W. Llewelyn Williams' introduction, p.xv, to the 1908 Everyman's edition of *The Itinerary Through Wales* and *The Description of Wales,* by Giraldus Cambrensis, Gerald wrote the *Itinerarium* while accompanying Archbishop Baldwin on his 1188 preaching crusade in Wales. Gerald's works are available in translation both in the Williams' edition of 1908, and Thomas Wright's 1863 edition of *The Historical Works of Giraldus Cambrensis,* republished in 1968 by AMS Press in New York.

[4]Eileen Power utilized an estate book, written between 811 and 826 by Abbot Irminon, for the Abbey of St. Germain des Prés, near Paris, as the prime source for her portrait of peasant life at Villaris.

the natural process of growing up. Parents would occasionally deliberately set aside time in order to teach their children a certain activity (as a mother might show her daughter how to squeeze the teats of a cow and aim the flow of milk into a wooden bucket), but neither parents nor children were aware that "education" was occurring. To their way of thinking, "education" meant schooling for the gentry or studying with a priest so as to learn how to become a priest.

Eileen Power's account of a day in the life of a ninth century Frankish peasant family shows .the boy learning his tasks from his father and provides a clear differentiation between men's and women's work. H. S. Bennett shows how tasks changed according to the season, an important "lesson" to be learned by the peasant child. Ernle's description of the self-sufficient rural village of the thirteenth century describes still other tasks, some performed by men and their sons in the evenings and others performed by the women, to be learned by the children of rural or agricultural families. Finally, the thirteenth century listing of manorial officers' duties which are included in this chapter indicate, albeit only partially, the hierarchical structure of roles which rural children needed to come to understand.

1. The Peasant Bodo

Eileen Power

When we turn up the pages in the estate book dealing with Villaris, we find that there was a man called Bodo living there. He had a wife called Ermentrude and three children called Wido and Gerbert and Hildegard; and he owned a little farm of arable and meadow land, with a few vines. And we know very nearly as much about Bodo's work as we know about that of a smallholder in France today. Let us try and imagine a day in his life. On a fine spring morning towards the end of Charlemagne's reign Bodo gets up early, because it is his day to go and work on the monks' farm, and

From *Medieval People* by Eileen Power (London: Methuen & Co., 1924; 10th ed., 1963). Reprinted by permission. This selection appears on pages 23-24 and 26-28 of the 1968 paperback edition published by Barnes & Noble, New York.

he does not dare to be late, for fear of the steward. To be sure, he has probably given the steward a present of eggs and vegetables the week before, to
keep him in a good temper; but the monks will not allow their stewards to
take big bribes (as is sometimes done on other estates), and Bodo knows
that he will not be allowed to go late to work. It is his day to plough, so he
takes his big ox with him and little Wido to run by its side with a goad, and
he joins his friends from some of the farms near by, who are going to work
at the big house too. They all assemble, some with horses and oxen, some
with mattocks and hoes and spades and axes and scythes, and go off in
gangs to work upon the fields and meadows and woods of the seigniorial
manse, according as the steward orders them. The manse next door to Bodo
is held by a group of families: Frambert and Ermoin and Ragenold, with
their wives and children. Bodo bids them good morning as he passes. Frambert is going to make a fence round the wood, to prevent the rabbits from
coming out and eating the young crops; Ermoin has been told off to cart a
great load of firewood up to the house; and Ragenold is mending a hole in
the roof of a barn. Bodo goes whistling off in the cold with his oxen and his
little boy; . . . he ploughs all day and eats his meal under a tree with the
other ploughmen. . . .

Bodo certainly *had* plenty of feelings, and very strong ones. When he got
up in the frost on a cold morning to drive the plough over the abbot's acres,
when his own were calling out for work, he often shivered and shook the
rime from his beard, and wished that the big house and all its land were at
the bottom of the sea (which, as a matter of fact, he had never seen and
could not imagine). Or else he wished he were the abbot's huntsman, hunting in the forest; or a monk of St. Germain, singing sweetly in the abbey
church; or a merchant, taking bales of cloaks and girdles along the high
road to Paris; anything, in fact, but a poor ploughman ploughing other
people's land. . . .

Nevertheless, hard as the work was, Bodo sang lustily to cheer himself
and Wido. . . .

It is certain too that Bodo agreed with the names which the great Charles
gave to the months of the year in his own Frankish tongue; for he called
January "Winter-month," February "Mud-month," March "Spring-
month," April "Easter-month," May "Joy-month," June "Plough-month,"
July "Hay-month," August "Harvest-month," September "Wind-month,"
October "Vintage-month," November "Autumn-month," and December
"Holy-month."

And Bodo was a superstitious creature. The Franks had been Christian
now for many years, but Christian though they were, the peasants clung to
old beliefs and superstitions. On the estates of the holy monks of St. Germain you would have found the country people saying charms which were

hoary with age, parts of the lay sung by the Frankish ploughman over his bewitched land long before he marched southwards into the Roman Empire, or parts of the spell which the bee-master performed when he swarmed his bees on the shores of the Baltic Sea. Christianity has coloured these charms but it has not effaced their heathen origin; and because the tilling of the soil is the oldest and most unchanging of human occupations, old beliefs and superstitions cling to it and the old gods stalk up and down the brown furrows, when they have long vanished from houses and roads. So on Abbot Irminon's estates the peasant-farmers muttered charms over their sick cattle (and over their sick children too) and said incantations over the fields to make them fertile. If you had followed behind Bodo when he broke his first furrow you would have probably seen him take out of his jerkin a little cake, baked for him by Ermentrude out of different kinds of meal, and you would have seen him stoop and lay it under the furrow and sing:

> Earth, Earth, Earth! O Earth, our mother!
> May the All-Wielder, Ever-Lord grant thee
> Acres a-waxing, upwards a-growing,
> Pregnant with corn and plenteous in strength;
> Hosts of grain shafts and of glittering plants!
> Of broad barley the blossoms,
> And of white wheat ears waxing,
> Of the whole land the harvest. . . .
>
> .   .   .
>
> Acre, full-fed, bring forth fodder for men!
> Blossoming brightly, blessed become!
> And the God who wrought with earth grant us gift of growing
> That each of all the corns may come unto our need.

Then he would drive his plough through the acre.

The Church wisely did not interfere with these old rites. It taught Bodo to pray to the Ever-Lord instead of to Father Heaven, and to the Virgin Mary instead of to Mother Earth, and with these changes let the old spell he had learned from his ancestors serve him still. It taught him, for instance, to call on Christ and Mary in his charm for bees.

2. Ermentrude's Day is Filled with Chores

Eileen Power

Ermentrude is busy too; it is the day on which the chicken-rent is due—a fat pullet and five eggs in all. She leaves her second son, aged nine, to look after the baby Hildegard and calls on one of her neighbours, who has to go up to the big house too. The neighbour is a serf and she has to take the steward a piece of woollen cloth, which will be sent away to St. Germain to make a habit for a monk. Her husband is working all day in the lord's vineyards, for on this estate the serfs generally tend the vines, while the freemen do most of the ploughing. Ermentrude and the serf's wife go together up to the house. There all is busy. In the men's workshop are several clever workmen—a shoemaker, a carpenter, a blacksmith, and two silversmiths; there are not more, because the best artisans on the estates of St. Germain live by the walls of the abbey, so that they can work for the monks on the spot and save the labour of carriage. But there were always some craftsmen on every estate, either attached as serfs to the big house, or living on manses of their own, and good landowners tried to have as many clever craftsmen as possible. Charlemagne ordered his stewards each to have in his district "good workmen, namely, blacksmiths, goldsmiths, silversmiths, shoemakers, turners, carpenters, swordmakers, fishermen, foilers, soapmakers, men who know how to make beer, cider, perry, and all other kinds of beverages, bakers to make pasty for our table, netmakers who know how to make nets for hunting, fishing, and fowling, and others too many to be named." And some of these workmen are to be found working for the monks in the estate of Villaris.

But Ermentrude does not stop at the men's workshop. She finds the steward, bobs her curtsy to him, and gives up her fowl and eggs, and then she hurries off to the women's part of the house, to gossip with the serfs there. The Franks used at this time to keep the women of their household in a separate quarter, where they did the work which was considered suitable for women. . . . If a Frankish noble had lived at the big house, his wife would have looked after their work, but as no one lived in the stone house at Villaris, the steward had to oversee the women. Their quarter consisted of a little group of houses, with a workroom, the whole surrounded by a thick hedge with a strong bolted gate, like a harem, so that no one could come in without leave. Their workrooms were comfortable places, warmed by stoves, and there Ermentrude (who, being a woman, was allowed to go

From *Medieval People* by Eileen Power (London: Methuen & Co., 1924; 10th ed., 1963). Reprinted by permission. This selection appears on pages 24-26 of the 1968 paperback edition published by Barnes & Noble, New York.

in) found about a dozen servile women spinning and dyeing cloth and sewing garments. Every week the harassed steward brought them the raw materials for their work and took away what they made. Charlemagne gives his stewards several instructions about the women attached to his manses, and we may be sure that the monks of St. Germain did the same on their model estates. "For our women's work," says Charlemagne, "they are to give at the proper time the materials, that is linen, wool, woad, vermilion, madder, wool combs, teasels, soap, grease, vessels, and other objects which are necessary. And let our women's quarters be well looked after, furnished with houses and rooms with stoves and cellars, and let them be surrounded by a good hedge, and let the doors be strong, so that the women can do our work properly." Ermentrude, however, has to hurry away after her gossip. . . . She goes back to her own farm and sets to work in the little vineyard; then after an hour or two goes back to get the children's meal and to spend the rest of the day in weaving warm woollen clothes for them. All her friends are either working in the fields on their husbands' farms or else looking after the poultry, or the vegetables, or sewing at home; for the women have to work just as hard as the men on a country farm. In Charlemagne's time (for instance) they did nearly all the sheep shearing. Then at last Bodo comes back for his supper, and as soon as the sun goes down they go to bed; for their hand-made candle gives only a flicker of light, and they both have to be up early in the morning.

3. Growing Seasons Determine Rural Activities.

H. S. Bennett

. . . let us assume that we are dealing with an energetic and reasonably successful peasant who has thirty acres under the three-field system, and follow him throughout the year as he works upon them. First, the ten acres of fallow. These present a comparatively simple problem. As we have seen, they form part of one of the common fields and are open to all to feed upon, and the peasants turn their cattle out upon them, in part to manure them, in part to graze upon the scanty vegetation that they supply, each acre of which should be sufficient to support two sheep at the very least. From time to time, however, preparations for the coming crop have to be made,

From *Life on the English Manor* by H. S. Bennett (Cambridge: Cambridge University Press, 1937). Reprinted by permission. This selection appears on pages 79-85 of the 1962 paperback edition.

and the field is ploughed on three occasions. April is a good time for this first ploughing, Walter of Henley tells us, for then the earth breaks up well, and it is good to do it again in a couple of months' time, taking care not to plough too deeply, but just sufficiently to destroy the thistles. After this it can be left until the autumn, and then in October it is ploughed for the last time before the winter corn* is sown. This time the plough should go some two finger lengths deeper than before, "then the plough will find sure ground, and clear and free it from mud, and make fine and good ploughing."

The other two fields, however, took up much of the peasant's time. In January he could do little upon them, save perhaps cart out manure or spread marl** ready to be ploughed in as soon as the weather was suitable. These were his main means of fertilising the soil and were most important. The straw of the previous year's harvest was carefully saved, and was used in the cowsheds and stables during the winter, and then piled up outside and mixed with earth, or even thrown in roads and paths for a time. Before the drought of March it was carted on to the fields, and ploughed into the earth; and so valuable was it considered that we are told that the straw kept for this purpose was worth half the price of the corn. The peasant, therefore, did his best to have some of this precious manure ready for his fields, even though his lord had exercised his rights of folding his cattle for part of the year, and thus deprived him of part of this most valuable fertiliser. Marl was less commonly used, and it must have been an exceedingly laborious and slow business to cart the large quantities required on to the land, break it up sufficiently small and then spread it about.

Ploughing in the early spring kept the peasant busy on his strips, and once this was done, harrowing and then the sowing of the spring corn (oats, barley) or the peas and beans followed. Something has already been said about the problem of co-operation among the peasants, but a few more words may be added. The plough was a comparatively light and simple affair, and in many types of soil did not require a large plough team. There is abundant evidence to show that it was possible to manage with only a yoke of oxen or pair of horses, and this, it is arguable (at the least) is what many men did do. They had, or could assemble, a plough with two beasts to pull it, and with this could quite well plough their strips. It is true that the ploughing was not very deep, but it was all the ploughs of those days could manage.

Once the ground was ready the seeds were sown. These were brought on to the field in a sack, and then a quantity from this was placed in a wooden

Editor's Notes:
*"Corn" is a generic term used to refer to any edible cereal plant such as wheat, rye, oats, or Barley.
**"Marl" is a calcium-rich clay used to fertilize lime-deficient soil; frequently this loamy clay contained shell particles.

basket or box slung round the sower's neck, or tied round the waist. This box was called a seed-lip, or hopper, and from it the sower took seed and scattered it abroad with a rhythmic movement of the body.... At other times a kind of apron was worn instead of the seed-lip, and the seed scattered from this. Peas and beans, on the other hand, were "dibbled:" a small hole was made with a pointed stick, and the seeds at once dropped in — a task which, as it seems, was usually performed by women.

After the sowing came the harrow — "or els crowes, doves, and other byrdes wyll eate and beare away the cornes"; else, as Walter of Henley says, "to pull the corn into the hollow" which is between the two ridges. The harrow was much as we know it to-day, if we follow the illustration in the *Luttrell Psalter.* There is pictured a solid cross-barred wooden frame with teeth projecting on its under side. It is drawn by a horse, and a boy follows, scaring off the birds by the use of a sling and stones. No doubt many peasant farmers could not afford so expensive a thing, and made use of a rude bush-harrow, formed of blackthorn or whitethorn which was dragged across the ground at the tail of a horse, and served its purpose reasonably well. Sometimes on hard clotted ground where the harrow could make but little impression it was necessary for the peasant to break up the clods with wooden mallets....

Once all this was finished the peasant's labours were not so pressing, and he could turn to the many other secondary jobs waiting to be done. If the land was heavy, draining operations were constantly necessary and worth while; ditches wanted digging out after the winter floods, and the good earth put on to the land again; hedges and enclosures round the little home or any private bit of enclosure required attention, and so on. Then, as we have seen, it was time for the first ploughing of the fallow field, and the busy activities in the garden where such vegetables and fruits as were then available were grown.

So the days went by with plenty to occupy men till the end of May. The coming of June saw them making renewed efforts. The haymaking called for all their strength: first, there were the numerous compulsory days which they had to spend in getting in the lord's hay; and, as well as this, there was their own crop waiting in the enclosed meadows which had been carefully guarded and reserved for this purpose since Christmas. The mowers used a long scythe.... With this they appear to have mowed not more than one acre in a day.

After the haymaking, the strips again called for much attention. Thistles had to be uprooted, but this was not done before St. John's Day (June 24) as a country tradition asserted that thistles cut before this would but multiply threefold. The fallow ground was also ploughed up again to destroy weed — the "second-stirring," or *rebinatium,* as it was called in the books.

Hemp and flax were gathered by the good-wife, and dried before being spun into yarn for thread, rope or linen yarn. Both of these plants were pulled up by the roots, not cut like corn, and then laid out on the ground to dry a little before being put into a convenient stream to rot away the fleshy part. This was vigorously rubbed away, and the remainder dried thoroughly, and then beaten so as to get the fibres clean and separate. Then it was ready to hang up in "strikes" to finish drying, before it was combed out and ready for the spinning-wheel. Meanwhile the men-folk were busy weeding in the two fields under cultivation; they used two long sticks, the one held in the left hand had a forked end, while the other had a small curved blade. With these they worked up and down their strips, cleaning the corn of dock and other weeds.

With the coming of August the peasant's activities reached their climax. Once again the demands made upon him by this lord were often very heavy. He had to appear in person again and again to gather in the lord's crops — and, although he usually worked one or two days more a week from August to Michaelmas than at other times in the year, this was not enough, and he had to give several extra days of his time as a boon or gift to his lord. And further, he had to come with all his family: everyone able to work, save perhaps the housewife, was pressed into service for so many days. This made the getting-in of his own crops a more difficult and anxious matter, and work during these crucial weeks must have been wellnigh unending. The scythes were at work mowing down the barley, rye, oats, peas and beans, but the wheat was cut with a reap-hook or sickle as in recent times. The ear was cut off high up on the stalk leaving the straw standing. . . . Gloves were worn to protect the hands while at work, and these were usually issued freely by the lord to his men.

After the corn was cut and put into sheaves the Church's portion — the tithe — had to be selected. . . .

Now the heaviest part of the year's work was over, and the strips in the common fields all stood bare, and once again the cattle wandered over them to seek what they could. This they were allowed to do until the time came for the autumn ploughing. Then they were moved away from the field that had stood fallow for a twelvemonth and there a third and last plough-ing preluded the planting of the wheat and other seed for the coming year. On the other fields manuring or marling were all that was necessary, and the peasant then turned towards home and to making provision for the coming winter. First, such fruits and nuts as were available were gathered and stored; then, the supply of winter fuel had to be assured. The right of taking timber from the nearby woods was jealously controlled, and it was only such dead wood or timber not exceeding a certain dimension that was at the peasant's disposal. The cutting down of oak or ash, without permission, meant a fine at the Manor Court; and, in general, the lord's officers were here, there and everywhere, on the look out for over-zealous appropriators of wood. Yet wood was essential, not only for fuel to help pass the long winter nights, but also for the thousand and one things about the medieval home.

Even when the wood-pile was large enough, and turves or peat had been stored wherever possible, much remained to be done. In some parts (especially in East Anglia) the sedge was cut, for this was well known to make the very best thatch; bracken was gathered in great quantities to be used as bedding for the cattle in the coming winter. The stubble, which had been left standing when the corn was cut, was now gathered, either for thatching or bedding, or to be cut and mixed with hay as fodder. If it was not thus wanted, it was often ploughed in and allowed to rot and thus nourish the soil.

In wet weather there was always plenty to do in threshing the corn. The lord, of course, was able to have his done in his great barn, but the peasants probably made shift with the more cramped space under a lean-to against their house, or anywhere which was dry and sufficiently large to allow of the easy swinging of the flail. This was made of two pieces of wood (frequently thorn) tied one to the other by a leathern thong. The worker stood over a pile of corn and by a rhythmical circular motion brought one end of the flail down smartly on to the ears, thus dislodging the grains of corn. Once this had been done, it was necessary to separate the chaff and straw from the grain. This they did either by winnowing the whole with a fan so that the lighter husks of the chaff were blown away leaving the grain, or by tossing it up in the air near the door of the barn so that the breeze could catch and bear away the chaff, leaving the grains of corn to fall to the ground. The chaff itself was not wasted, but swept up and mixed with damaged corn and used as food for the beasts.

The advent of Christmas saw the bad weather bringing work in the fields to a standstill; and, once the peasant had made his preparations outlined above and threshed his corn, he could estimate what return he had received for all these exacting labours throughout the year.

4. No Spare Time for Villagers Living in Isolated Rural Areas.

Rowland E. Prothero, Lord Ernle

Thirteenth century rural villages were isolated and self-supporting. The inhabitants had little need of communication even with their neighbours, still less with the outside world. The fields and the live-stock provided their necessary food and clothing. Whatever wood was required for building, fencing, and fuel was supplied from the wastes. Each village had its mill, and nearly every house had its oven and brewing kettle. Women spun and wove wool into coarse cloth, and hemp or nettles into linen; men tanned their own leather. The rough tools required for cultivation of the soil, and the rude household utensils needed for the comforts of daily life, were made at home. In the long winter evenings, farmers, their sons, and their servants carved the wooden spoons, the platters, and the beechen bowls. They fitted and riveted the bottoms to the horn mugs, or closed, in coarse fashion, the leaks in the leathern jugs. They plaited the osiers and reeds into baskets and into "weeles" for catching fish; they fixed handles to the scythes, rakes, and other tools; cut the flails from holly or thorn, and fastened them with thongs to the staves; shaped the teeth for rakes and harrows from ash or willow, and hardened them in the fire; cut out the wooden shovels for casting the corn in the granary; fashioned ox-yokes and bows, forks, racks, and rack-staves; twisted willows into scythe-cradles, or into traces and other harness gear. Travelling carpenters, smiths, and tinkers visited detached farmhouses and smaller villages, at rare intervals, to perform those parts of the work which needed their professional skill. But every village of any size found employment for such trades as those of the smith and the carpenter, and the frequency with which "Smiths Ham" appears among field names suggests the value which the inhabitants attached to the forge and the anvil. Meanwhile the women plaited straw or reeds for neck-collars, stitched and stuffed sheepskin bags for cart-saddles, peeled rushes for wicks and made candles. Thread was often made from nettles. Spinning-wheels, distaffs, and needles were never idle. Home-made cloth and linen supplied all wants. Flaxen linen for boardcloths, sheets, shirts or smocks, and towels, as the napkins were called, on which, before the introduction of forks, the hands were wiped, was only found in wealthy houses and on special occasions. Hemp, in ordinary households, supplied the same necessary articles, and others, such as candle-wicks, in coarser form. Shoethread, halters, stirrup-thongs, girths, bridles, and ropes were woven from the "carle" hemp; the finer kind, or "fimble" hemp,

From *English Farming, Past and Present* by Rowland E. Prothero, Lord Ernle, 3rd ed. (New York: Longmans, Green & Co., 1922), pp. 29-30. Reprinted by permission.

supplied the coarse linen for domestic use, and "hempen homespun" passed into a proverb for a countryman. Nettles were also extensively used in the manufacture of linen; . . . The formation of words like spinster, webster, lyster, shepster, maltster, brewster, and baxter indicated that the occupations were feminine, and show that women spun, wove, dyed, and cut out the cloth, as well as malted the barley, brewed the ale, and baked the bread for the family.

5. Seneschal's Guide Book Indicates Manorial Responsibilities.

Anonymous

The seneschal of lands ought to be prudent and faithful and profitable, and he ought to know the law of the realm, to protect his lord's business and to instruct and give assurance to the bailiffs who are beneath him in their difficulties. He ought two or three times a year to make his rounds and visit the manors of his stewardship, and then he ought to inquire about the rents, services, and customs, hidden or withdrawn, and about franchises of courts, lands, woods, meadows, pastures, waters, mills, and other things which belong to the manor and are done away with without warrant, by whom, and how: . . .

The seneschal ought, at his first coming to the manors, to cause all the demesne lands of each to be measured by true men, and he ought to know by the perch of the country how many acres there are in each field, and thereby he can know how much wheat, rye, barley, oats, peas, beans, and dredge one ought by right to sow in each acre, and thereby can one see if the provost or the hayward account for more seed than is right, and thereby can he see how many ploughs are required on the manor. . . .

The seneschal has no power to remove a bailiff or servant who is with the lord, and clothed and kept by him, without the special order of the lord. . . .

The seneschal should not have power to sell wardship, or marriage, or escheat, nor to dower any lady or woman, nor to take homage or suit, nor to sell or make free a vilein without special warrant from his lord. . . .

The seneschal ought, on his coming to each manor, to see and inquire how they are tilled, and in what crops they are, and how the cart-horses and avers, oxen, cows, sheep, and swine are kept and improved. And if

From "Seneschaucie," author unknown; translated by Elizabeth Lamond in *Walter of Henley's Husbandry* (London: Longmans, Green & Co., 1890), pp. 86-117.

there be loss or damage from want of guard, he ought to take fines from those who are to blame, so that the lord may not lose. . . .

The bailiff ought to rise every morning and survey the woods, corn, meadows, and pastures, and see what damage may have been done. And he ought to see that the ploughs are yoked in the morning, and unyoked at the right time, so that they may do their proper ploughing every day, as much as they can and ought to do by the measured perch. And he must cause the land to be marled, folded, manured, improved, and amended as his knowledge may approve, for the good and bettering of the manor. He ought to see how many measured acres the boon-tenants and customary-tenants ought to plough yearly, and how many the ploughs of the manor ought to till, and so he may lessen the surplus of the cost. And he ought to see and know how many acres of meadow the customary-tenants ought to mow and make, and how many acres of corn the boon-tenants and customary-tenants ought to reap and carry, and thereby he can see how many acres of meadow remain to be mowed, and how many acres of corn remain to be reaped for money, so that nothing shall be wrongfully paid for. And he ought to forbid any provost or bedel or hayward or any other servant of the manor to ride on, or lend, or ill-treat the cart-horses or others. And he ought to see that the horses and oxen and all the stock are well kept, and that no other animals graze in, or eat their pasture. . . .

The bailiff must see that there be good watch at the granges over the threshers, and that the corn be well and cleanly threshed, and that the straw be well saved in good stacks or cocks well covered, and that no forage be sold from the manor, but let the forage and fern, if there be any, be thrown in marshy ground or in roads to make manure. And no stubble should be sold from the manor, but let as much as shall be wanted for thatching be gathered together, and the rest remain on the ground and be ploughed with the ploughs.

And the bailiff ought to oversee the ploughs and the tillage, and see that the lands are well ploughed with small furrows, and properly cropped, and well sown with good and pure seed, and cleanly harrowed. . . .

Let nothing on the manors which ought to be sold be taken by the people, but let it be sent to fairs and markets at several places, and be inspected and bargained for and whoever will give the most shall have it. . . .

And the bailiff ought, after shearing, to cause all the skins of all the sheep killed in the larder or dead of murrain to be brought before him, and then he can see how many are fresh and which are flayn without leave and inspection; and then he must see that all the skins of the sheep are of one mark and that the wool and the skins match, and that the skins be not changed or bought, and then sell the skins with the wool. And the wool ought to be sold by sack or by fleece, according as he shall see there is the greatest profit and advantage. . . .

The provost ought to be elected and presented by the common consent of the township, as the best husbandman and the best approver among them. And he must see that all the servants of the court rise in the morning to do their work, and that the ploughs be yoked in time, and the lands well ploughed and cropped, and turned over, and sown with good and clean seed, as much as they can stand. And he ought to see that there be a good fold of wooden hurdles on the demesne, strewed within every night to improve the land.

And he ought to see that he have a good fold for wethers, and another for ewes, and a third for hogs, according as there are sheep. . . . The provost ought to see that the corn is well and cleanly threshed, so that nothing is left in the straw to grow in thatches, nor in manure to sprout. The husks, and the trampled corn, and the refuse of the winnowing, may be put together and threshed, and then winnowed and put with the other. And the provost must take care that no thresher or winnower shall take corn to carry it away in his bosom, or in tunic, or boots, or pockets, or sacks or sacklets hidden near the grange. . . .

And the provost ought often to see that all the beasts are well provided with forage and kept as they ought to be, and that they have enough pasture without overcharge of the other beasts, and he ought to see that the keepers of all kinds of beasts do not go to fairs, or markets, or wrestling-matches, or taverns, by which the beasts aforesaid may go astray without guard, or do harm to the lord or another, but they must ask leave, and put keepers in their places that no harm may happen; and if harm or loss do come about, let the amend be taken from the keepers and the damage made good. . . .

The hayward ought to be an active and sharp man, for he must, early and late, look after and go round and keep the woods, corn, and meadows and other things belonging to his office, and he ought to make attachments and approvements faithfully, and make the delivery by pledge before the provost, and deliver them to the bailiff to be heard. And he ought to sow the lands, and be over the ploughers and harrowers at the time of each sowing. And he ought to make all the boon-tenants and customary-tenants who are bound and accustomed to come, do so, to do the work they ought to do. And in haytime he ought to be over the mowers, the making, the carrying, and in August assemble the reapers and the boon-tenants and the labourers and see that the corn be properly and cleanly gathered; and early and late watch so that nothing be stolen or eaten by beasts or spoilt. . . .

The lord ought to love God and justice, and be faithful and true in his sayings and doings, and he ought to hate sin and injustice, and evil-doing. The lord ought not to take counsel with young men full of young blood, and ready courage, who know little or nothing of business, nor of any juggler,· flatterer, or idle talker, nor of such as bear witness by present, but he ought to take counsel with worthy and faithful men, ripe in years, who have seen much, and know much, and who are known to be of good fame, and who never were caught or convicted for treachery or any wrong-doing. . . .

The lord ought to command and ordain that the accounts be heard every year, but not in one place but on all the manors, for so can one quickly know everything, and understand the profit and loss. . . .

The lord ought to inquire by his own men and others on his manors as many as there are, about his seneschal and his doings, and the approvements he has made since his coming; in the same way he ought to inquire about profits and losses from the bailiff and provost, and how much he will have to seek from both. He ought to ask for his auditors and rolls of account, then he ought to see who has done well and who not, and who has made improvement and who not, and who has made profit and who not, but loss, and those he has then found good and faithful and profitable, let him keep on this account. And if anyone be found who has done harm and is by no means profitable, let him answer for his doing and take farewell. . . .

The auditors ought to be faithful and prudent, knowing their business and all the points and articles of the account in rents, in outlays, in returns of the grange and stock, and other things belonging thereto. And the accounts ought to be heard at each manor, and then one can know the profit and loss, the doings and approvements of the seneschal, bailiff, provost, and others, for as much as they have done of profit or loss can be seen by the account in a day or two, and then can soon be seen the sense or the folly of these said seneschals, bailiffs, and provosts; and then can the auditors take inquest of the doings which are doubtful and hear the plaints of each plaintiff and make the fines.

The ploughmen ought to be men of intelligence, and ought to know how to sow, and how to repair and mend broken ploughs and harrows, and to till the land well, and crop it rightly; and they ought to know also how to yoke and drive the oxen, without beating or hurting them, and they ought to forage them well, and look well after the forage that it be not stolen nor carried off; and they ought to keep them safely in meadows and several pastures, and other beasts which are found therein they ought to impound. And they and the keepers must make ditches and build and remove the earth, and ditch it so that the ground may dry and the water be drained. And they must not flay any beast until some one has inspected it, and inquired by what default it died. And they must not carry fire into the byres for light, or to warm themselves, and have no candle there, or light unless it be in a lantern, and for great need and peril.

The waggoner ought to know his trade, to keep the horses and curry them, and to load and carry without danger to his horses, that they may not be overloaded or overworked, or overdriven, or hurt, and he must know how to mend his harness and the gear of the waggon. And the bailiff and provost ought to see and know how many times the waggoners can go in a day to carry marl or manure, or hay or corn, or timber or firewood, without great stress; and as many times as they can go in a day, the waggoners must answer for each day at the end of the week. No waggoner or other shall cause a cart-horse or aver to be flayn without inspection and the command of his superior, until it be known why and for what default it died, as is said above. And no waggoner shall carry fire or candle into the stables, unless the candle be in a lantern, and this for great need, and then it must be carried and watched by another than himself. Each waggoner shall sleep every night with his horses, and keep such guard as he shall wish to answer for without damage; and so shall the oxherds sleep in the same way with their oxen.

The cowherd ought to be skilful, knowing his business and keeping his cows well, and foster the calves well from time of weaning. And he must see that he has fine bulls and large and of good breed pastured with the cows, to mate when they will. And that no cow be milked or suckle her calf after Michaelmas, to make cheese of rewain; for this milking and this rewain make the cows lose flesh and become weak, and will make them mate later another year, and the milk is better and the cow poorer.... And every night the cowherd shall put the cows and other beasts in the fold during the season, and let the fold be well strewed with litter or fern, as is said above, and he himself shall lie each night with his cows.

The swineherd ought to be on those manors where swine can be sustained and kept in the forest, or in woods, or waste, or in marshes, without sustenance from the grange; and if the swine can be kept with little sustenance from the grange during hard frost, then must a pigsty be made in a marsh or wood, where the swine may be night and day....

Each shepherd ought to find good pledges to answer for his doings and for good and faithful service, although he be companion to the miller. And he must cover his fold and enclose it with hurdles and mend it within and without, and repair the hurdles and make them. And he ought to sleep in the fold, he and his dog; and he ought to pasture his sheep well, and keep them in forage, and watch them well, so that they be not killed or destroyed by dogs or stolen or lost or changed, nor let them pasture in moors or dry places or bogs, to get sickness and disease for lack of guard. No shepherd ought to leave his sheep to go to fairs, or markets, or wrestling matches, or wakes, or to the tavern, without taking leave or asking it, or without putting a good keeper in his place to keep the sheep, that no harm may arise from his fault.

Let all the lord's sheep be marked with one mark, and let no ewes be milked after the feast of our Lady, for they will mate more tardily another year, and the lambs shall be worth less. . . .

The dairymaid ought to be faithful and of good repute, and keep herself clean, and ought to know her business and all that belongs to it. She ought not to allow any under-dairymaid or another to take or carry away milk, or butter, or cream, by which the cheese shall be less and the dairy impoverished. And she ought to know well how to make cheese and salt cheese, and she ought to save and keep the vessels of the dairy, that it need not be necessary to buy new ones every year. And she ought to know the day when she begins to make cheese and of what weight, and when she begins to make two cheeses a day, of how much and of what weight. . . .

The dairymaid ought to help to winnow the corn when she can be present, and she ought to take care of the geese and hens and answer for the returns and keep and cover the fire, that no harm arise from lack of guard.

PART II

Chivalric Education

THE Knight and Squire who accompanied Chaucer's Pilgrims wending their way to Canterbury possessed many of the characteristics highly prized during the age of chivalry: courtesy, strength, horsemanship, combat success, respect for the ladies, and loyalty to one's liege lord. The cultivation of these virtues and skills began early in a boy's life. Young boys spent their first seven years or so in the company of women (usually in the lady's bower) where they learned to speak gently and to behave properly in the company of their superiors. From about seven to fourteen the young boy served as a page to a nobleman and he performed menial tasks and learned how to serve at the table of his lord. (Chaucer's squire was already skilled in carving before his father, the knight, at table.) Much of the page's time was spent either with the household serving staff or with women, who supervised the servants. Training in running, climbing, fighting, physical endurance, the use of weapons and horsemanship were the major emphases in the last seven-year training period as the young squire sought to become worthy of knighthood. During his tutelage as both a page and squire, the young knight-to-be was also schooled in the elaborate etiquette of courtly love and the poetical and musical skills needed to demonstrate such love as well as in the ethic of fidelity to both God and his lord.

There exists an ample romantic literature on the age of chivalry, including Malory's *Morte D'Arthur, The Romance of the Rose, Sir Gawain and the Green Knight,* and even Froissart's *Chronicles;* the materials chosen for this chapter will attempt to dispel some of the romanticism surrounding knighthood, while attempting to stress the importance of moral education as well as physical training in the education of knights.

Edith Rickert's translation of *The Babees' Book,* which had been written around 1475 with advice to young children on the behavior expected of them when in the presence of noblemen, indicates that quiet, respectful table manners were of primary concern in the early stages of a child's preparation for knighthood. William Stearns Davis paints a portrait of the training of young Aimery, a French nobleman's son at the time of Philip Augustus (1220), who learns to become a knight. Sidney Painter distinguishes three ideals in chivalry (feudal chivalry, with its emphasis upon physical prowess and courtesy between knights; religious chivalry, in which knighthood becomes imbued with religious ceremonies and symbolism, particularly as knights depart for crusades labelled "holy"; and the chivalry of courtly love in which the knight's skills as a lover, composer of verse, and jouster become more important than his fidelity to either the combat of war or the defense of Christianity), the first two of which are included here. Painter also provides an account of a thirteenth century critic of chivalric education, Ramon Lull, who wished to see the training of knights become more dignified by becoming more intellectual. Incidentally, Davis argues elsewhere in his book that devotion to chivalry frequently disguised a major feature of a nobleman's pursuit of war, namely, fighting to avoid boredom.

Herbert J. Muller points out that the knightly ideal of courteous behavior on the battlefield, so celebrated by Froissart, was often breached in practice. Lewinsohn criticizes the courtly love ideal, arguing that, with chivalry, adultery became an amusing pastime for members of the aristocracy.

Just as the devotion to brotherly comradeship and the maintenance of high standards of craftsmanship which began with the early gilds gave way to selfish economic interests, and much as the pious devotion to asceticism and the desire for God of the early monastic orders and convents gave way to dissolution, so, too, did the ideals underscoring chivalric education eventually crumble when knights no longer had a "noble cause" for which to fight. But, as Arthur remarks to the young Tom Malory at the conclusion of the musical version of "Camelot," what was important about the age of chivalry was not that it failed, but that the attempt was made. Such had been the aim of chivalric education.

6. How Children Should Behave in Noble Households: Advice from *The Babees' Book*.

And first of all, I think to show how you babies who dwell in households should behave yourselves when ye be set at meat, and how when men bid you be merry you should be ready with lovely, sweet, and benign words. . . .

When you enter your lord's place, say "God speed," and with humble cheer greet all who are there present. Do not rush in rudely, but enter with head up and at an easy pace, and kneel on one knee only to your lord or sovereign, whichever he be.

If any speak to you at your coming, look straight at them with a steady eye, and give good ear to their words while they be speaking; and see to it with all your might that ye jangle not, nor let your eyes wander about the house, but pay heed to what is said, with blithe visage and diligent spirit. When ye answer, ye shall be ready with what ye shall say, and speak useful things and give your reasons smoothly, in words that are gentle, but brief and to the point. . . . Take no seat, but be ready to stand until you are bidden to sit down. Keep your hands and feet at rest; do not claw your flesh or lean against a post in the presence of your lord, or handle anything belonging to the house.

From *Chaucer's World* by Edith Rickert (New York: Columbia University Press, 1948). Reprinted by permission. This selection appears on pages 104-107 of the paperback edition published in 1962.

Make obeisance to your lord always when you answer; otherwise, stand as still as a stone, unless he speak.

Look with one accord that if ye see any person better than yourself come in, ye go backwards anon and give him place, and in nowise turn your face from him, as far forth as you may.

If you see your lord drinking, keep silence, without loud laughter, chattering, whispering, joking, or other insolence.

If he command you to sit in his presence, fulfill his wish at once, and strive not with another about your seat.

When you are set down, tell no dishonest tale; eschew, also, with all your might, to be scornful; and let your cheer be humble, blithe, and merry, not chiding as if ye were ready for a fight.

If you perceive that your better is pleased to commend you, rise up anon and thank him heartily.

Advise you against taking so much meat into your mouth but that ye may right well answer when men speak to you.

When ye shall drink, wipe your mouth clean with a cloth, and your hands also, so that you shall not in any way soil the cup, for then shall none of your companions be loath to drink with you.

Likewise, do not touch the salt in the salt-cellar with any meat; but lay salt honestly on your trencher, for that is courtesy.

Do not carry your knife to your mouth with food or hold the meat with your hands in any wise; and also if divers good meats are brought to you, look that with all courtesy ye assay of each; and if your dish be taken away with its meat and another brought, courtesy demands that ye shall let it go and not ask for it back again.

And if strangers be set at table with you, and savory meat be brought or sent to you, make them good cheer with part of it, for certainly it is not polite, when others be present at meat with you, to keep all that is brought you and like churls vouchsafe nothing to others.

Do not cut your meat like field men who have such an appetite that they reck not in what wise, where or when or how ungoodly they hack at their meat; but, sweet children, have always your delight in courtesy and in gentleness, and eschew boisterousness with all your might.

When cheese is brought, have a clean trencher, on which with a clean knife ye may cut it; and in your feeding look ye appear goodly and keep your tongue from jangling, for so, indeed, shall ye deserve a name for gentleness and good governance, and always advance yourself in virtue.

When the end of the meal is come, clean your knives; and, look you put them up where they ought to be, and keep your seat until you have washed, for so wills honesty.

When ye have done, look, then, that ye rise up without laughter or joking or boisterous word, and go to your lord's table, and there stand, and pass not from him until grace be said and brought to an end.

Then some of you should go for water, some hold the cloth, some pour upon his hands.

7. Aimery Learns to Become a Knight.

William Stearns Davis

From earliest youth Aimery has had success in arms held before him as the one thing worth living for. True, he has been taught to be pious. He understands it is well that God has created priests and monks, who may by their ceremonies and prayers enable the good warriors to enter into paradise. But the squire has never had the slightest desire to become a cleric himself. He thanks his divine patroness, St. Genevieve, that Conon has not treated him as so many younger brothers are treated, and forced him into the Church. What is it to become a lazy rich canon, or even a splendid lord bishop, beside experiencing even the modest joys of a common sire with a small castle, a fast horse, good hawks, and a few stout retainers? Aimery has learned to attend mass devoutly and to accept implicitly the teachings of the priests, but his moral training is almost entirely based on "courtesy," a very secular code indeed. Hence he acts on the advice given him while very young: "Honor all churchmen, but look well to your money."

Another well-remembered warning is never to put trust in villeins. He cannot, indeed, refuse to deal with them. He must treat them ordinarily with decency, but never trust them as real friends. The ignoble are habitually deceitful. They cannot understand a cavalier's "honor." They are capable of all kinds of base villainies. A sage man will have comradeship only with his nobly born peers, and pride is no fault in a baron when dealing with inferiors.

Although he is to be a warrior, Aimery has been given a certain training in the science of letters. It is true that many seigneurs cannot read a word on the parchments which their scriveners interpret, draw up, or seal for them, but this is really very inconvenient. . . . Another reason for literacy is that delightful books of romantic adventure are multiplying. The younger brother has, therefore, been sent over to the school at the neighboring

Abridged from pp. 178-187 in *Life on a Medieval Barony* by William Stearns Davis. Copyright, 1923, by Harper & Row, Publishers, Inc.; renewed 1951 by Alice Redfield Davis. By permission of the publishers.

monastery, where (along with a few other sons of noblemen) he has had enough of the clerk's art switched into him to be able to read French with facility, to pick out certain Latin phrases, and to form letters clumsily on wax tablets—writing with a stylus something after the manner of the ancients.

Once possessed of this wonderful art of reading that Aimery had while yet a lad, he could delve into the wonderful parchments of romances which told him of the brave deeds done of old. Especially, he learned all about the Trojan War, which was one long baronial feud between North French cavaliers fighting for the fair Helen, imprisoned in a strong castle. His sympathy was excited for Hector as the under dog. He read of many exploits which had escaped the knowledge of Homer, but which were well known to Romance trouveres. He reveled in scenes of slaughter whereof the figures are very precise, it being clearly stated that 870,000 Greeks and 680,000 Trojans perished in the siege of that remarkable Trojan fortress.

Almost equally interesting was the history of Alexander, based on the version of the pseudo-Callisthenes. This was very unlike the accounts which other ages consider authentic. The names of the battles with Darius were altered, strange adventures with the Sirens crept into the narrative, and finally Alexander (the tale ran) died sorely lamenting that he could not conquer France and make Paris his capital.

The story of Caesar is also available, but it seems less romantic, although full of episodes of fairies and dwarfs.

For the history of France, Aimery has learned that the country was originally settled by exiled Trojans; later the Romans came, and some time later one meets the great Emperor Charlemagne, whose exploits entwine themselves with Charles Martel's defeat of the Saracens. Charlemagne, we gather, conducted a crusade to the Holy Land and took Jerusalem, although later the Infidels regained it. Recent French history remains very mixed in the young noble's mind until the great Council of Clermont (1095), which launched the First Crusade. In the century after that great episode, however, the events stand out clearly, and of course he knows all the history of the local baronial houses down to the story of the petty feud forty years ago between two Burgundian counts.

But when is monk's or jongleur's lore compared with the true business of a born cavalier? When he was only seven or eight, Aimery was fencing with a blunted sword. From ten onward he took more regular fencing lessons. . . . Equally early he had his horse, his hawks, and his dogs; he was taught how to care for them entirely himself, and was soon allowed to go on long rides alone into the dense forest in order to develop his resourcefulness, sense of direction, and woodcraft. Then, as he grew taller, his brother began to deliver long lectures for his betterment. . . .

One day Conon exhorted him in the style of the old County Guy advising his son Doon in the epic, "Doon of Mayence." "Ask questions of good men whom you know, but never put trust in a stranger. Every day, fair brother, hear the holy mass; and whenever you have money give to the poor—for God will repay you double. Be liberal in gifts to all, for a cavalier who is sparing will lose all in the end and die in wretchedness; but wherever you can, give without promising to give again. When you come to a strange house, cough very loudly, for there may be something going on there which you ought not to see. When you are in noble company, play backgammon; you will be the more prized on that account. Never make a noise or jest in church; it is done only by unbelievers. If you would shun trouble, avoid meddling and pretend to no knowledge you do not possess. Do not treat your body servant as your equal—that is, let him sit by you at table or take him to bed with you; for the more honor you do a villein the more he will despise you. After you are married by no means tell a secret to your wife; for if you let her know it you will repent your act the first time you vex her." . . .

Before he was fifteen Aimery had thus learned to read and write, to ride and hawk, to play chess, checkers, and backgammon, to thrum a harp and sing with clear voice, to shoot with the arbalist, and to fence with considerable skill. He was also learning to handle a light lance and a shield while on horseback. Then came his first great adventure—his brother sent him to the gentle Count of Bernon to be "nourished."

The higher the baron the greater his desire to have nobly born lads placed in his castle as *nourris,* to serve as his squires and be trained as cavaliers. Bernon had kept three squires simultaneously. . . . It is a friendly courtesy to send word to an old comrade in arms . . . , saying: "You have a fine son [or brother]; send him to be 'nourished' in my castle. When he is of ripe age I will give him furs and a charger and dub him knight." Of course, it was a high honor to be reared by a very great lord . . . ; but younger sons or brothers did not often enjoy such good fortune. Petty nobles had to send their sons to the manors of poor sires of their own rank, who could keep only one squire.

Once enrolled as squire to a count, Aimery soon learned that his master was a kind of second father to him—rebuking and correcting him with great bluntness, but assuming an equal responsibility for his training. Hereafter, whatever happened, no ex-squire could fight against his former master without sheer impiety. . . .

It is held that no father or brother can enforce sufficient discipline over a growing lad, and that "it is proper he shall learn to obey before he governs, otherwise he will not appreciate the nobility of his rank when he becomes a knight." Aimery in the De Bernon castle surely received his full share of discipline, not merely from the count, but from the two older squires, who took pains at first to tyrannize over him unmercifully, until they became knighted, and he gained two new companions younger than himself, with whom he played the despot in turn.

In his master's service Aimery became expert in the use of arms. First he was allowed to carry the count's great sword, lance, and shield, and to learn how the older nobles could handle them. Next he was given weapons and mail of his own, and began the tedious training of the tilt yard, discovering that a large part of his happiness in life would consist in being able to hold his lance steady while his horse was charging, to strike the point fairly on a hostile shield until either the tough lance snapped or his foe was flung from the saddle, and at the same time to pinch his own saddle tightly with his knees while with his own shield covering breast and head against a mortal blow. Couch, charge, recover—couch, charge, recover—he must practice it a thousand times.

Meantime he was attending the count as a constant companion. He rose at gray dawn, went to the stables, and curried down his master's best horse; then back to the castle to assist his superior to dress. He waited on his lord and lady at table. He was responsible for receiving noble guests, preparing their chambers and generally attending to their comfort. On expeditions he led the count's great war charger when the seigneur rode his less fiery palfrey; and he would pass his lord his weapons as needed. At tournaments he stood at the edge of the lists, ready to rush in and rescue the count from under the stamping horses if he were dismounted. He was expected to fight only in emergencies, when his master was in great danger; but Bernon was a gallant knight, and repeatedly in hot forays Aimery had gained the chance to use his weapons.

At the same time he was learning courtesy. He was intrusted with the escort of the countess and her daughters. He entertained with games, jests and songs noble dames visiting the castle. He learned all the details of his master's affairs. The count was supposed to treat him as a kind of younger self—intrust him with secrets, send him as confidential messenger on delicate business, allow him to carry his purse when he journeyed, and keep the keys to his coffers when at home. After Aimery became first squire he was expected also to assist the seneschal in a last round of the castle at night, to make sure everything was locked and guarded; then he would sleep at the door of the count's chamber. Beyond a doubt, since the count was an honorable and capable man, Aimery received thereby a training of enormous value. While still a lad he had large responsibilities thrust upon him, and learned how to transmit commands and to handle difficult situations. He was versed in all the ordinary occasions of a nobleman. When he became a knight himself, he would be no tyro in all the stern problems of feudal life.

Thus Conon's brother came within four years to be an admirable *damoiseau* (little lord), an epithet decidedly more commendatory than its partial equivalent "squire" (*ecuyer,* shield bearer).

Of course, his military training had proceeded apace. Soon he was allowed to tilt with his horse and lance at the *quintain.* This is a manikin covered with a coat of mail and a shield, and set on a post. The horseman dashes up against it at full gallop, and tries to drive his lance through shield and armor. There are many variations for making the sport harder. After Aimery could strike the *quintain* with precision he took his first tilt against an older squire. Never will he forget the grinding shock of the hostile lance splintering upon his shield; the almost irresistible force that seemed smiting him out of the saddle; the dismay when he found his own lance glancing harmlessly off the shield of his opponent, slanted at a cunning angle. But practice makes perfect. When he finally returned to St. Aliquis his own brother was almost unhorsed when they tried a friendly course by the barbican.

So Aimery completed his education. If he has failed to learn humility, humanity to villeins, and that high respect for women which treats them not merely as creatures to be praised and courted, but as one's moral and intellectual equals, he at least has learned a high standard of honor in dealing with his fellow nobles. The confidences his master has reposed in him have made it a fundamental conviction that it were better to perish a dozen times than to betray a trust. He believes that the word of a cavalier should be better than the oath of the ignoble. As for courage, it were better to die like Ganelon, torn by wild horses, than to show fear in the face of physical danger. He has been trained also to cultivate the virtue of generosity to an almost ruinous extent.

Free giving is one of the marks of a true nobleman. Largess is praised by the minstrels almost as much as bravery. "He is not a true knight who is too covetous." Therefore money is likely to flow like water through Aimery's fingers all his life. The one redeeming fact will be that, though he will be constantly *giving,* he will always be as constantly *receiving.* Among the nobles there is an incessant exchanging of gifts—horses, armor, furs, hawks, and even money. All wealth really comes from the peasants, yet their lords dispose carelessly of it even though they do not create it. Even the villeins, however, will complain if their masters do not make the crowds scramble often for coppers—never realizing that these same coppers represent their own sweat and blood.

8. Feudal Chivalry: The Ideals of Prowess, Loyalty and Courtesy

Sidney Painter

The seeds at least of the knightly ideals of prowess, loyalty, and generosity existed in the cultural tradition of the noble class and needed only the nourishment provided by twelfth-century France to spring into full flower, but another chivalric ideal, courtesy, seems to have grown directly out of the feudal environment. Now courtesy as used by mediaeval writers had a wide variety of meanings.... Here our interest must be confined to courtesy as applied to the relations between noblemen. As the heritability of fiefs became firmly established in the tenth and eleventh centuries it led to the stabilization of the feudal class and to the development of class consciousness. In time the idea appeared that nobles deserved special consideration from their fellows. One result of this feeling was the growth of interest in courtesy in its narrowest sense, ordinary politeness in conversation and social relations. All chivalric writers agree that a good knight should be polite to his fellows. But the class consciousness of the nobles showed itself in more practical forms of courtesy. By the twelfth century feudal opinion seems to have required that the hardships of war should be ameliorated through mutual consideration shown to noble by noble. This tendency appears in some of the cruder *chansons de geste*. When Gaydon had cut off the head of his opponent in a duel, he laid two swords crosswise on his foe's body. This moved the Emperor Charles to cry "Ha! God, how courteous this duke is!" In *Raoul de Cambrai* Bernier had by devious stratagems persuaded his enemy to step naked into a fountain while he himself stood by armed, yet he refused to kill the helpless man. Such a deed would cause him to be an object of scorn and reproach all his days. This belief that it was unethical to attack an unarmed man is illustrated throughout the *chansons de geste* and is one of the few courteous principles mentioned in this literature. The Arthurian works of Chrétien de Troyes show these ideas in a more developed form. When the hero of a tale overthrows a villainous knight, he practically always spares his life and releases him on parole. No one attacks an unarmed man. Two knights never set upon one. Even bands of robbers who meet an adventuring knight are careful to assault him one by one. While this picture of the most wicked knights scrupulously observing the requirements of courtesy may be regarded as rather fanciful, there seems little doubt that feudal propriety demanded that knights fight each other on essentially equal terms and that the van-

From *French Chivalry* by Sidney Painter (Baltimore: Johns Hopkins Press, 1940). Copyright 1940 by The Johns Hopkins Press. Reprinted by permission. This selection appears on pages 32-34 of the 1965 paperback edition (Cornell University Press).

quished be treated with consideration. In Froissart's opinion a true knight would show every possible courtesy to his noble prisoners, would quickly release them on parole, and would set their ransoms at sums easily within their means. All this was merely the courtesy one knight owed to another.

9. Religious Chivalry

• Sidney Painter

On the day before he was to be dubbed a knight the young noble confessed. That night he passed in the church fasting and praying. In the morning he attended mass and listened to a sermon. The actual dubbing was performed while the squire knelt before the altar. The knight who was receiving him into the order girded on the novice's sword, kissed him, and gave him the ceremonial blow. Then the new knight rode through the town so that all could see him. That same day he gave a great feast for everyone who had attended the ceremony. Finally he and the knights who had dubbed him exchanged gifts and the heralds were duly feed.... The men of the Middle Ages were devoted to symbolism, but nowhere did this taste flourish more magnificently than among the ecclesiastical writers on chivalry. Every article of knightly equipment, even every part of an article, had its significance. True, no two writers were likely to attach the same meaning to an article, but this merely gave freer rein to the creative imagination. One of the earliest complete systems of symbolism for knightly arms was produced by Robert of Blois in his *Enseignement des princes*. A few examples must suffice. The sword is clear and well polished—the knight should be honest and straight. The shield represents charity which covers many sins. The lance which pierces the foe before he gets near symbolizes foresight. Lull began his discussion of this subject by pointing out that every article of priestly vestments had its symbolic significance. Hence as knights were an order similar to the clergy, their equipment should also have a meaning. The sword is shaped like a cross. This signifies that knights should use the sword to slay foes of the cross. The sword has two edges to remind the knight that he should defend chivalry and justice. The shield symbolizes the office of a knight. As a knight places his shield between himself and his enemy, so a knight stands between prince and people. The

From *French Chivalry* by Sidney Painter (Baltimore: Johns Hopkins Press, 1940). Copyright 1940 by The Johns Hopkins Press. Reprinted by permission. This selection appears on pages 82-84 of the 1965 paperback edition (Cornell University Press).

knight should receive the blows aimed at his lord as his shield wards off those aimed at him. The lance represents truth, and its pennon marks the fact that truth fears not falseness. There is no need to go further. Enough has been said to show the general nature of this fascinating if rather fruitless pastime of inventing symbolic significance for the various pieces of a knight's equipment.

10. Ramon Lull's Criticism of the Training of Knights

Sidney Painter

Lull expressed dissatisfaction with the contemporary method of training young nobles. The son of a knight was placed in a noble household where he acquired his knightly education while serving as page and squire. Lull criticized this eminently practical apprentice system not for inefficiency but for lack of dignity. Other professions, such as the religious, law, and medicine, were learned from books, and the military was entitled to equal consideration. He wanted the knowledge that was requisite for a knight reduced to writing so that aspirants could study it in schools of chivalry. On the basis of these statements Lull has been charged with expressing the utterly silly idea that skill in arms could be learned from books, but this does not seem justified. He did not want to abolish the period of apprenticeship. He merely wished to add to it some formal study in books. Furthermore it is clear from the early part of *Le libre del orde de cauayleria* that he considered this work a suitable textbook for young nobles who aspired to be knights. He did not conceive of having squires read books on the care of horses— such things they would learn by practice. It was the history of the chivalric order, its proper function in society, and the ethical principles which governed true knights that he wished the squires to study. In short Lull was partly the author encouraging the reading of his book and partly the enthusiast seeking to propagate an ideal. After his term of service as page and squire Lull wished the young noble to attend a school of chivalry where he would learn the duties and qualities of a true knight by reading *Le libre del orde de cauayleria*.

From *French Chivalry* by Sidney Painter (Baltimore: Johns Hopkins Press, 1940). Copyright 1940 by The Johns Hopkins Press. Reprinted by permission. This selection appears on pages 81-82 of the 1965 paperback edition (Cornell University Press).

11. Knighthood: Glorified Violence

Herbert J. Muller

Bloodshed...was made honorable by the institution of chivalry, which ritualized violence. By origin a Germanic warrior, the medieval knight was given a Roman ancestry; poets discovered that Romulus was the founder of chivalry. The genuine knightly virtues of courage and fidelity were likewise bedecked with Christian and courtly ideals: the knight became Sir Galahad and Sir Lancelot, or a squire of the Virgin, while other poets made the Archangel Michael the father of chivalry. Nevertheless the knight remained at heart a rude warrior, who fought chiefly for the love of fighting, not of God or of ladies, and whose chivalrous code extended only to his peers. The medieval chronicles devoted to his valorous exploits are full of casual examples of his cruelty, lust, and greed, and his habit of pillaging or slaughtering the peasantry. In time he became a professional soldier or a simple mercenary. But from the outset war was commonly fought over trivial causes, involving personal animosities rather than principles. Its absurdity was accentuated by the Truce of God, through which the Church sought to maintain peace at least on holy days and over week ends.

12. The Immorality of Knightly Morals

Richard Lewinsohn

...the Middle Ages were more tolerant in matters of sex-life than many earlier and later ages. No one except priests, monks and nuns—who constituted, indeed, a considerable fraction of the population—was required to repress his sexual impulses. They were not to be driven out, as the Fathers of the Church had wanted, only concealed. Subject to this condition, people could, in practice, do as they liked. If it is permissible to characterize a

From *The Uses of the Past* by Herbert J. Muller. Copyright ©1952 by Oxford University Press, Inc. Reprinted by permission. This selection appears on pages 242-43 of the 1960 paperback edition (New York: The New American Library of World Literature).

Abridged from pp. 135-136, (hardbound edition) in *A History of Sexual Customs* by Richard Lewinsohn, translated by Alexander Mayce. English translation copyright ©1958 by Longmans, Green & Co., Ltd. and Harper & Row, Publishers, Inc. Original edition in German ©1956 by Rowohlt Verlag GmbH, Hamburg, under the title *Eine Weltgeschichte der Sexualitat*. By permission of the publishers. This selection is from pages 127-28 of the 1964 paperback edition (Greenwich, Conn.: Fawcett Publications).

period so long and so changeful with a simple phrase, we may say: the essential was dissimulation. This applied to politics, and also to sex-life. On the surface, everything centered round loyalty. The entire feudal system depended on the fidelity of the vassal to his liege lord, and family life on a marital fidelity which left no place for other relationships. But the elaboration of the conception of fidelity brought with it as its corollary the elevation of infidelity into a fine art.

An act of infidelity was no disgrace, always provided that one preserved the forms of polite society and was prepared to draw the sword and if necessary (this was not often the case) to die for one's heart's passion. The art of adultery used the same terminology as the official code of morals: honour, purity, virtue, loyalty were part of the popular vocabulary of the heroes who seduced other men's wives. Any knight who contented himself with wedding a maiden before having himself grown practised in adultery and carried off several trophies of the chase was unworthy of his spurs. Adultery was a social diversion among the upper classes. A knight had to have a "lady" whom he worshipped, to whom he devoted himself, and the lady had to be married, if possible to a husband of slightly higher rank than the lover, for in knightly love the eye was always turned upward. Everything was pure, delicate and noble—*honi soit qui mal y pense*.... Church and State alike tolerated the adulterous relationship between the young knight and the baronial lady. A cavalier might even bring religion into his affairs of the heart. It was the thing to choose a celestial patroness, and the usual practice, incredible though it sounds, was to invoke the Virgin Mary to patronize the liaison and soften the lady's heart towards her suppliant.

The Virgin Mary had been definitely recognized as *Theotokos*, The Mother of God, by the Council of Ephesus in 431. Since then, the cult of the Virgin had passed through many phases. She was more than a mortal woman; divine honours were paid her. In the period of transition from heathendom to Christianity she was identified in the East with Rhea-Cybele, the Great Goddess of the Greco-Roman pantheon. In Italy she borrowed the features of Ceres, the harvest goddess; in northern Europe she took the place of the goddess Freya. Presently, however, the faithful installed her on a still higher throne as *Regina Coeli*, Queen of Heaven. It was only in the later Middle Ages that she became more humanized and was made the symbol of motherhood. Never before, however, had mankind committed such blasphemy as to make the Virgin the patroness of organized adultery—for the knightly *minne* service, divested of its romantic trappings, was just that.

PART III

Monastic Education

MONASTERIES during the medieval period were institutions designed essentially for religious purposes; they were communities of men who gathered to pray, to glorify God, and to discover ways of serving Him and making His presence central to their lives. Christian monasteries were not a peculiarly medieval institution. Rather, as J. M. Hussey[1] points out, the origins of monasticism trace far back in Christian experience to Egypt and the

---

[1]"The *coenobium* (literally "common life"—*koinos bios*) or monastery *par excellence* in the western sense, grew up in Egypt at the same time as the eremitic life. Its founder was an Egyptian, the pagan soldier Pachomius who became converted to Christianity. After a trial run as a hermit, Pachomius realized that this made demands beyond the powers of most, and he organized corporate ascetic life at Tabennisi on the Nile in the early fourth century. So rapidly did the movement grow that when Pachomius died he had under him a congregation of eleven houses (two of which were for women). Pachomius was the head of his community, as well as the general superior over the whole group of houses. The main essentials of daily life stand out: prayer and services in common, private meditation and devotions, the bare minimum in the way of meals (usually eaten together in the refectory), manual labour and the performance of necessary domestic and administrative duties." Reprinted by permission from J. M. Hussey, *The Byzantine World* (New York: Harper & Row, 1961), p. 115.

Patristic era, when a distinction was made between two traditions of ascetic life. One is the eremitic tradition in which hermits or anchorites retire to the desert to meditate, contemplate God, and, in silence and solitude, seek to discover religious wisdom and divorce themselves from the temptations of the world. Occasionally such eremitic monks congregated around a more experienced ascetic monk for minor instruction, but typically the eremitic tradition is one of solitude, of silent worship, and of contemplation. The second is the cenobitic tradition which emphasizes the corporate life, the congregation or group of ascetic monks seeking to perform their prayers and the divine office in common, to eat in common, to contemplate alone but in the company of others, and to work together. It is the cenobitic tradition that became established in the monasticism of Western Europe. What is important, in terms of a derivative from this early Egyptian experience, is the emphasis upon prayer, contemplation, and silence whether alone or in the company of others. This is the ascetic experience emphasized again by St. Benedict as he founded Monte Cassino, the first important monastery in medieval Europe. Monte Cassino, built on the location of the ruin of a temple of Apollo in Italy in 529, served as the model for subsequent European monasteries.

The Rule formulated by Benedict to govern the community of cloistered monks at Monte Cassino extended the Egyptian emphasis upon prayer, contemplation, and silence by developing the principle that idleness was to be shunned as sinful and that monks should use their time profitably in the service of God, both by manual labor and in reading sacred literature. So important was this Rule that the two important monastic reform movements of the medieval period can be viewed not so much as objections to Benedict's ideas as attempts to correct Benedictine practice. [2]

[2]The Cluniac reform movement, led by St. Odo (926-942) and St. Odilo (994-1049), both Abbots of Cluny, multiplied and lengthened the number of services which the monks chanted together. It extended the artistic elaboration of the Christian liturgy, which was now expressed not only through music but also through Romanesque architecture. The order's services to the poor were expanded. Whereas the decentralized independent houses of the Benedictines had been subject to the governance and periodic inspection of local bishops, monasteries were now placed organizationally under Rome. The move towards centralization not only strengthened the authority of the Holy See, but was also taken as a measure to

During the medieval period some men entered the cloistered life by choice as adults; often, however, parents seeking to assure their sons of a secure position (particularly second sons who could not inherit property from their fathers under the primogeniture rules governing inheritance) would give their children to the monasteries to be trained for the vocation of monk. Both Benedictine and Cluniac monks used this method of recruitment up until the twelfth century.[3] The boys so given to monasteries were known as *oblati*. It was incumbent upon the monasteries receiving these children at about the age of ten to find some way of training them to be able to chant the Divine Office, to perform their religious obligations, and to carry out St. Benedict's injunction that they read sacred literature. To accomplish these ends, the monasteries ran "schools" for the *oblati*. Olga Tomkeieff portrays their communal life and education as follows:

> Lanfranc legislated for these "children of the cloister." They were in the overall care of a child master, responsible for their education and training. They were tonsured like the monks. They shared the same dormitory. They must never be alone together nor speak together. They shared the service of the church and were invaluable in the choir singing. Slight allowance only was made for their tender years. They were excused the first service, at about 2 a.m., and they seem to have been allowed breakfast during the monks' chapter. The children had their own chapter, a replica of that of the monks. The Abingdon Chronicle relates a story of Queen Edith, wife of the Confessor, visiting the monastery while the children were at breakfast—of dry bread. She made a gift of property to the monastery, earmarked for the provision of morning milk for the children.[4]

There is considerable controversy amongst scholars as to the extent to which the monasteries functioned as educational centers;

---

bring about wider conformity in the practice among the several monasteries. The Cistercian movement, led by St. Bernard of Clairvaux (b. 1091-d.1153), reemphasized the monkish virtues of fasting, abstinence, and simplicity in the furnishings of the abbey churches as befitting those whose "regulated life" insisted upon the rule of poverty.

[3]The practice of oblation became illegal in 1216, largely due to criticism by the new orders which insisted that monastic life should be entered into only by freely choosing and freely consenting adults, according to Tomkeieff, p. 90.

[4]O. G. Tomkeieff, *Life in Norman England*, pp. 89-90.

there are primarily two lines of discussion: one intellectual, the other religious. First of all, it has been asserted by many that monasteries preserved the flickering flame of learning that threatened to be extinguished as the barbarian hordes poured over Europe following the collapse of Rome and the dissolution of the Graeco-Roman world. More especially it is alleged that between the fifth and eleventh centuries, the Christian monasteries were the *only* important educational (teaching) institution and that they also served the function of preserving, particularly through the scriptorium, the learning and wisdom of the pagan world. From this perspective, it is claimed that although many people point to the development of scholasticism and the intellectual ferment of the universities as the major intellectual and educational innovation of the medieval period, the universities would never have come into being in the later middle ages (thirteenth and fourteenth centuries), had not the monasteries patiently preserved the learning ultimately incorporated into university studies. On the other hand, there are those who argue that the very asceticism of the monasteries was itself a major reason for the lack of intellectual effort and the lack of education to be found in the monasteries. Perhaps characteristic of this second view is that of William Boyd, the noted British historian of education from the University of Glasgow, who claims:

> Monasticism was a movement which attracted to itself earnest men of the most diverse character and attainments, and the forms it assumed were correspondingly diverse. But even granting the possibility of exceptional cases, it may be safely said that the ascetic spirit which dominated the movement was generally unfavourable to educational work. Men who had left the world to seek salvation in seclusion from their fellows were little likely to be interested in learning for themselves, or to be desirous of imparting it to others.[5]

The second issue requiring examination regarding monasteries has to do with the religious life, for it is claimed by some—and Chaucer was by no means either the first or last—that the monks, despite their professed devotion to God and an ascetic ideal, were

[5] William Boyd, *The History of Western Education*, p. 102.

wanton, dissolute, gluttonous, rapacious, given to excesses, vulgar, and even guilty of displays of worldliness in terms of dress by wearing brightly colored sashes, rings and bells, and other ornaments of secular life. From this point of view, monks are characterized as being not especially pious, but especially privileged, as preying upon the simple people with whom they came in contact, as being worldly in their appetites, as having political ambitions of their own or as serving the political interests of the nobility—in short, as being hypocrites who professed vows of poverty, obedience, and chastity and lived quite differently. Needless to say, the alternate view holds that the vast majority of monks were devoted to God, seeking constantly for ways of glorifying him not only in deeds but in the arts of manuscript illumination and chant composition, ascetic at table by having a meager diet of small portions, often abstaining from flesh and fowl by eating only vegetables or bread and wine, and devoting themselves to Christian service to their fellow man through acts of charity, praying for the souls of the laity, and caring for the diseased as well as the insane in monastic hospitals.

Materials included in this chapter concern the controversy about both dimensions of the education of monks in medieval monasteries: (1) intellectuality and (2) religiosity.

William Boyd had argued that there was a basic disinterest in education in the continental monasteries which contrasted sharply with a keen interest in intellectual and educational matters manifested by the Irish monasteries. Supplementing Boyd's view of the Irish monasteries is material provided by Roger Chauviré. Helen Cam's discussion of the early English monasteries, and particularly of the teaching style of Aelfric, Abbot of Eynsham, indicates that the English were also keenly interested in education. So impressed was Charlemagne with the quality of English scholarship that he invited Alcuin of York to come to his court and set up a "palace school" for the education of himself and his retinue. The respect which Charlemagne had for competent monastic instruction, as well as his criticism of poor scholarship in monasteries, is clearly revealed in his letter to Abbot Baugulf.

R. W. Southern claims that in order to follow the Church calendar, to compute Church hours, and to compose music necessary for the performance of the Divine Office, monks required a specialized education.[6]

Dom Knowles in his discussion of English monasteries notes that the community of monks required a fair number of administrative officials in order to fulfill the supervisory tasks .connected not only with running a school for novices, but also with maintaining cooking and living facilities for the monks and guests visiting the abbot, and with the various workshops which supplied the tools and implements for tilling the manorial estate upon which the monastery was built. Knowles argues that the "horarium" of the monastery was based upon a conception of time, silence, and work quite foreign to the contemporary reader. Since conversations were sharply restricted in the cloistered environment, monks were forced to rely upon a sign language in order to communicate their wishes. The Sign Language of the Monastery of Syon indicates the complexity of that language; Giraldus Cambrensis is reported to have found the use of similar sign-language by the monks at Canterbury in 1180 more comical than pious.[7]

G. G. Coulton has pieced together an account of the young oblate's tonsuring and daily activities on the basis of the Custumal of Bec and the Custumal of St. Benigne at Dijon. Evans's discussion of monastic daily life at Cluny makes clear that discipline meted out by the Chapter also served to teach the monks lessons of piety and obedience.

Having characterized the monastic writers as either (1) those composing treatises on philosophy, theology, or sermons; (2) those writing histories, chronicles, or biographies; or (3) "literary monks, men of wit, poets, especially satirists, troubadours clad in the robe, and therefore, one must add, very irregular monks," Luchaire sharply lambastes the monastic writers for their preoccupation with

[6]Tomkeieff (*Life in Norman England,* pp. 119-120) argues that many monastic communities in healing their fellows and artistically glorifying God in manuscripts and monastery chapels became centers for studying medicine and painting.

[7]Evans (*Monastic Life at Cluny,* pp. 82-85) indicates that Sundays and Feast Days required even greater attention to religious services on the part of the cloistered community than did the ordinary horarium.

literary symbolism and wordplay. He also contends that monasteries were not always havens for those seeking to glorify God, but that they also served as a place for parents to rid themselves of crippled and burdensome children. Further, Luchaire argues that monasticism often differed in practice from its ascetic theory. Both Evans and Knowles call attention to the importance of copying manuscripts and public as well as private reading as learning experiences. Knowles argues that the scriptorium provided opportunities for concentrated work and study, as well as an occasion for learning a highly disciplined calligraphic art form. Evans claims that the monks at Cluny were exposed to reading both communally and in their private hours of study when they had recourse to the monastery's library.

It is to a present-day monk that the final selections of this chapter turn for an evaluation of medieval monasteries as educational institutions. In *The Love of Learning and the Desire for God*, Dom LeClercq claims that intellectuality and religiosity were never competitive principles in the monasteries (contrary to Boyd's initial assertion); that the monasteries encouraged learning for the purpose of better loving and better understanding God. While it is true that the monks were ascetic and contemplative, this did not mean that they were anti-intellectual; indeed, LeClercq argues, contemplation is a refined intellectuality and produced not only able scholars of classical literature but a mystical religious literature as well. LeClercq describes the method of studying classics in monasteries; he also offers some interesting observations about the kind of learning and theology to be found in contemplative monastic experiences as contrasted with the active ecclesiastical preparation of the "schools." [8]

---

[8] *The Love of Learning and the Desire for God*, pp. 238-243.

13. Intellectuality Fostered at Irish Monasteries

Roger Chauviré

The Irish monasteries, Clonard, Clonmacnois, Armagh, then later Bangor and Lindisfarne, were centers not only of spiritual, but also of intellectual, life; they were in a sense the universities of their day. Being surrounded in their own country with religious respect, and protected by distance from the great barbarian invasions and the relapse into savagery which they caused, they were the only lights still burning in the night which had come down over the West; for two centuries Ireland, being thus privileged, was truly to be the teacher of Europe. Her wide-spread fame for learning and piety brought her a host of disciples: according to the tradition, no less than three thousand had gathered round St. Finnian at Clonard, and Armagh was so swarming with English students that it had a special Saxon quarter. The Merovingian king Dagobert possibly was educated at Slane. Travelers would also pay visits; Adamnan, of Iona, wrote his *De Locis Sanctis* at the dictation of a bishop of Gaul, one Asculf, who had returned from the Holy Land. Theological speculation was no doubt the most important study, to which the name of John Scotus Eriugena (this name says twice that he was an Irishman) bears witness; but it was nevertheless a monk, Dicuil, who composed a universal geography, *De mensura orbis terrarum,* while Fergal, the Abbot of Aghadoe, was even in those far-off days teaching that the earth is round.

The intellectual advance which Ireland felt she had on a barbaric Europe, and the charity with which she was animated for the peoples who had sunk or were still pagan, filled her with zeal. She applied herself eagerly to the conquest of minds and souls. In her view the work of evangelization must go *pari passu* with the bringing of light. The Carolingian renaissance owed much to her. The bold theologian John Scotus taught for twenty-five years in the schools of Laon, under Charles the Bald. Fergal of Aghadoe is the same as Virgil, Bishop of Salzburg, whose dangerous teaching about the antipodes did not prevent him from being later canonized by the Holy See. Along with the men of learning, there were missionaries and their missions: St. Fursa at Peronne *(Peronna Scotorum),* St. Fiacre near Meaux, St. Cilian at Wurzburg, and one will find others as far away as Taranto and Kiev. The most famous of all was St. Columban, who "in order to win a

From *A Short History of Ireland* by Roger Chauviré (Old Greenwich, Conn.: The Devin-Adair Company). Copyright ©1956 by The Devin Adair Company. Reprinted by permission. This selection is from pages 31-32 of the 1965 Mentor Book paperback edition (New York: The New American Library).

heavenly fatherland through exile," left Bangor, and having founded Luxeuil in Gaul, was then deported by the wicked King Thierry II; instead of returning to Ireland he escaped, and having left his disciple, St. Gall, at Riechenau, Switzerland, finished his course in what was to be the best-known house of his order, Bobbio, in 615. The Ireland of those days had every cause to be known as "the isle of saints and scholars."

A fact which contributed to her spiritual expansion was that with the coming of Christianity Latin had become her second language. It went near to being the first: a cleric such as Adamnan, for instance, had nothing but disdain for the vernacular tongue, and Gaelic was only able to maintain its position through the love borne it by the *filidh*. But Irish thought was eventually able to find its way to all parts of the known world, under the wing of Latin, the universal language. Ireland took her cultural vocabulary also from Christianity and from Rome, as her words for *priest, book, to write,* etc., testify, and from Rome she also received her form of writing, that lovely *oncial* which has survived in the Gaelic characters down to our own day.

14. Early English Monasticism

Helen Cam

No picture of English life in the Middle Ages is complete that leaves out monasticism. Of all the communities of medieval England the religious were those which were for some eight centuries, most completely taken for granted as an integral part of society. Yet in origin the monks were fugitives from society. . . .

The missionaries who came to Kent in 597 were monks from a Roman monastery, and Pope Gregory who sent them was himself a monk. Within ten years they had founded a monastery in Canterbury, St. Augustine's. Meanwhile the missionaries from Iona had brought another type of monasticism to Northumbria—a monasticism that had come from France to Scotland by way of Ireland and was "more austere, less humane and more eremitical" than the Benedictine. Lindisfarne in the north, Glastonbury in the south, drew their inspiration from Celtic sources. In the pagan and barbarous England of the seventh century the monasteries were the bases

From *England Before Elizabeth* by Helen Cam (New York: Harper & Row, 1950). This selection appears on pages 123-127 of the 1960 paperback edition. Reprinted by permission.

for evangelism, and as Christianity spread, they became the nurseries of the church leaders and the centres of learning, art and culture. Bede tells how the Gregorian chants, the starting point of medieval music, were used and taught in the churches of Kent and Northumbria. Vernacular Christian poetry ... was born at Whitby Abbey; the Lindisfarne gospels are here today to show what the monastic artist of the eighth century could achieve. Bede's writings bear witness to the well-stocked library of Jarrow. The education given in the monasteries was for children dedicated to the religious life by their parents; they learnt their letters and their psalter at the same time, following the monastic routine, though with a milder discipline. Alcuin writing from the court of Charlemagne to his former teachers at York thanks them for their patience and the fatherly care with which they chastised the heedless boy who preferred Vergil to the psalms, and "made a man of him"....

"For nearly three hundred and fifty years," wrote Alcuin in 793 when he heard of the sack of Lindisfarne by the Danes, "have we dwelt in this fairest of lands, and never before has such terror come on England as we are now enduring. St. Cuthbert's church, the most venerable in all Britain, sprinkled with the blood of priests and robbed of its ornaments, has become the spoil of the heathen." This was but the first wave of the tempest that swept away not only the treasures of the monasteries but monasticism itself. Every monastery north and east of the Watling Street was utterly destroyed and, when Alfred became king, those of the south-west that survived no longer observed the Rule, but had become either the property of a layman or the lodgings of married clerics, like Glastonbury when Dunstan was a boy. Alfred, who had read Bede and knew what monasticism could be, founded Athelney as a house for monks and Wilton and Shaftesbury for nuns, but Athelney soon ceased to exist, and if the Rule was kept in the two nunneries it is probable that they and St. Augustine's in Canterbury were alone in preserving the regular life in England in the days when it was being revived on the Continent at Cluny and Fleury.

English monasticism was refounded by Dunstan who, like St. Augustine, was a scholar before he was a saint. Though there were no monks at Glastonbury it was a shrine to which pilgrims came, some of them learned men from Ireland, and the monastic library was still in existence. At first a student and later a member of Athelstan's household, Dunstan found himself called to the religious life, and when King Edmund made him titular abbot of Glastonbury in 943 he set to work to create a true monastery there, collecting disciples and instructing them in the Benedictine Rule. One of his monks, Aethelwold, was given the derelict abbey of Abingdon a year before Dunstan was banished by Edmund's son. In exile Dunstan saw for himself the reformed monasticism in Ghent, and when Edgar recalled him in 957 and made him first Bishop of Worcester and London, and then Archbishop of Canterbury, he was able to bring about a rebirth of monasticism throughout England south of the Humber. The three monk-bishops, Dunstan, Oswald and Aethelwold, with King Edgar's whole-hearted support, refounded ancient abbeys like St. Albans, Peterborough and Malmesbury, and founded new houses like Ramsey and Sherborne.

It was a renaissance not only of the regular life but of the arts and letters associated with it in the past. Dunstan himself was a composer, an illuminator and a metal-worker, who according to the traditions of Abingdon abbey made two great bells for them with his own hands. Aethelwold was also a skilled craftsman, and the monks of Ely were workers in gold and silver. The two Winchester monasteries gave their name to the school of illumination whose exquisite designs and beautiful lettering are as famous as the fresh and lively line drawings inspired by the famous Utrecht Psalter. The same freshness and liveliness appears in the writings of Aelfric, Abbot of Eynsham, not only in the vernacular homilies already mentioned, but in the Latin dialogues which he composed for the children of the monastery. He was clearly a born teacher: to help the boys to acquire a good Latin vocabulary he makes them take the part of different workers—the ploughman, the carpenter, the shoe-maker, the shepherd, the oxherd, the baker, the salter, the cook, the hunter, the fowler, the fisherman and the merchant, and finally pits them against each other in a debate as to which is the most important craft. The boy who impersonated the fisherman must have enjoyed answering the question, "Do you wish to catch a whale?" as much as the merchant who is asked if he sells his goods at the same price for which he bought them overseas, or the cook who says, "Without my craft you would not be able to bite your food." And the boy who is asked "Have you been beaten today?" and replies "No, I was careful," and then to the question "How about the other boys?" replies indignantly "Why do you ask me? I can't tell you our secrets," is no remote figure. We learn also from him that the monastery children, though beating was in the Middle Ages an indispensable instrument of education, were treated tenderly in other respects. "I still eat meat, because I am a child." When he becomes a monk, the Rule will forbid meat-eating.

15. Letter to Abbot Baugulf: The Importance of Monastic Studies

Charlemagne

Charles, by the grace of God, King of the Franks and Lombards and Patrician of the Romans, to Abbot Baugulf and to all the congregation, also to the faithful committed to you, we have directed a loving greeting by our ambassadors in the name of the omnipotent God.

Be it known, therefore, to your devotion pleasing to God, that we, together with our faithful, have considered it to be useful that the bishoprics and monasteries entrusted by the favor of Christ to our control, in addition to the order of monastic life and the intercourse of holy religion, in the culture of letters also ought to be zealous in teaching those who by the gift of God are able to learn, according to the capacity of each individual, so that just as the observance of the rule imparts order and grace to honesty of morals, so also zeal in teaching and learning may do the same for sentences, so that those who desire to please God by living rightly should not neglect to please him also by speaking correctly. For it is written: "Either from thy words thou shalt be justified or from thy words thou shalt be condemned." For although correct conduct may be better than knowledge, nevertheless knowledge precedes conduct. Therefore, each one ought to study what he desires to accomplish, so that so much the more fully the mind may know what ought to be done, as the tongue hastens in the praises of omnipotent God without the hindrances of errors. For since errors should be shunned by all men, so much the more ought they to be avoided as far as possible by those who are chosen for this very purpose alone, so that they ought to be the especial servants of truth. For when in the years just passed letters were often written to us from several monasteries in which it was stated that the brethren who dwelt there offered up in our behalf sacred and pious prayers, we have recognized in most of these letters both correct thoughts and uncouth expressions; because what pious devotion dictated faithfully to the mind, the tongue, uneducated on account of the neglect of study, was not able to express in the letter without error. Whence it happened that we began to fear lest perchance, as the skill in writing was less, so also the wisdom for understanding the Holy Scriptures might be much less than it rightly ought to be. And we all know well that, although errors of speech are dangerous, far more dangerous are errors of understanding. Therefore, we exhort you not only not to neglect

From *The Medieval Pageant* by Norton Downs, pp. 67-68. ©1964 by Litton Educational Publishing, Inc. By permission of Van Nostrand Reinhold Company. Originally published in *De litteris colendis* (Philadelphia: University of Pennsylvania Translations and Reprints, 1899) Vol. VI, No. 5.

the study of letters, but also with most humble mind, pleasing to God, to study earnestly in order that you may be able more easily and more correctly to penetrate the mysteries of the divine Scriptures. Since, moreover, images, tropes and similar figures are found in the sacred pages, no one doubts that each one in reading these will understand the spiritual sense more quickly if previously he shall have been fully instructed in the mastery of letters. Such men truly are to be chosen for this work as have both the will and the ability to learn and a desire to instruct others. And may this be done with a zeal as great as the earnestness with which we command it. For we desire you to be, as it is fitting that soldiers of the church should be, devout in mind, learned in discourse, chaste in conduct and eloquent in speech, so that whosoever shall seek to see you out of reverence for God, or on account of your reputation for holy conduct, just as he is edified by your appearance, may also be instructed by your wisdom, which he has learned from your reading or singing, and may go away joyfully giving thanks to omnipotent God. Do not neglect, therefore, if you wish to have our favor, to send copies of this letter to all your suffragans and fellow-bishops and to all the monasteries. (And let no monk hold courts outside of his monastery or go to the judicial and other public assemblies. Farewell).

16. Monastic Tasks Require Certain Studies

R. W. Southern

At the beginning of our period, the continuity of organized study with few exceptions (among which the most important was medicine, with its long tradition of study at Salerno) depended on the existence of monasteries and other collegiate bodies such as the cathedral churches. The Benedictine monasteries stand out among all these bodies as the inheritors of a mature and well-ordered tradition. Elsewhere there were perhaps greater possibilities of development, precisely because purposes were less clearly defined and habits less distinctly formed. But we must start with the monasteries.

[With]...the complex round of church services which was developed in the monasteries during the tenth and eleventh centuries...the arrangement of these services raised many difficulties, which required a varying

From *The Making of the Middle Ages* by R. W. Southern (New Haven: Yale University Press, 1953). Reprinted by permission. This selection is from pages 185-88 of the 1967 paperback edition.

degree of learning for their solution. The time was long past when the ordering of the church year had been a matter which called for a high degree of technical skill and scientific knowledge: the main task of calculating in advance the occurrence of Easter had long been accomplished, and the results digested in the form of "perpetual calendars," with which each church would be supplied. But, in detail, much remained to be done, especially as the number of saints' days observed by special forms of service grew rapidly, and the taste for elaboration in liturgical matters became more widely shared. Apart from the task of writing the necessary books for these elaborate services, itself a work of high skill and scholarship, there was a demand for original compositions—for saints' lives, hymns, antiphons, the arrangement of suitable lectionaries, and so on. And there was the equally important task of setting the words to music. In all this, there was great scope for local talent and learning. No two monasteries were alike and even those which started more or less alike soon developed wide differences of practice. Hence, throughout Europe, sparsely in the tenth century, but in increasing numbers throughout the eleventh, there were in the monasteries men, perhaps of no more than local fame, whom the ever-increasing elaboration of Church services had made into historians, prose writers, poets and composers.

This was work which might well occupy the best talent in a monastery, and if the products of all this activity appear to us very much on a level of mediocrity, it appeared otherwise to contemporaries: they rated these compositions among the notable achievements of their time. Orderic Vitalis, for instance, found room in the midst of his great History to commemorate the artists and authors who were responsible for the service books which he and his fellow-monks of St. Evroul handled every day. Looking back to the time of Abbot Osbern (1061-6)—at least half a century before the time when he was writing—he records the names of five or six men whose products were part of his daily life. There was Witmund, a scholar and musician, who had written antiphons and responses to go with the Legend of St. Evroul. Then there was Arnulf, the author of the Legend or series of Lessons for the patronal Feast. He had been precentor of Chartres and a pupil of the famous Bishop Fulbert, and he had not only written the words but taught the manner of chanting them to two monks whom the abbot sent to Chartres for the purpose. There was also Rainald the Bald who had composed the response in praise of the Lord, which the monks used at Vespers, as well as seven antiphons which (says Orderic) you will find in the Antiphonar of St. Evroul; and there was Roger of Le Sap who was the author of several hymns in honour of the patron saint of the monastery. This passage in Orderic shows well the co-operative activity and the combination of literary, poetical and musical gifts which lay behind the rich solemnities of monastic life. These activities required a foundation of learning, and they encouraged the growth of centres where this learning could be had; they brought this rather obscure Norman monastery—like many others—in touch with the great school of Chartres which owed its fame to Bishop Fulbert.

There were other tasks which kept the monastic communities constantly alive to the world of learning—even, for example, the humble task of seeing that the services began at about the right time. There were no clocks, the times of the services varied with the seasons, and in the early morning at least the sequence was so rapid that any considerable miscalculation would cause a grave interruption of the monastic day. The problem required careful thought, and the following passage will show one way in which it was solved:

> On Christmas Day, when you see the Twins lying, as it were, on the dormitory, and Orion over the chapel of All Saints, prepare to ring the bell. And on Jan. 1st, when the bright star in the knee of Artophilax (i.e., Arcturus in Bootes) is level with the space between the first and second window of the dormitory and lying as it were on the summit of the roof, then go and light the lamps.

This comes from the instructions for the night-watchman at a monastery near Orleans in the eleventh century. The monastery must have had someone watching the stars in a more than casual way. He knew their names, their courses, the times of their rising and setting, he could distinguish between the planets and the fixed stars. He had the elements of a simple cosmology. All this required study and teaching. It was not much, but it was by such small things that contact was maintained with the stock of ancient learning, and a curiosity to know more was born.

Another science which made its way forward rapidly in the eleventh century under the pressure of daily needs—this time as much secular as religious—was the science (or practice, it would be perhaps more accurate to say) of arithmetic. The only numerals known in the West at the time when our story starts were Roman numerals, and the inconvenience of doing complicated sums in these numerals will be appreciated by anyone who tries to add £ mcmlxxxvii xixs. ivd. to £ mmcccxcix ivs. xid. Yet monasteries as well as kings had estates which brought in large revenues, and bailiffs who presented accounts not above suspicion. There was urgent need for the development of some device which would make calculation easy, and many heads in the eleventh century were occupied with the problem. Gerbert had made a start in reintroducing to the West the study of the ancient calculating board known as the abacus. He and his successors spent a great deal of energy in working out the complicated processes of multiplication and division with the aid of this board. It had the charm of a scientific toy as well as the promise of usefulness. When abbot Odilo of Cluny lay dying in 1049, we are told that he turned to the monastery's expert on the abacus and asked him to calculate the number of masses he had celebrated during his long abbacy. But the machine had sterner uses: by the early twelfth century in England it had given its name to that session of the king's court which became the first Department of State. The Exchequer, so-called from its abacus or chequer cloth, was the centre of the most relentless financial system in Europe.

It is sometimes difficult to realize how much effort was needed to reconstitute the bodies of knowledge such as those of astronomy and arithmetic as they had been known in the ancient world. It was not a question of going beyond the ancients—the impulse to "research," in the sense of extending the boundaries of scientific knowledge, was only faintly stirring even in the twelfth century—but simply to learn what had been known, and what the world had since lost, was a stupendous task, demanding the labours of many scholars through the whole course of our period. The regaining of this ground in the eleventh century was not specially a task of monastic scholarship, though it was one in which Benedictine scholars played a large part. Partly the needs of their daily life, partly the urge to conserve and to restore, which lay behind so much of the Benedictine achievement throughout the centuries, made the monasteries centres for the accumulation of scientific information on which the work of later scholars could be based.

17. The Horarium of Medieval Monasteries

Dom David Knowles

The monks and children of the cloister slept in a common dormitory, wearing by night the habit, without the scapular. Rising a little after two, the monks proceeded to choir in their night shoes, recited certain prayers, and then waited while the children entered and repeated the same prayers. The fifteen gradual psalms were then recited, followed by Nocturns (or, as they are now called, Matins) and prayers for the royal house. Then, after a short interval, Matins (the modern Lauds) were begun, perhaps about five o'clock, and were followed by various prayers, and by Lauds of All Saints and of the dead. Prime followed immediately if the day had already dawned, otherwise there was a wait till the light came. This, a reasonable procedure in southern France and Italy, where the rising of the sun varies

From *The Monastic Order in England* by Dom David Knowles (London: Cambridge University Press, 1940; 2nd ed. 1963), pp. 450-51. Reprinted by permission.

less, must have led to inconvenient periods of waiting in England. After Prime came three psalms, followed by the seven penitential psalms, litanies and prayers. If Prime began at six, the whole cannot have ended before a quarter to seven at the earliest. From thenceforward till eight o'clock was a time for reading in the cloister, and perhaps for the private Masses of such as were priests; at eight the monks returned to the dormitory, washed, and put on their day shoes; they then returned to choir for Terce and the morrow Mass. This would have ended a little before nine; it was followed immediately by the chapter, at which a spiritual conference was often given, and faults confessed and punished; it closed with five psalms for the dead. The end of chapter would have come between half-past nine and ten; next came a long stretch of work, manual, intellectual or artistic, lasting till about half-past twelve, when Sext was recited, with other prayers, followed by the sung High Mass. Then, while the community remained in choir, the servers and readers of the refectory broke their fast with a small quantity of bread and beer; when they returned to the church, None was recited, and then all went to dinner, at about two o'clock or a little later. Dinner was followed by the second long period of reading, from a little before three till about five. Then came Vespers, and Vespers and Matins of the dead, after which the monks put on their night shoes and performed the Maundy. Next, after a drink in the refectory, there was a short public reading in choir, followed by Compline, and at a little before seven they retired to the dormitory.

It will be seen at once that there was very little time during the day which was not occupied by liturgical or community duties of one kind or another. The only times for private reading or work were an hour in the early morning, some three hours between chapter and Sext, and something over two hours in the afternoon. Even this average of five hours, which on some ferial days may have been increased, must often in practice have been greatly curtailed, both by the elaborations of chant and ceremonial on feast days and by the numberless pieces of necessary personal business to be done by each individual, to say nothing of conversations. It is, indeed, quite impossible to calculate the time which was occupied by the ceremonies and chant, sung lessons and responds, "farced" Common and Proper of the Mass, and the rest. At Cluny and the greater Cluniac houses we know from first-hand evidence that on all feasts (and feasts were of extremely frequent occurrence) partically the whole day was filled up,* and the manuscripts of chant which remain, even those which date from before the Conquest, and the elaborate regulations of Lanfranc's *Statuta*, show that the greater houses, at least, practised an extremely rich liturgical life.

*Editor's Note:
Joan Evans provides an excellent account of the complexities surrounding Cluniac feast days in her work, *Monastic Life at Cluny*, pp. 82-85 of the 1968, Archor Books, edition.

18. Sign Language from the Monastery of Syon

Abbess—Make the sign for age, and also for a woman.

Aged—Draw down thy right hand straight over thy hair and over thy right eye.

Ale—Make the sign of drink and draw thy hand displayed before thine ear downward.

Bed—Make the sign of a house and put thy right hand under thy cheek, and close thine eyes.

Bedes—Fumble with thy thumb upon the forefinger in manner of parting of beads in prayer.

Book—Wag and move thy right hand in manner as thou shouldest turn the leaves of a book.

Bread—Make with thy two thumbs and two forefingers a round compass. And if thou wilt have white make the sign thereof (of white) and if brown touch thy cowl sleeve.

Butter or other Fats—Draw thy two right upper fingers to and fro on thy left palm.

Candle—Make the sign for butter with the sign for day.

Cheese—Hold thy right hand flatways in the palm of thy left.

Church—Make the sign of a house, and after make a benediction.

Chiming—Make a sign as if ye smote with a hammer.

Cloister—Make a round circle with your right forefinger toward the earth.

Clothe—Rub up and down the ends of all thy right fingers upon thy left.

Cold—Make the sign of water trembling with thy hand or blow on thy forefinger.

Drink—Bow thy right forefinger and put it on thy nether lip.

Eggs—Make a token with thy right forefinger upon thy left thumb to and fro as though thou shouldest peel eggs.

Eating—Put thy right thumb with two forefingers joined to thy mouth.

Enough—Close thy fist together and hold up thy thumb, and this may serve for *I know it well.*

Fish—Wag thy hand displayed sideways in manner of a fish tail.

Girdle—Draw the forefingers of either hand round about thy middle.

Glass—Make the sign of a cup with the sign of red wine.

Hot—Hold the side of thy right forefinger fast into thy mouth closed.

I wot never—Move easily the fingers of thy right hand, flatways and from thee and it serveth for *nay.*

Incense—Put thy two fingers into thy two nostrils.

From *Life in the Middle Ages* by George Gordon Coulton (Cambridge: Cambridge University Press, 1967) Part IV, pp. 322-24. Reprinted by permission.

Keeping—Put thy right hand under thy left armhole.

King—Put all thy finger-ends closed together on thy forehead.

Man—Put and hold thy beard in thy right hand.

Mass—Make the sign of a blessing.

Mustard—Hold thy nose in the upper part of thy right fist and rub it.

Red colour—Put thy forefinger to the red place of thy cheek.

Ringing—Make a token with thy fist up and down as thou shouldest ring.

Salt—Fillip with the right thumb and forefinger over the left thumb.

Saucer—Make a round circle in thy left palm with thy right little finger.

Silence—Put thy forefinger sideways to thy mouth and draw it up and down.

Sleeping—Put thy right hand under thy cheek and forthwith close thine eyes.

Text or Pax—Kiss the back of thy left hand, with a cross on thy breast with thy right thumb.

Vinegar—Make the sign of wine and draw thy forefinger from thine ear to thy throat.

Washing—Rub thy right hand flatways upon the back of thy left hand.

Water—Join the fingers of thy right hand and move them downward droppingly.

19. The Tonsuring and Life of the Oblate

Custumal of the Abbey of Bec

When any boy is offered for the holy Order, let his parents bring him to the altar after the Gospel at Mass; and, after the Cantor hath offered as usual, let the boy also make his offering. After which let the Sacristan take the offering, and let the parents, drawing near, wrap the boy's right hand in the altarcloth. Then, having kissed it thus enveloped, let them give it into the hands of the priest, who shall receive the boy and make the sign of the cross over his head. If they wish to make him a monk on that same day, let the Abbot bless his crown, saying: *Let us pray, beloved Brethren;* then let him pour holy water on his head and, making the sign of the cross over it, crop his hair with the shears round his neck. While the boy is being shorn, let the Cantor begin the antiphon, *Thou art He Who wilt restore,* the Psalm *Preserve me, O God* (another antiphon is *This is the generation*

From *Life in the Middle Ages* by George Gordon Coulton (Cambridge: Cambridge University Press, 1967), Part IV, pp. 98-101. Reprinted by permission.

and the Psalm *The earth is the Lord's*); then let him pray, *Grant, we beseech Thee, Almighty God*, then let the Abbot bless his cowl, saying the prayer, *Lord Jesu Christ, by Whom the garment*. After this aspersion and benediction, let the boy be stripped of his clothes, and the Abbot say, as he strips him, *May the Lord strip thee;* then let him clothe him in the cowl and say, *May the Lord clothe thee,* and say over him as a prayer, *Lord, be present at our supplications.* . . . When the boy be come to the age of reason, let him make his profession after the same order as the other monks, except for the benediction of the cowl, which he hath already received as an Oblate. . . .

At Nocturns, and indeed at all the Hours, if the boys commit any fault in the psalmody or other singing, either by sleeping or such-like transgression, let there be no sort of delay, but let them be stripped forthwith of frock and cowl, and beaten in their shirt only . . . with pliant and smooth osier rods provided for that special purpose.

And because, so long as the Abbot is in his bed in the dormitory, none may make the sound whereby the Brethren are awakened to rise in the early morning . . . therefore the Master of the Boys should rise very softly and just touch each of the children gently with a rod, that he may awake from sleep; then let them rise as quickly as possible, and, leaving the dormitory, wash and comb and say their prayers. . . .

Let the masters sleep between every two boys in the dormitory, and sit between every two at other times, and, if it be night, let all the candles be fixed without on the spikes which crown the lanterns, that they may be plainly seen in all that they do. When they lie down in bed, let a master always be among them with his rod and (if it be night) with a candle, holding the rod in one hand and the light in the other. If any chance to linger after the rest, he is forthwith smartly touched; for children everywhere need custody with discipline and discipline with custody. And be it known that this is all their discipline, either to be beaten with rods, or that their hair should be stoutly plucked; never are they disciplined with kicks, or fists, or the open hand, or in any other way. . . .

When they wash, let masters stand between each pair at the lavatory. . . . When they sit in cloister or chapter, let each have his own tree-trunk for a seat, and so far apart that none touch in any way even the skirt of the other's robe . . . let them wipe their hands as far as possible one from the other, that is, at opposite corners of the towel. . . .

If any of them, weighed down with sleep, sing ill at Nocturns, then the master giveth into his hand a reasonably great book, to hold until he be well awake. . . . Nor doth one ever speak to the other except by his master's express leave, and in the hearing of all who are in the school. . . . When there is in the refectory a loving-cup of piment or other drink, then the

refectorer-master, if he be of mature age and manners, may let the boys
hold out cups and pour them out some drink.... One reporteth whatsoever he knoweth against the other; else, if he be found to have concealed
aught of set purpose, both the concealer and the culprit are beaten.... [At
Matins] the principal master standeth before them with a rod, until all
are in their seats, and their faces well covered. At their uprising likewise,
if they rise too slowly, the rod is straightway over them. After Matins, when
they are to sleep again, if it be not yet dawn, then the master standeth
before them as they take off their clothes, with a rod in his right hand and
a candle in his left, and they are quickly in their places.... In short, that I
may make an end of this matter, meseemeth that any king's son could
scarce be more carefully brought up in his palace than any boy in a well-
ordered monastery.

20. The Chapter Teaches the Wayward Monk

Joan Evans

The Chapter was usually held after the morning Mass, in the chapter-
house. In the time of Abbot Hugh this was forty-five feet long and thirty-
four feet wide, lit by seven windows, with three rows of seats all round.
The Abbot presided, seated on his throne. Only the brethren had the right
to be present, though the Abbot might exceptionally admit a distinguished
stranger. After prayer and the reading of a chapter of the Benedictine Rule
(whence the assembly took its name), or the giving of a homily on a feast-
day, the Chapter proceeded to business: the admission of novices, the
expulsion of an unworthy monk, the punishment of sin, the exchange or
leasing of properties, the borrowing of money, the acceptance of gifts, the
reading of obituary rolls, and, exceptionally, the revision of the statutes.
The monks were free to express their opinion on any matter, provided it
was given with humility, but they might not argue with the Abbot; he in
his turn had to listen to them and consider their views, but was free to act
in opposition to them.

At the Chapter the Abbot accused the brethren of any public sin, and
dealt with any secret fault that had been confessed to him privately. The
culpable monk came in with his arms outside the sleeves of his woollen

From *Monastic Life at Cluny* by Joan Evans (London: Oxford University Press, 1930).
Reprinted by permission. This selection is from pages 85-87 of the 1968 edition (Hamden,
Conn.: Archon Books).

robe, ready to receive his punishment; when the moment for justice came, he rose and asked pardon once and once only; but each time a new accusation was brought he had to ask pardon afresh. If he was convicted of a venial sin the Abbot ordered him to be beaten with a rod. After his chastisement he had to remain prostrate before the altar during the services, shut out from participation in the rites, excluded from the common table, until one of the brothers came from the Abbot to whisper in his ear, "You are absolved." If his sin was more serious—drunkenness, anger, swearing, quarrelling, calumny, pride, envy, covetousness, the possession of private property, perjury, absence from the monastery precincts without leave, malingering, speech with a woman, or other grave dereliction of the Cluniac rule—the culprit had to stand at the chapter-house door barefoot, his scapular and cape off and folded under his left arm, his robe undone, a bundle of rods in his right hand. When allowed to approach, he laid his garment and the rods on the floor, and prostrated himself to ask pardon. Then he was chastised until the Abbot said, "It is enough"; went out and put on his garments; returned and abased himself once more. When the Abbot bade him go, he went to the place assigned as his prison, where he remained alone. During the offices and regular hours he had to stand at the church door, his face hidden by his cowl, until the Psalms began, and then had to abase himself on the pavement until the last brother had left the church. He had to hear the two daily Masses from a corner of the chapterhouse; and during the Chapter had once more to prostrate himself on the ground. The monk who brought his food might not speak to him; the culprit's only speech was with the brethren the Abbot sent to him to reason with him and exhort him. These, when they were assured of his penitence, asked pardon for him in Chapter. If it was granted, he was once more admitted, once more chastised, and after prostrating himself to ask pardon before each one of the brethren, was readmitted on sufferance to the community. He had the last place in church, refectory, and dormitory; he was not admitted to communion or to the kiss of peace; he was not on the roster for reading aloud. He might, however, perform baser duties— act as cook, and wash the feet of the brethren. He had to ask pardon after every office and each daily Chapter; until finally, after an exhortation from the Abbot, he was reinstated. Then, lest any pride should be encouraged among the brethren who had not thus sinned, all bowed before him.

If a grave sin had been committed in the presence of laymen it was publicly punished, and the culprit was beaten in the open space before the narthex of the church. For a venial sin so committed the culprit had to stand barefoot and bareheaded at the door of the church on Sunday morning, when all the citizens came to church, with a servant standing beside him to answer their questions concerning his misdeeds.

21. The Scriptorium

Dom David Knowles

Throughout the early Middle Ages, as is well known, the copying of manuscripts was the fundamental claustral employment of the black monks: that is to say, it was the one regular work which all were capable of performing, and which all did in fact perform unless or until they were transferred to some other form of activity. The boys of the cloister, and at a later period the novices, were instructed in all the technical details of the preparation of ink and parchment, and trained to follow with exactitude the particular form of script common at the time, and in due course were given a fixed task of copying to carry through.

The proportion of those actually engaged on this work varied from period to period. In the first decades of the revival under Dunstan, and again during the first decades after the Norman plantation, when the monasteries were devoted to a very intense intellectual effort, and when this and the ever-growing number of monks created a lively demand for books of every kind, the writing of manuscripts must have occupied the time and energies of a very large fraction of the total monastic population. When, on the other hand, numbers dwindled, or when, as in the later twelfth century, administrative duties absorbed so much of the energies of the monks, the task of copying books no doubt fell solely upon the young monks and a few incapable or not desirous of other employment.

The straightforward hack-work of writing was, however, only one of the departments of the scriptorium. Above it was the more careful writing of Bibles and service-books and the picking out of initial and capital letters in gold or colours; above this again, and the province of those with gifts purely artistic, was the painting and illumination of designs and miniatures; a corresponding occupation of those with exceptional literary talent was the composition and transcription of original work, or the compilation of a chronicle. At the head of all was the precentor, for in origin the chief business of writing had been concerned with books for the choir and altar; it was his duty to assign the work to be done and to provide the necessaries with which to do it, though it is natural to suppose that the senior monks pursued lines of their own, and had under them small groups of the younger.

In epochs of expansion the need for the multiplication of books was very great, and especially of service-books for the Office, Chant and Mass, and of Bibles for use in the choir and refectory; however solidly bound,

From *The Monastic Order in England* by Dom David Knowles (Cambridge: Cambridge University Press, 1963), pp. 518-22. Reprinted by permission.

these would often need renewing if in constant use. There was, besides, a need for the commonest text-books of instruction for the children, and when, after the Conquest, all transactions were recorded by charter and almost all official letters were both carefully written and copied, the routine work of this kind, and the compilation of cartularies and registers, implied a steady output of manuscript volumes. All the evidence goes to show that the diffusion of certain types of book at different periods was very rapid and widespread; thus Bibles and Gospels containing the Continental text and based on a Winchester tradition, and all written within a few years of the entry of the monks into the Old and New Minsters, are known to have been soon in the possession of many of the newly founded monasteries. Under Lanfranc, Bibles and texts of canon law were broadcast, and a little later there was great activity in the writing of large and sumptuously illuminated Bibles; later still, shortly after the death of Becket, and due in part to his influence and that of his biographer, the monk of Christ Church, Herbert of Bosham, the scholastic text of the Scriptures, together with the Glosses of Peter the Lombard and of the school of Anselm of Laon, was diffused throughout the monastic body. The researches of specialists have already shown how often the impulse to a particular method or pursuit came from a single centre, and how often books of the same family can be shown to derive from a common ancestor and from a single scriptorium or school of illumination, and without question further investigation will identify more and more of such centres of intellectual life.

Where the demand for books was great it was sometimes necessary to add the work of paid scribes to that of the monks. Paul of St. Albans, faced with the necessity of building up a collection of books for a community of English monks unable to write, or at least unable to write script that would satisfy a Norman, employed paid labour; thirty years later Faricius of Abingdon (1100-17), who was responsible for a great increase in the numbers of his abbey, imported scribes for the servicebooks, while apparently reserving for the monks the transcription of theological and medical works. Later, perhaps owing to the numerous other occupations which drew the monks off from the work, almost every great abbey had one or more permanent writers with a fixed corrody; it is possible that these executed much of the purely routine and secretarial writing of the house.

The training in writing demanded of the learner an exact conformity to the style of hand current at the time; all individuality was excluded, so much so, indeed, that at the period when the culture of western Europe was most homogeneous during the first half of the twelfth century, not only the personal, institutional and regional individuality of the scribe disappeared, but even traces of national influence distinguishing England

and France are very rare, and the differences of hand between Citeaux and Durham are often so small as to be hard to detect.

At the revival under Dunstan the formal Carolingian minuscule came into the monasteries of England, and gradually displaced the pointed English hand. The latter was retained for the native language till the Conquest, though it became firmer and more square under the influence of the foreign script which was used for all liturgical and Latin writing. With the Conquest the entry of the Continental minuscule was complete; in the early days a special variety of this, radiating from Canterbury, was common in the monasteries. Perhaps Lombardic in origin and brought north by Lanfranc, it certainly came to England from Bec under the influence of the archbishop; it has been called the "prickly" style on account of the many sharp and elongated points on the letters, and is usually found together with a peculiar shade of colour in the decoration. In time, however, all such peculiarities tended to disappear, and the typical style of the twelfth century was evolved in France and England. This, which was largely the product of the scriptoria of the black monks, is probably the most exact and beautiful form of writing that has ever existed as common property to be used for all purposes. The scribes throughout north-western Europe produced work of almost incredible regularity and perfect legibility, in which contractions were few and clearly indicated and every letter was formed separately. The writing was never suffered to deteriorate, whatever the subject-matter, and charters and cartularies of the time are as beautifully and clearly written as service-books or Malmesbury's autograph of his own work, so much so that the reader takes the excellence of the calligraphy for granted much as he would the clearness of modern print, and is only reminded of the quality of the work when he turns to a page added to the same volume in a hand of the fourteenth or fifteenth century. In England especially this style attained a perfection unrivalled in other countries, and the work of the great monastic scriptoria supplies almost all the surviving examples. As the century wore on, the absolute uniformity tended to disappear; together with a general tendency to a smaller writing, and with the beginnings of a "Gothic" appearance, minute pecularities of the individual schools appear, and in the thirteenth century it becomes possible to attribute a book to Canterbury or St. Albans from considerations of calligraphy alone.

The production of books included their binding. This at first was elaborate only in the case of the books for the church, the most precious of which were encased in ornamental bindings, enriched with metals and gems, which were the work of artist craftsmen. Later, binding in thick parchment or vellum, or in boards covered with leather, became general for all books.

The work of writing was normally done in the north walk of the cloister: the walk, that is, that lay nearest to the church. If it happened, as at Christ Church and elsewhere, that the church lay to the south of the cloister garth, the walk of the cloister against the building was still used as the workplace of the monks, though the north aspect must have made it both cold and dark. References to the cold, and to the impossibility of working in winter, are not wanting; in pre-Conquest days, as has been seen, work was done in the room where there was a fire, and it is difficult to suppose that this practice was abandoned so long as the cloisters had no glass. At St. Albans there is mention of a special room built as a scriptorium, and such may have been the case elsewhere. Later, when the windows were glazed and wooden carols were provided, a walk with a southern aspect, in the lee of a great church, would not often have been intolerably cold; the first mention of carols is in the thirteenth century, but they may have existed towards the end of the twelfth.

22. Reading at Cluny

Joan Evans

The reading of books was a part of the daily life of the monastery, and brought into its tradition an element of literary culture. According to the Benedictine Rule the monks read in the cloister from the fourth to the sixth hour between Easter and October, and after Sext might either read in the cloister or rest on their beds. In the short winter days there was only time for an hour's reading; but with Lent the time was again increased. On Sundays reading was permitted at any time between the offices and meals.

At Cluny, besides private reading, there was much reading aloud both in church, refectory, and chapter-house. At Septuagesima, Genesis was begun for the night office, and finished in a week; Exodus followed at Sexagesima, and it and the succeeding books of the Bible were read in both church and refectory, so that the first eight books of the Old Testament were finished by Ash Wednesday. Augustine on the Psalms was read at Nocturns during Lent; the Prophecies of Jeremiah in the first days of Holy Week; part of the Acts of the Apostles during the octave of Easter; Revelation and the Epistles in the fortnight following. The Acts were continued from Ascen-

From *Monastic Life at Cluny* by Joan Evans (London: Oxford University Press, 1930). Reprinted by permission. This selection is from pages 98-102 of the 1968 edition (Hamden, Conn.: Archon Books).

sion to Whitsun, but as the nights were getting shorter less was read at Nocturns and more in the refectory. The books of Kings, the Song of Solomon, the books of Job, Tobit, Judith, Esther, Esdras, and Maccabees were read during the summer. In November with lengthening nights more was read at Nocturns. Ezekiel lasted until Martinmas; Daniel, the twelve minor prophets, and Gregory's commentary on Ezekiel were read between then and Advent. During Advent, Isaiah was read, together with the epistles of Pope Leo on the Incarnation, and the Commentary of Augustine. After Christmas came the Epistles of St. Paul, with Chrysostom's treatise on the Epistle to the Hebrews if there was time for it. At the Chapter part of the Benedictine Rule was read and commented on every morning, and every evening there was more reading, generally from the *Collationes* of the Fathers, the study of which St. Benedict had recommended to all those who would seek perfection.

The library at Cluny was kept in a closet called the *Armarium*, opening off the cloister. A list of some of the books in the time of Odilo includes a remarkable number of books on the Lives and Passions of the Saints. A later and fuller catalogue shows the library to have been unusually rich. Naturally it contained the books needed for the daily life of church and cloister: Old and New Testaments, homilies, sermons, and lives of saints, the works of Gregory, Augustine, and Chrysostom. Its collection of the Fathers was fairly complete: Orosius, Basil, Tertullian, Eusebius, Ambrose, Jerome, Priscian, Isidore, Cassian, Origen, Caesarius, Hilary, Cassiodorus, and their successors the pseudo-Dionysius, Hrabanus Maurus, Walafrid Strabo, Bede, Alcuin, Anselm of Bec, and Lanfranc. It contained copies of all the chief coenobitic and eremitic Rules of early times: Basil, Pachomius, Fructuosus, Faustus, Isidore, and Columban, and Smaragdus' *Diadema Monachorum*, and of the usual grammatical works, Priscian, Donatus, Macrobius, Servius, and Martianus Capella.

Civil and Canon Law were represented by a book of Papal decrees, another of decrees of Church Councils, the Decretals, Theodosius' manual of Roman Law, the Institutes of Gaius, and a copy of the Salic Law. Other books of practical use were Boethius on Arithmetic, Guy of Arezzo on Music, and a treatise on medicaments. The historical section was rich and varied. It naturally included writings concerning Cluny—the works of Odo, Maiol, Odilo and Peter the Venerable, and their lives; the letters of Peter Damian, Fulbert, Bernard of Clairvaux and others—but its scope was much wider than this. It included a history of the Franks, the chronicle of Ado, Archbishop of Vienne, a history of the Vandal and Lombard Church, the *Historia tripartita*, the *Vita Karoli*, the Chronicle of Bishop Friculf, the *Origo et gesta francorum* up to the time of William of Aquitaine, and a history of the Lombards in **seven** books; and a fairly representative collection of classical historians: Livy, Suetonius, Sallust, Josephus, Pompeius Trogus, and a book on the lives and deaths of the Emperors from Augustus to Theodosius. Science was represented by Pliny, Solinus, Vitruvius on Architecture, Serenus on medicine, and the *Physiognomon*. A surprising number of the works of the orators and poets of antiquity was to be found on its shelves: the *Bucolics, Georgics,* and *Aeneid,* with the commentary of Servius; a remarkably complete collection of the works of Cicero; two copies of Horace; Juvenal; three copies of Terence; Ovid, *de arte amatoria* and *de remedio amoris;* Statius; Lucan; Claudianus; Apuleius; the Fables of Avianus; the *Somnium Scipionis;* a life of Alexander of Macedon; the romance of Apollonius of Tyre, and *libri mythologiarum.* Philosophy was represented by Chalcidius' translation of the *Timaeus,* with its commentary, by the *Ten Categories* of Aristotle, by Boethius on the *Consolations of philosophy,* and by a treatise of Philo the Jew.

The Rule of St. Benedict prescribed that each monk should read one book during Lent, and at Cluny books were issued to the brethren at that season by the precentor, who had charge of the library. Every year on the second day of Lent a brother demanded the return of those already issued, and, list in hand, checked those which each monk laid on the table before him. If the book returned had not for any reason been read, pardon had to be asked. The list of books given out in Lent in 1042 or 1043 has survived, and includes, besides theological and devotional works, several books of history—Eusebius, Orosius, Bede, Josephus, and Livy. A later list, that for 1252, includes a herbal, a book of prognostications, a history of the kings of Britain and Jerusalem, a book "de pictura rote," a book on animals, a work in Hebrew, and a book in verse, not otherwise specified. The register of borrowers ends with a list of eleven missing books. Books were lent not only within the monastery but also to other houses of the Order; the list of 1252 shows no less than 128 works to have been so lent. Books were borrowed and lent even outside the Order, but Abbot Hugh made a rule that no book should be so lent except on receipt of an adequate surety.

Naturally such reading as was carried on at Cluny encouraged theological studies. Peter the Venerable has left us a portrait of the monkish theologian in his description of Brother Gregory. He was the one truly happy man that Peter knew; for all his life was passed in theological speculation, and all his being found satisfaction in it. He went round the Cluniac houses working in their libraries, collating texts, discovering difficult questions in order that he might have the pleasure of answering them.

"Wherever the business of the Order calls me," wrote Peter, "in all our houses and even in their darkest corners, I find Gregory with his Sermons, Gregory with his Epistles, Gregory with treatises, with a pile of

books and notes. I see you everywhere, and everywhere in the same sur-
roundings; the lap of your robe is full of books, your knees give way
beneath their weight."

But the library at Cluny gave encouragement not only to theological
studies. Many of the brethren were not altogether unversed in profane
literature, and could profit by the study of the classics. When Abbot Odo
was a canon of Tours he studied Virgil, until he had a dream of a vase
beautiful in form but filled with serpents, which he interpreted as a symbol
of the pernicious doctrines which Virgil poetically expressed; and so re-
nounced him for the study of the Gospels and Prophets. Maiol, again,
studied the classics at Lyons before he came to Cluny; and we are told that
when he was appointed Librarian, "having himself read the philosophers
of old and the lies of Virgil, he no longer desired either to read them himself or to let others do so." Hugh also studied Virgil until his scruples were
aroused. One night, as he fell asleep, he seemed to see a heap of serpents
lying under his head. He woke in horror and could not sleep, until he found
a volume of Virgil under his pillow. Casting it out, he fell asleep, and
awoke convinced of the poisonous nature of poetic fictions.

Such stories in themselves show the charm that the classics had for
Cluniac minds, and it is not surprising that the Cistercians upbraided the
Cluniacs for their classical learning. In the "Dialogue between a Cluniac
and a Cistercian" the Cistercian says: "By your speech, by your quotations
from the poets, I recognize a Cluniac, for you and your brethren take so
much pleasure in the lies of poets, that you read, study, and teach them
even in the hours which St. Benedict has definitely reserved for the reading
of the Scriptures and manual labour." The Cluniac justifies the practice
as a means to an end: "If we read the books of the pagans, it is to make
ourselves perfect in their language, and thus to fit us better to understand
the Scriptures; for in our Order, as you know, the reading of sacred books
and prayer succeed each other without intermission. From reading we pass
to prayer, and from prayer we return to reading."

23. Literary Symbolism: A Monkish Preoccupation

Achille Luchaire

All that is evident from the confused mass is that the minds which compiled it were endowed with a remarkable capacity for abstraction and a curious passion for the most bizarre subtilities. It was a time when they strove to find an allegorical and mystical meaning in every word of the Holy Scriptures—the golden age of subtile paraphrase, of Byzantine commentary. The monk employed in this work treasures of ingenuity and patience. He did not always subtilize in solitude on parchment, for his own pleasure alone. When he was a preacher, as he frequently was toward the end of the twelfth century, he shared with the faithful his refinement of ideas, and the auditor, whether he comprehended or not, went into ecstasies.

Among the innumerable commentaries on the Canticles which the middle ages have bequeathed to us, that of a Cistercian monk, named Thomas, is one of the chief works of allegorical interpretation. This monk already employed symbolism, and the most skilled symbolists of after times doubtless had some difficulty in rising to his level. Each of the expressions of living tenderness, of which the Canticles are full, gives the occasion for a dissertation, according to rule, where the abstractive and analytical mania rages without limit and without check. The nature of the subject and the candor with which the author undertakes the grossest explanations makes citation difficult. One example will suffice.

In the first verse of the Canticle, the wife says to her husband, *Osculetur me osculo oris sui* (Let him kiss me with the kisses of his mouth), and this passionate appeal Thomas the Cistercian explains thus:

> It is the cry of the Jewish nation, which knows that Christ must come into the world, as it has been told by the angels, and by the prophets. This is why, desirous of seeing Him, she cries *Osculetur me,* that is to say, she longs for Christ to come, instruct, and save her. He must not send His angels, patriarchs, or prophets; He must come Himself in person. And what is this kiss which she desires, *osculum ejus?* It is the knowledge which issues from His own lips. Let Him come then, that I may learn from Him what I ought to know.

There follows a very long disquisition on the kiss, of which the author distinguishes four species. Then he even analyzes the kiss, learnedly decomposing it into its physiological elements; finally, comes a study of the

From *Social France at the Time of Philip Augustus* by Achille Luchaire, trans. Edward Benjamin Krehbiel (New York: Henry Holt & Co., 1912). This selection is from pages 190-92 of the 1967 paperback edition (New York: Harper & Row).

diverse ways in which it is given—all defined, subdivided, rigorously classified, and symbolically interpreted. By this one can judge the rest. The
allegorical commentary on the tenth verse is also very interesting, but it
defies translation.

It will suffice to glance over the sermons of the preachers then most in
vogue—the abbot of Sainte-Geneviève, Stephen of Tournai, Absalon, the
abbot of Saint-Victor, the Abbot Adam of Perseigne, and Alain of Lille,
who has been called the "Universal Doctor,"—to discover the current
allegories and the popular symbolisms. They handed them on from pulpit
to pulpit, and the audience heard them over and over, always with pleasure.
. . . The "spiritual chariot" is that which conveys the soul of the just. It has
four wheels: the two front wheels are the love of God and fellowman; the
two rear wheels are the incorruptibility of the body and the integrity of
the soul. In the first wheel the hub is the knowledge of the Lord, the spokes
which radiate from it are meditation, and the tire of the wheel is devotion.
And thus with the other wheels. The axle which joins the back wheels
represents the peace of God, and that joining the front wheels represents
the uprightness of intention. The bullocks which draw the chariot are the
angels yoked to the beam by the bonds of the love of man. In order that
the chariot may not jostle on the stones of the road, it must have before it
the thought of the presence of God, behind it the scorn of the world, to
the left strength of mind in adversity, to the right good use of prosperity.
And whither goes this allegorical chariot? To the celestial Jerusalem. . . .

Scholastic education left an ineffaceable trace on the monk. Instilling
into him from infancy the love for playing on words, of antitheses, of
metaphors, of bad taste, and extravagant allegory, it gave him an intellectual malady which the long reflections in the leisure moments of monastic
life brought to an acute state.

24. Cloistered Havens for the Crippled

Achille Luchaire

Finally, one must add to this diverse category of voluntary and invol-
untary monks all the disinherited of the world, whom infirmities or defec-
tive physique did not permit to lead a normal life. When a father had

From *Social France at the Time of Philip Augustus* by Achille Luchaire, trans. Edward
Benjamin Krehbiel (New York: Henry Holt & Co., 1912). This selection is from pages 222-23
of the 1967 paperback edition (New York: Harper & Row).

crippled children he made them clerics or monks, so that the church was obliged to take steps to avoid becoming merely a vast association of defectives. She required of her priests, canons, and especially of her bishops certain qualifications in the way of health and esthetic appearance, and opposed the admission of persons who had weak constitutions or were subject to ridicule into the sacerdotal body. In a time when bodily strength was so honored and physical beauty so appreciated among the nobles, it was important that the ministers of God should not have a grotesque or repulsive appearance. On principle, then, rules were established on this point, which were, however, often violated: it could not be otherwise. The church was always less particular about the monks, because in theory they would have but little contact with the world, and because infirmities hidden in the depth of the cloister were not likely to arouse laughter or scandal. The monasteries were also the natural refuge of a number of men who, for physical reasons, were not able to lead the hardy existence of a knight and of a number of non-marriageable women. It was a necessity which certain abbots found hard to accept. One of them, Peter Mirmet, a contemporary of Philip Augustus, became abbot in 1161 and was charged with management of the abbey of Andres, near Boulogne-sur-Mer. "On entering the monastery," says a chronicler of the time, "he drew back in horror before the deformity of the band which he was called to lead. Some monks were lame, others were one-eyed or cross-eyed or blind, and others one-armed." A reaction was necessary. During the thirty-two years in which he was abbot, Peter Mirmet refused admittance into his monastery to all persons having any bodily defect. That was, perhaps, going to the other extreme.

25. Worldliness Rather Than Asceticism

Achille Luchaire

...In the time of Philip Augustus, the monks not only found it very convenient and exceedingly profitable to allow laymen to come to the church in multitudes, but they themselves voluntarily left their cloister and went out into the profane world. In spite of canonical prohibitions and the severity of the rules, they were to be seen everywhere, upon every

From *Social France at the Time of Philip Augustus* by Achille Luchaire, trans. Edward Benjamin Krehbiel (New York: Henry Holt & Co., 1912). This selection is from pages 179-82 and 185-87 of the 1967 paperback edition (New York: Harper & Row).

road. Philip of Harvengt, abbot of Bonne-Espérance and a contemporary of Philip Augustus, indignantly complains of it:

> Where is the road, the village, where is the crowded thoroughfare, in which one does not see the monk on horseback? Who is now able to leave his house without stumbling upon a monk? Is there a feast, a fair, or a market-place where monks do not appear? They are to be seen in all assemblies, in all battles, in all tourneys. Monks swarm everywhere that knights assemble for battle. What do they in the midst of the shock of bucklers and the crash of furious lances, and wherefore are they authorized to go out thus and ride about? . . .

. . . monks were employed in politics and business and how princes and kings little hesitated to take them from their cloisters and intrust them with the most diverse missions. They were discreet, clever men, understanding how to do things. The respect which their robes inspired permitted them, more than any others, to go about without fear. As negotiators and as messengers to the court and to the armies, one frequently sees them taking their places in the entourage of the Capetians and the Plantagenets.

. . . Monks were good for everything, and sovereigns imposed upon them. It was not always of their own free will that the monks left the monastery to journey afar in a time when long journeys were as uncomfortable as perilous. . . .

The wandering foot *(acedia)*, that incurable spleen, that mystical conception which all preachers condemned, is only a passionate desire to leave the monastic prison to live at large and at liberty among people who act and talk. One of the most celebrated contemporaries of Philip Augustus, the philosopher and theologian, Alain of Lille, spoke of it in no uncertain terms:

> The *acedia* makes one rebel against the severity of the rule in the cloister. They wish to eat more delicately, to sleep on softer beds, to lessen the watching, to observe the rule of silence less, or even break it entirely. It is this which nourishes vice, and takes the monk away from his abbey. . . .

There are other monks, and they are numerous, who leave the abbey to study in the schools, especially in Paris, where the student life, as we have seen, was not without its charms. These latter gave excellent reasons to justify their absence and their travels: they needed to study medicine, to heal their sick brethren, and law, to conduct the lawsuits of the community with good results. But the monk-scholars soon became legion: so that ecclesiastical authorities became worried, and finally took measures to keep the cloisters from being further deserted. Already the council of Tours, in 1163, had pronounced with severity against them. It prohibited the study

of law and medicine, especially to those who had made profession of monastic life. Orders were given them to repair to their abbeys in two months,
under pain of excommunication, and those who returned should have the
last place among the monks in the choir, in the chapter, in the refectory,
and should lose all hope of promotion to any dignity unless the mercy of
the Holy See disposed otherwise. This prohibition was renewed in 1213
at the council of Paris. And in his famous bull *Super speculam,* 1219,
which prohibited the study of law in the university of Paris, Pope Honorius
III had a very harsh word for those monks who became students: "They
no longer endure," said he, "the monastic silence. They repulse the law of
God which converts souls, that law which they should love more than gold
or precious stones." And why this flood of monks in the great schools?
It is because they liked to mingle with the crowd, to reap the applause of
the vulgar, and to amuse the ladies'-maids, *"ad pedisequas amplectandas."*
It is a pope who says this. To the monks who vainly multiplied objections
and gave plausible reasons to justify their absence in the schools, Pope
Honorius wished to have the penalty, decreed by the council of Tours,
rigorously applied: excommunication without heed of an appeal to Rome.

26. The Study of the Classics in Medieval Monasteries

Jean Leclercq

How were these authors studied, and what procedures were used? By
what channels did they penetrate medieval monastic psychology? There
were three principal ways: the introduction to the authors, commentary or
explanation of the texts, and lastly, copying. No author was taken up
without preparation. This introduction was effected through preparatory
notes on each which were called *accessus ad auctores.* . . .

The *accessus* is a short literary history which takes up for each author
the following questions: the life of the author, title of the work, the writer's
intention, the subject of the book, the usefulness of its contents and, finally, the question as to what branch of philosophy it belongs to. This whole
procedure which was used by the lawyers (both the Canonists and the
civilians), theologians, rhetoricians and philosophers, seems to stem from
a much more elaborate technique for commentaries on the works of

From *The Love of Learning and the Desire for God* by Jean Leclercq, O.S.B., trans. Catherine Misrahi (New York: Fordham University Press, 1961), pp. 144-45; 149-52. Reprinted
by permission. The author's footnotes have been deleted.

Aristotle. In scholasticism, it was also applied to Holy Scripture; it is practically the same as the one used by Peter Lombard in the prologue to his commentary on St. Paul. But the underlying intention which inspires these texts is patristic in origin. St. Jerome, who did not follow the system of the *accessus* in his Prologues to the different books of the Bible, had, however, shaped the direction it was to follow by framing and applying the two postulates on which all this literature rests: optimism with regard to the pagan authors and the necessity of giving them an allegorical interpretation. . . . allegorical interpretation of the texts could be undertaken but on condition that it would not become merely literary history. Unlike the practice of today, these texts were not studied solely as evidence of the past or as dead documents. A practical end was sought: to educate young Christians, future monks, to "introduce" them to Sacred Scripture and guide them toward Heaven by way of *grammatica*. To put them in contact with the best models would, at one and the same time, develop their taste for the beautiful, their literary subtlety, as well as their moral sense. To succeed in this they used practical, not scientific methods: they interpreted. Certainly in the writings of the Fathers and of the medieval monks there is no lack of statements condemning the immorality of certain texts, Ovid's for example; he was known to be dangerous. But once it had been decided to study him, they wished to make him acceptable. There was no difficulty over the things he had said which were right, but as for the rest, he had to be brought into conformity with Holy Scripture in order to safeguard his prestige and authority.

The result of this kind of pedagogy was to set free the consciences of both teachers and pupils with regard to the pagan authors and to develop in all, a power of enthusiasm and the capacity for admiration. It also made possible an amazing contact with ancient literature. The vital use they made of it is something that we can no longer achieve in our times. Ovid, Virgil, and Horace *belonged* to these men as personal property; they were not an alien possession to which to refer and quote with reverence—and with bibliographical references. Medieval men claimed for themselves the right to make the authors conform to usage, to the actual needs of a living culture. Each of these authors was quoted freely and from memory and even without acknowledgement. The important thing was not what he had said or meant, nor what he was able to say in his own time and place, but what a Christian of the tenth or twelfth century could find in him. Wisdom was sought in the pages of pagan literature and the searcher discovered it because he already possessed it; the texts gave it an added luster. The pagan authors continued to live in their readers, to nurture their desire for wisdom and their moral aspirations. Through the *accessus* method, the writers of antiquity were made comprehensible and useful to men who lived in an environment totally different from their own, but who were not resigned to possessing only a bookish, scholarly knowledge of them. The authors had really, in the words of Rhabanus Maurus, been "converted" to Christianity.

GLOSSES

Another component of the method of initiation into the classics was the commentary. Many of the classical texts have come down to us in manuscripts surrounded by scholia, marginal and particularly interlinear glosses, explaining various words and phrases. While the *accessus* was a general introduction to each author and to each work, the gloss is a special explanation of each word of its text.

ORAL COMMENTARY

To the gloss, a written commentary, was added the oral commentary. It was given by the teacher at whose feet a child learned to "read," which means, not merely learning the letters of the alphabet—this had already been the subject of elementary instruction—but understanding the words, learning the rules which determined their use, and understanding the meaning of sentences. What was called *legere ab aliquo,* to "read with" a grammar master, was to listen to him read and explain the texts, to receive his "lessons." His oral explanations were concerned not only, as was the written gloss, with the meanings of the words but with their grammatical forms. He taught how to "decline," that is, to produce the "derived" forms of each word subject to varying inflections in the different cases, numbers, moods and tenses. This *declinatio,* as the ancients understood it, implied both what is called today "declension," and "conjugation." . . . With gifted individuals, this very precise method when practiced under such masters and in such an atmosphere could produce astonishing results: it fixed forever in the pupil's memory the letter of the text studied, and obliged him to make close contact with language at its best; and for that very reason, it taught him not only how to read the ancients but also how to write well. . . .

27. Monastic Studies are Spiritual Exercises

Jean Leclercq

...the monk was expected to have some knowledge of letters and a certain proficiency in doctrine. In the secular schools the *auctores* studied, particularly the poets, are full of mythology, hence the danger which these studies, however necessary, present for Christians. In the monastic school, teaching is concerned mainly — but not exclusively — with the Scripture and its commentaries. Thus the monastic school resembles at once the classical school because of the traditional method of *grammatica,* and the rabbinical school because of the nature of the text to which this method is applied. Furthermore, education is not separated from spiritual effort; even from this viewpoint, the monastery is truly a "school for the service of the Lord," *dominici schola servitii.*

Indeed the one end of monastic life is the search for God. It is clear to anyone who is acquainted with the *Rule* of St. Benedict that monastic life has no other purpose than *quaerere Deum.* In order to obtain eternal life, of which St. Benedict speaks so often as the only end which has any importance, one must become detached from all immediate interests, devoting oneself in silence and in withdrawal from the world to prayer and asceticism. All of the monk's activities, including his literary activity, can have no motivation other than spiritual, and spiritual motives are always called upon to justify all his actions. If, for example, the monk obeys, it is "because he wishes to make progress toward eternal life." According to St. Benedict, monastic life is entirely disinterested; its reason for existing is to further the salvation of the monk, his search for God and not for any practical or social end which, incidentally, is never even mentioned. The *conversatio* of the monk is presumed to be a *conversio* similar to St. Benedict's which entails total renunciation with the intention of pleasing God alone. The whole organization of monastic life is dominated by the solicitude for safeguarding a certain spiritual leisure, a certain freedom in the interests of prayer in all its forms and, above all, authentic contemplative peace.

From *The Love of Learning and the Desire for God* by Jean Leclercq, O.S.B., trans. Catherine Misrahi (New York: Fordham University Press, 1961), pp. 23-24. Reprinted by permission. The author's footnotes have been deleted.

PART IV

The Education of
Craftsmen and Merchants

SPECIALIZED laborers and craftsmen, such as millers, wheel-wrights, coopers, bootmakers, masons, carpenters, and gold-smiths, had practiced their trades during the feudal period of the early Middle Ages, but were usually tied to a particular rural parish, manor, or abbey. Indeed, some of the monks were specialized craftsmen; other monasteries hired local craftsmen to perform those tasks for which none among those cloistered were qualified. Noble-men maintaining fighting forces on their estates also required the services of blacksmiths, armorers, saddlers, and bladesmiths to ready their men for battle.

However, the craftsmen came into their own as feudalism de-clined and the cities began to develop.[1] By moving into the city, the craftsmen were able to be closer to their market (whether they sold finished goods wholesale or retail, or whether they worked on only one part of the manufacturing of finished items—much as the fullers

[1]See Henri Pirenne's *Medieval Cities* for a good analysis of the growth of urban areas.

prepared cloth for use by others such as hatters and clothiers, and the tanners prepared hides for use by shoemakers) and closer to their own source of materials. In short, buying and selling was made easier for the craftsman as he clustered with others of his craft along the same streets and sections of the newly emerging cities.

Paralleling the merchants who had banded together for physical protection from attack along the trade routes and within the confines of the city as well as for setting prices and conditions governing their sales, the specialized craftsmen organized themselves into "gilds" or "corporations" or "companies" or "misteries." The early gilds were composed of two sorts of craftsmen: (1) those who were not only sufficiently skilled, but also sufficiently affluent, to operate independently as "masters," and (2) those known as "journeymen" who were skilled but had to work in the service of a master.

One became a journeyman, and ultimately a master, by demonstrating competence in the technical performance of the craft. Typically this competence was acquired through a period of apprenticeship (usually lasting seven years but varying from as few as two to as many as fifteen years depending upon the complexity of the craft to be learned), in which the neophyte lived with a master and was taught by him all the skills necessary to the craft. Masters were responsible not only for the technical education of their apprentices, but also for their physical well-being and moral instruction. Contracts of indenture in which, for a certain sum of money, the master agreed to train the apprentice and provide him with food and lodging and the apprentice was obliged to work for the master, were drawn between a master and the father of an apprentice. Proof of the acquisition of skilled competence came when the apprentice presented his "master piece"—which was to be the climactic manifestation of all he had learned from his master. Frequently the gild members judged the technical quality of the "master piece" work of a particular apprentice before permitting him to join the fellowship of the organized gild.

As labor became more specialized with the growth of cities and trade, labor organizations or gilds became limited only to masters, with journeymen excluded from membership. (Apprentices had always been so excluded.) Not surprisingly, such a situation led to the economic exploitation of the journeymen (who were, technically speaking, employees) by the masters who employed them, until the journeymen also organized to protect their economic rights.[2]

Craftsmen gilds were not exclusively *economic* associations; the gilds took on social and religious significance as well. Gildsmen would not only drink together and have dinners commonly when apprentices were about to be admitted to the status of "master," but they also acted as burial societies should one of their members perish; they helped to support the widows and orphans of members who died unexpectedly through mishap; not infrequently they hired a chantry priest to sing masses for the souls of their departed members; they acquired "patron saints" and celebrated their feast days; and in addition to decorating churches by donating money or labor, say, for a stained glass window commemorating their craft, they also joined in religious festivals, parades, and the performance of miracle, mystery, and morality plays. The medieval citizen loved pageantry; and gildsmen helped to contribute to that pageantry whenever possible.

Gilds were frequently chartered by royalty or city government, and in their charter specifically enjoined to behave in certain fashions. Cities found it necessary to legislate against gilds, on occasion, in order to protect the health, safety, and purse of the citizenry. Furthermore, the very *in loco parentis* responsibility of the master towards his apprentice occasionally led to suits and court appearances when either master or apprentice failed to fill his side of the contracted bargain.

While all craftsmen required technical training as well as moral education, some were also taught reading, writing, and basic computational skills. This minimal "academic" education, however, would prove to be insufficient for most merchants; consequently, merchants tended to send their sons to school for more formal instruction before teaching them the complexities of buying and investing, profit calculation, monetary systems, weights and measures,

---

[2]P. Boissonnade's discussion of the formation of masters' and journeymen's gilds in his study, *Life and Work in Medieval Europe* (translated by Eileen Power in 1927) is valuable here.

and the trade routes. The gilds of merchants served many of the social, economic, and religious functions performed by the craftsmen's gilds; but typically they did not train apprentices. Merchants did, however, contribute to education not only by their own emphasis upon "lernyng" for themselves and their sons and daughters, but also in their interest—however desultory it might have been—in encouraging the growth of book publishing and book circulation. Moreover, the merchant gilds were frequently the political stronghold of the city, and served as the agencies of city government.

In the selections which follow, the legal chartering of gilds is manifested in a royal grant to London weavers; the social service function of the gilds is indicated by the description of the Holy Trinity of Lynn's customs as well as the ordinances of the whiteleather dressers of London; the relationship between master and apprentice is described by L. F. Salzman and evidence is provided from London of the abuse of apprentices; the conditions under which apprentices prepare their master pieces is discussed; an illustration of the complexity of glassmaking is indicative of the sorts of skills which the apprentice glazier would have to acquire during his training period; and, finally, the moral education of merchants is examined.

28. Royal Grant to the Weavers of London, 1154-1162

Henry II

Henry, by the grace of God, king of England, duke of Normandy and Aquitaine, count of Anjou, to the bishops, justiciars, sheriffs, barons, and all his servants and liegemen of London, greeting. Know that I have granted to the weavers of London to have their gild in London with all the liberties and customs which they had in the time of King Henry, my grandfather. Let no one carry on this occupation unless by their permission, and unless he belong to their gild, within the city, or in Southwark, or in the other places pertaining to London, other than those who were wont to do so in

From *English Historical Documents, 1042-1189*, Vol. II, edited by David C. Douglas and George W. Greenaway. Oxford University Press, New York, 1953. Reprinted by permission.

the time of King Henry, my grandfather. Wherefore I will and firmly order that they shall everywhere legally carry on their business, and that they shall have all the aforementioned things as well and peacefully and freely and honourably and entirely as ever they had them in the time of King Henry, my grandfather; provided always that for this privilege they pay me each year 2 marks of gold at Michaelmas. And I forbid anyone to do them injury of insult in respect of this on pain of 10 pounds forfeiture, Witness: Thomas of Canterbury; Warin fitz Gerold. At Winchester.

29. The Gild of the Holy Trinity of Lynn: Caring for the Bretheren

If any of the aforesaid bretheren shall die in the said town or elsewhere, as soon as knowledge thereof shall come to the alderman, the said alderman shall order solemn mass to be celebrated for him, at which every brother of the said gild that is in town shall make his offering; and further, the alderman shall cause every chaplain of the said gild, immediately on the death of any brother, to say thirty masses for the deceased.

The alderman and skevins of the said gild are by duty obliged to visit four times a year all the infirm, all that are in want, need, or poverty, and to minister to and relieve all such, out of the alms of the said gild.

If any brother shall become poor and needy, he shall be supported in food and clothing, according to his exigency, out of the profits of the lands and tenements, goods and chattels of the said gild.

No born serf or one of such like condition, nor any apprentice can be received, and if any one of such like condition should be received into the said gild, the alderman and his bretheren not knowing it, when it is truly and lawfully proved, such a one shall lose the benefit of the gild.

30. The Ordinances of the White-Leather Dressers of London — 1346

In honor of God, of Our Lady, and of all saints, and for the nurture of tranquillity and peace among the good folks, the megucers, called white-

From *Translations and Reprints from the Original Sources of European History* by E. P. Cheyney (Philadelphia, n.d.), vol. II, pp. 14-20. This selection is from pages 178-79 of *The Medieval Town* by John H. Mundy and Peter Riesenberg (Princeton: Van Nostrand Co., 1958).

From *Readings in English History Drawn from the Original Sources* by E. P. Cheyney (Boston: Ginn & Co., 1908), p. 211.

tawyers, the folks of the same trade have, by assent of Richard Lacer, mayor, and of the aldermen, ordained the points underwritten.

In the first place, they have ordained that they will find a wax candle, to burn before Our Lady in the church of Allhallows, near London wall.

Also, that each person of the said trade shall put in the box such sum as he shall think fit, in aid of maintaining the said candle.

Also, if by chance any one of the said trade shall fall into poverty, whether through old age or because he cannot labor or work, and have nothing with which to keep himself, he shall have every week from the said box 7*d.* for his support, if he be a man of good repute. And after his decease, if he have a wife, a woman of good repute, she shall have weekly for her support 7*d.* from the said box, so long as she shall behave herself well and keep single.

And if anyone of the said trade shall have work in his house that he cannot complete, or if for want of assistance such work shall be in danger of being lost, those of the said trade shall aid him, that so the said work be not lost.

And if any one of the said trade shall depart this life, and have not wherewithal to be buried, he shall be buried at the expense of their common box. And when any one of the said trade shall die, all those of the said trade shall go to the vigil and make offering on the morrow. . . .

31. The Master-Apprentice Relationship

L. F. Salzman

Apprenticeship was from quite early times the chief, and eventually became practically the only, path to mastership. The ordinances of the London leather-dressers, made in 1347, and those of the pewterers, made the next year, give as alternative qualifications for reception into the craft the completion of a period of apprenticeship, or the production of good testimony that the applicant is a competent workman. A similar certificate of ability was required of the dyers at Bristol, in 1407, even if they were apprentices, but as a rule the completion of a term of apprenticeship was a sufficient qualification. That term might vary considerably, but the custom of London, which held good in most English boroughs, eventually fixed it

From *English Industries of the Middle Ages* by L. F. Salzman (Oxford: The Clarendon Press, 1923), pp. 340-43. Reprinted by permission.

at a minimum of seven years. This would often be exceeded, and we find, for instance, a boy of fourteen apprenticed to a haberdasher in 1462 for the rather exceptional term of twelve years; but in this case the master had undertaken to provide him with two years' schooling, the first year and a half to learn "grammer," and the next half year to learn to write. In the same way a goldsmith's apprentice in 1494 agreed to serve ten years instead of nine provided his master would keep him one year at a writing school. A certain amount of teaching, apart from technical training, was usually stipulated for in indentures of apprenticeship. A weaver at Taunton agreed to give his apprentice "instruction in the language of Britanny," while conversely a London carpenter was allowed "to have home hys prentys tyll he can speke better engleys," to obey the city laws serves as a reminder that the apprentice, not being a full member of the gild, was under the charge of the city authorities to some extent. Indentures of apprenticeship had as a rule to be enrolled by the town clerk, and in London the transfer of an apprentice from one employer to another was not legal unless confirmed by the city chamberlain. Besides having his indentures enrolled, and paying a fee to the craft gild, the apprentice, or rather his friends, had to give a bond for his good behaviour. Masters had the right of correcting their apprentices with the rod, within reason, and the city authorities would have little mercy on such young men as John Richard, who, when his employer wished to chastise him "as reson and comon usage is" for divers offences, "of very malice and cursednesse as an obstinat apprentis to his master" picked up an iron bar and threatened to kill him. The rights of the apprentice, on the other hand, were probably always guarded by a right of appeal to the wardens of his craft: this was certainly the case at Coventry in 1520, the masters of the cappers being obliged to go once a year to all the shops of their craft and call the apprentices before them, and if any apprentice complained three times against his master for "insufficient finding," they had power to take him away and put him with another master. As a master's interest in his apprentice was transferable to another master, so it was possible for an apprentice to buy up the remainder of his term after he had served a portion. He could not, however, be received into his gild as a master until the whole of his term had expired, and although it would seem that he could set up in business by himself, probably he might not employ workmen, and as a rule he no doubt spent the unexpired portion of his term as a journeyman.

The journeymen, working by the day *(journee)*, either with their masters, or in their own houses, as opposed to the covenant servants, who were hired by the year, and lived in their employer's house, constituted the fluid element in the industrial organization, and were composed partly of men who had served a full apprenticeship but lacked funds or enterprise to set up independently, and partly of others who had either served only a brief apprenticeship or had picked up their knowledge of the craft in other ways. Although they were more or less free to work for what employers they would, practically all gild regulations contained a stringent order against the employment of any journeyman who had broken his contract or left his late master without good reason.

32. Abuse of Apprentices, 1371, Recorded in the Plea and Memoranda Rolls of the London Corporation

Thomas and William Sewale, sons of Thomas Sewale of Canterbury, who had been apprenticed by their father to John Sharpe, came into court and complained that their master had been for a long time in Newgate and was unable to instruct them, and that his wife Margery had fed them insufficiently, had beaten them maliciously, and had struck William on the left eye so violently that he lost the sight of that eye, wherefore they prayed the court to be discharged from their apprenticeship. Evidence having been given that the master was in prison and that neither he nor his wife could support the boys, and as it appeared from a corporal examination that they had been cruelly beaten, the court exonerated them altogether from their apprenticeship.

33. Creating a Master Piece

Paul Lacroix

When apprentices or companions wished to become masters, they were called *aspirants,* and were subjected to successive examinations. They were particularly required to prove their ability by executing what was termed a *chef-d'oeuvre.* which consisted in fabricating a perfect specimen of whatever craft they practised. The execution of the *chef-d'oeuvre* gave rise to many technical formalities, which were at times most frivolous. The aspir-

From *Chaucer's World* by Edith Rickert (New York: Columbia University Press, 1948). Reprinted by permission. This selection is from pages 107-8 of the 1962 paperback edition.

From *Manners, Customs and Dress During the Middle Ages and During the Renaissance Period* by Paul Lacroix (London, Bickers & Son, n.d.), pp. 289-90.

ant in certain cases had to pass a technical examination, as, for instance, the barber in forging and polishing lancets; the wool-weaver in making and adjusting the different parts of his loom; and during the period of executing the *chef-d'oeuvre*, which often extended over several months, the aspirant was deprived of all communication with his fellows. He had to work at the office of the association, which was called the *bureau*, under the eyes of the jurors or syndics, who, often after an angry debate, issued their judgment upon the merits of the work and the capability of the workman.

On his admission the aspirant had first to take again the oath of allegiance to the King before the provost or civil deputy, although he had already done so on commencing his apprenticeship. He then had to pay a duty or fee, which was divided between the sovereign or lord and the brotherhood, from which fee the sons of masters always obtained a considerable abatement. Often, too, the husbands of the daughters of masters were exempted from paying the duties. A few masters, such as the goldsmiths and the clothworkers, had besides to pay a sum of money by way of guarantee, which remained in the funds of the craft as long as they carried on the trade.

34. What the Apprentice Glazier Needed to Learn

J. J. Bagley

. . . both London and York had celebrated gilds of glaziers. The medieval glassmaker melted his metal in small iron pots, and had difficulty in producing pieces which were uniform in thickness or much bigger in area than a square foot. To colour the glass he added metallic oxides to the molten mixture. Silver oxide gave him yellow glass, iron compounds different shades of green, copper compounds either blue-green or ruby, and the vagaries of chance unexpected colours, often treasured beyond all others. Pure white glass was rare: most mixes produced a yellow or blue tinge, which the glassmaker could not eradicate, but could increase in intensity by reheating. The artist painted the design on the pieces of coloured glass with paints made from a mixture of ground copper and glass, or, in the later Middle Ages, from various metallic oxides mixed with gum arabic and vinegar. Later artists sometimes covered the pieces of glass with a wash of

Reprinted by permission of G. P. Putnam's Sons from *Life in Medieval England* by J. J. Bagley, pp. 139, 141. Copyright © 1960 by J. J. Bagley.

paint, and then scratched their design on the dried surface. If the basic glass were white or lightly-coloured, this technique allowed more light to enter the building, and the resulting two-colour design made a pleasant contrast from the neighbouring multi-coloured windows.... When the artist had finished his work by whatever process he wished, the glazier then fused the paint into the surface of the glass by reheating and slowly cooling the glass again in an annealing furnace. The many pieces which formed the window had then to be fitted together jig-saw wise on a table, and each piece fastened to its neighbours by strips of lead soldered together and folded over the edges of the glass. Finally, more strips of lead secured the finished window to the iron saddlebars, which the masons had previously tied into the stone work of the window spaces.

35. Moral Education of Merchants' Sons

Sylvia L. Thrupp

The church schools stressed the teaching of virtue along with that of grammar. To the merchant this was of supreme importance; at a pinch, his children could go through life without much knowledge of Latin, but it was essential that they be brought up virtuously, well instructed in bonis moribus. In his mind this referred not only to the inculcation of abstract moral values but also to a training in all those social attitudes that were by convention suited to their role in the community. The two kinds of training had to be interlinked, the one reinforcing the other. This part of the children's education, in the nature of the case, could not be surrendered entirely to priests or to any other schoolmasters, for it was carried on continuously through pressure exercised by all the older members of a household.

In the first place, the child had to learn that the world was organized by authority. Linked, through religious teaching, with the idea of divine authority, this was further impressed upon him by lessons in deference and obedience to elders and superiors, which were taught with rather more rigor than immediate disciplinary ends could always have required. The child's state of subordination, involving liability to corporal punishment,

From *The Merchant Class of Medieval London* by Sylvia L. Thrupp (Chicago: University of Chicago Press, 1948). Copyright ©1948 by The University of Michigan. Reprinted by permission. This selection is from pages 164-67 and 169 of the 1962 paperback edition (Ann Arbor: University of Michigan Press).

was prolonged throughout apprenticeship, the master's part in the matter being set out in the indentures as though chastisement of his charge was a duty rather than a right. Boys who wished to protest against ill-treatment had to prove that they had been beaten more constantly or with more severity than was considered reasonable. Whatever psychological complexities may have lurked in this particular relationship, there was obviously a sense of urgency in the teaching of respect for authority that would have served to give it broad social implications. The boy learned that there were gradations of status and that these had to be accepted.

Along these lines he was gradually led to comprehend his own role as member of a governing and employing class. One of the arts he had to acquire in this capacity, the art of good manners, depended primarily upon a sensitivity to differences in status. The code of good behavior was not elaborate; indeed, it could almost be summed up in the necessity of restraining the temper, especially before inferiors or superiors. Being an avoidance of the sin of anger, this restraint had a moral aspect. It had also the value of bestowing a personal dignity that the merchant felt to be peculiarly fitting to his station. In the presence of superiors, calmness of manner betokened respect; in the presence of inferiors, on the other hand, it symbolized superiority, for loud voices and undignified quarreling in public were typically associated with the lower classes. Any public quarreling among merchants was felt to be a disgrace to their companies. . . .

Self-control before the representatives of authority is here clearly assimilated to that character of prudence and discretion in which the merchant liked to conceive himself; the prudent man is always mindful of the opinion of others. At the same time, respect for authority is viewed in a strongly moral light, for rudeness shows "an unmeeke spirit," that is, a breach of Christian virtue. . . .

In private there was little formality in merchant manners, consciousness of minor differences in status being normally concealed under a jovial friendliness. Use of the French tongue bequeathed an ambiguous intermingling of the terms of love and friendship. Business letters from one merchant to another could begin, "Salut & bon amour Treschier amy. . . ." or "A son tres chier & grant amy—salus & Treschiers amistees. . . .," and members of an intimate circle would be dubbed "good frendes and lovers." Yet the smooth surface would break; it is significant that even the well-haved tailor, Master Derby, would have felt free to give way to his anger in a private interview and bandy what he called plain English. There was little originality in the merchants' language of abuse, which revolved about such points as probity, fortune, intelligence, ancestry, on which they felt themselves to be jockeying for public esteem. "Harlot" was the favorite, most inclusive epithet of insult. . . .

Much of the moral teaching addressed to the young was focused upon the need of making what was considered prudent use of money. The wasteful character was undeserving. A boy would be left a legacy, for example, on condition that he grow up "of good verite and sad governaunce" or that he be "thriving and toward the world and of no riotuose disposition." The same qualities would serve him in good stead when he was seeking a bride with a good dowry, for parents and guardians preferred to intrust these only to promising businessmen. As one draper directed in his will, his daughters were to be married to "suche sadde and discrete persones. . . . as seme convenyent and profitable."

Although thoughts thus tended to gravitate to the making of money, the medieval merchant class does not seem to have generated a gospel of hard work. It was probably the practice to keep apprentices well occupied in waiting upon customers and carrying messages, but there was no great pressure of office work, to harass them, nor were they enjoined to spend all their days on earth at labor.

Nor was there any extreme puritanical ban upon amusement, although there were strong reservations on the score of expense. The love of hunting has been referred to already, and the love of pageantry and theatricals is too well known for comment. Commercialized amusements, however, were looked on with distrust as so many incitements to extravagance, and there was grave concern lest young men grow up in habits of dissipation. . . .

There was a very acute fear of the temptation of gambling. Apprentices were forbidden to play with cards or dice, but these and other forms of gambling retained their fascination. . . .

The discipline that was exercised over apprentices included prohibition of sexual relations. The indentures drawn for a Cirencester boy who was apprenticed to Drew Barentyn, wealthy goldsmith, in 1382, specified that he should not commit fornication either in his master's house or elsewhere, that he should not marry, and that without his master's permission he should not even become engaged. Nor was he to play at tables or chess or other forbidden games or to go to taverns except on business for his master. A tailor brought an apprentice into his company's court to be reproved for the waste of time that was consequent on falling in love; he "used the company of a woman which was to his grete losse and hynderyng for asmoch as he was so affectionate and resorted daily unto hyr," and the drapers punished an apprentice's misconduct with a maidservant by a cermonial flogging in the company hall, inflicted by masked men.

PART V

School and University Education

AFTER a period of florescence during the eighth, ninth, and tenth centuries, the decline of feudalism set in motion a number of events which ultimately culminated in the establishment of universities. Feudalism, an economic system based upon manorial land cultivation with carefully defined social/legal relationships between the workers and the manorial overlords (be they abbots or noblemen), crumbled as mercantilism and craftsmanship created a new urbanized social order. The craftsmen left the fief to move closer to the market areas where they could both sell made goods and buy materials. Cities developed in those areas which had been market sites and the major crossings for inland trade routes and ports for water trade routes. The returning warriors from the Holy Crusades against the Moslem "infidels" in Jerusalem came home bearing silks, spices, and jewels from the Orient. They were not eager to return from such high adventure to the stolid placidity of an agricultural life, and thus they further aided the development of cities.

Much as the manor estates and monasteries had needed to defend themselves from the barbarian hordes, the city's residents discovered that they needed to defend themselves from rival cities, private brigands seeking to lay siege to the city's wealth, and from rough-necks within the city population. A number of steps were taken; many cities built walls around the cities, girding themselves with fortresses as the feudal castles had been protected by walled moats. In addition to such physical fortification of the city, diplomatic, social, and police protection was also sought Negotiations between cities produced treaties to reduce the threat of war. Gilds of both merchants and craftsmen were created to protect their members' economic security, to establish territories for selling, to establish standards for controlling the quality of work, and to provide mutual physical protection from abuse and attack as well as burial societies for their members.

The wandering scholars (or *gyrovagi*) who, during feudalism, had moved from monastery to monastery, from manor to manor, and from cathedral school to school in expectation of welcome (usually food, drink, and lodging), of an opportunity to swap stories, verses,[1] songs, and gossip with each other, of the opportunity to study with a resident scholar of renown (in cloisters, cathedral schools, or palace courts) moved into the cities at about the same time as did the merchants and craftsmen. These wandering students found it desirable to organize into student gilds, initially to protect them-selves from physical abuse and attack within the city,[2] but also to

---

[1]The wandering scholars created a remarkable collection of Latin verse. One of the best studies of the wandering scholars (some of whom were called "jongeleurs" because the verse was not only recited, but often sung) is Helen Waddell's *The Wandering Scholars*. She notes that the composition of Latin verse was not a new phenomenon during the eleventh and twelfth centuries (such verse writing had been going on for some time) but that the popularity of these poetic outpourings reached a zenith during this time. Professor Waddell notes that while the wanderers helped to spread verse, they were not the only ones to write it. A number of abbots who did not wander from the cloister were versifiers. She distinguishes two sorts of verse: "the scholar's verse in the classical metres of Hildebert and Alphanus of Salerno and the school of Liège, and the cantilena, the rhythmus, which the young men sang at the cor-ners, 'pleasant,' says dear old Tetbald de Vernon who wrote the St. Alexis, 'because of its sound like a bell.' " (The *Wandering Scholars* originally published in 1927 by Constable and Co. Ltd., London; this citation is drawn from the 6th edition, Anchor Paperback, Pub-lished by Doubleday and Co., in Garden City, New York, 1961, p99.)

[2]The records of universities are replete with incidents of town/gown disorders in which the students fought it out with the youngbloods from the merchant and craftsmen classes. As a matter of fact, with the development of "nations" of students, the students often fought amongst themselves.

protect themselves from the sort of price-gouging they suffered at the hands of townspeople as the students privately purchased food and lodging for themselves.[3] The students also sought to hire teachers in the city who would teach them the subjects they wished to learn, under conditions stipulated by the students. These early student organizations were known as "universities."

It did not take long for the professors who were competing with each other to acquire students to realize that in order to protect themselves from outrageous demands on the part of the students they also needed to organize. Professors' organizations were known as "universities" in some cities and "colleges" in others. Once organized, the professors set the conditions under which one might enter the scholars' association. Modelling themselves on the craftsmen's gilds which stipulated the conditions under which one progressed from apprentice to journeyman to master craftsman, the professors stipulated that entry into their organization was to be won through a course of studies moving from bachelor to master to doctor and that the "master piece" of the scholar was to be demonstrated in the defense of a thesis as the culmination of scholarly skills. The universities began, then, as a group of students and scholars who met in cities and established, collectively, the conditions under which they would teach and study. Housing and classroom space was rented privately; it was not until later in the development of the university that there was dormitory living and college-owned classroom space. Communal living at college, more typical of both Cambridge and Oxford than of the French or Italian universities, shares a background similar to the development of student residences in the Northern European university cities during the fourteenth and fifteenth centuries. Whether residence halls were provided under the impetus of the university (as in England) or by the Brethren of the Common Life (as in many Northern European cities), the residence halls' existence reflected growing concern for the immorality encountered by young students as they left their families

---

[3]The writings of Alexander Neckham, as edited by Urban Tigner Holmes, provide a glimpse of the relatively simple lodgings required by students—a bed, a slop chamber, a candle stand, and a writing desk and chair.

or the cloisters to study in the cities. Dicing, whoring, drunkenness, fighting, and other temptations of the flesh were believed to deter the young student (and a few old ones as well!) from his earnest pursuit of wisdom and his attendance at religious services. Residence halls provided relatively safe, sanitary, economical, and religiously secure housing for students under the supervision of adults.

Universities were not chartered at their inception, and, thus, it is very difficult to state at precisely what date any given university began. [4] Some time after students and professors had come together and conducted classes on a regular basis, a charter was issued by a bishop, cathedral rector, or the Pope. The formal recognition of the existence of the university was usually from ecclesiastical rather than civil authority. Conditions governing the task of the university were stipulated in statutes. As the university became more complex and attracted students from wide geographical distances, it became necessary to regulate student life. As clerics, university students were not held subject to civil legal procedures; university discipline of students was at the hands of ecclesiastical authority. The stipulations against various forms of immoral conduct indicate the existence of such practices amongst students. The punishments for university misdemeanors varied from the severity of excommunication for those who professed or clung to heretical beliefs to fines and/or assessments of wine rations for all in the college as punishment for relatively minor offenses. The university student body was also subdivided into groupings known as nations, usually based upon the student's place of birth or residence, which served confraternity and mutual benefit purposes as well as having a role in the administration of the university through the election of the university rector. [5]

---

[4] The most authoritative study of medieval universities' history of development is Hastings Rashdall's *The Universities of Europe in the Middle Ages,* published in 1895. The work has been edited by F. M. Powicke and A. B. Emden, and republished in three volumes by Oxford University Press (1936).

[5] Pearl Kibre's, *The Nations in the Mediaeval Universities,* published in 1948 by the Mediaeval Academy of America, Cambridge, Massachusetts, is the most detailed and complete account of the variations between universities in the pattern of the "nations." At some universities, notably Bologna, the "nations" were only for students who did not come from the city in which the university was located. Elsewhere the entire student body was divided into nations which frequently included masters and students and cut across faculty lines, so that law

Intellectual studies at the university were organized into four major areas—arts, theology, medicine, and law, both canon and civil. The arts faculty concentrated on the seven liberal arts of grammar, rhetoric, logic, arithmetic, geometry, astronomy, and music. Various universities became famed for one faculty rather than another so that Paris was renowned for theology, Salerno for medicine, and Bologna for law.

The instructional method of the university came to be termed "scholastic" and involved learning how to offer reasoned argument to support one's position and how to destroy conflicting theses through the use of logic, clearly stipulated definitions of terms, and reliance upon "authorities" such as the Bible, writings of the Fathers, and classical literature. The method is best exemplified in the writings of St. Thomas Aquinas. Many students took great pleasure in listening to disputations, lectures, and debates amongst scholars. Judging from extant records, books were not readily available and any given student probably had very few in his possession, although he may have swapped and shared books with his fellows. Students created notes filled with explanations of passages and arguments employed by their professors. Since students came from a variety of countries in which vernacular languages were spoken, Latin (the universal language of the Church) was adopted as the language of instruction. Robert Ulich[6] claims that such reliance upon Latin created an intellectual group which tended to be cosmopolitan rather than nationalistic in its world-view; a cosmopolitan (albeit Christian) outlook that permitted a cultural unity in Western Europe. Other scholars question how well understood was the Latin spoken at the university, suggesting that many students could not really speak, read, or write Latin well and that they tended to rely upon

students and arts students might be in the same nation. Professor Kibre discusses the officers of nations, their administrative responsibilities, and the various functions served by the "nationa" at the universities of Paris, Bologna, Padua, Pisa, Perugia, Naples, Montpelier, Orléans, Angers, Poitiers, Aix, Valence, Bourges, Salamanca, Lérida, Oxford, Cambridge, Prague, Vienna, Heidelberg, Leipzig, Frankfort on the Oder, Louvain, St. Andrews, Glasgow, and Aberdeen.

[6]See Ulich's chapter, "The Middle Ages" in his book, *The Education of Nations*, published in 1962 by the Harvard University Press.

glosses for their studies and stock phrases in their own intellectual conversations.

In addition to a group of teachers and students addressing themselves in a common language to various intellectual concerns, university life was also marked by a garb which distinguished the community of scholars from other clerics and townspeople. It was believed that, marked by intellect, and, thus, set apart from ordinary men, the scholars (be they teachers or students) should be set apart by dress as well. Bachelors wore the simple tonsure of a cleric as well as an academic gown; masters' gowns were somewhat more complex, having long pointed draping cuffs in the sleeves; doctors were marked by special hoods in addition to gowns. When conferring the doctorate, the candidate received not only the hood, but also a special ring, signifying his achievement.

Since the universities were "fed" by the students who had learned their basic lessons in literacy and literature in the schools (be they grammar schools or cathedral schools), it is appropriate to look first to these institutions. Readings concerned with school education in this chapter include: William of Tournai's prescriptions for the proper education of children; a description of the cathedral and grammar schools run by secular clergy; the Bishop of Exeter's directive to his archdeacons in 1356 that they see to the improvement of the grammar schools; a description of the physical and intellectual competitiveness found amongst English grammar school boys; Hugh of St. Victor's extended discussion of Logic, Grammar, and Argument which formed the basis of much cathedral school curriculum; the rowdy play of schoolboys once released from their studies; and the reflections of Hugh of St. Victor concerning his boyhood education.

A picture of university education emerges from readings. Chaucer's portrait of the Oxford cleric is the paradigm of religious devotion to teaching. Letters written by students as well as manuals prepared to help them write letters indicate that students found travelling to school difficult; once they arrived at school housing accommodations were frequently meager; other problems—particularly ones requiring money from home for their solution—are mentioned in student letters; advice is offered to students or writing materials and the proper care of books; and the young scholars are reminded that humility is a virtue. Rules from the University of Paris describe the relations between students and masters and conditions of study; the lecture method is prescribed at Paris as the appropriate instructional technique. Additional information is offered regarding university study methods and the importance of disputation; the work of St. Thomas Aquinas is quoted to show the refinement achieved in this scholastic method of argument. Teachers are excoriated by thirteenth century preachers for their failure to set good examples of the scholarly, Christian life; degree requirements are set forth; and a set of regulations from Paris describes the way students were supposed to behave. Proclamations at the University of Heidelberg[7] indicate that students frequently misbehaved, and this is borne out by the thirteenth-century Paris preachers' sermons protesting the students' excesses. One town gown controversy in Rome is reported as well as the account of battling and murderous students at Oxford and Cambridge. Hugh of St. Victor's judgment that "many study, few find knowledge" seems an apt conclusion for the discussion of student life at Western European universities. The establishment of colleges in the Muslim world occurred prior to the establishment of universities in Western Europe and an indication of their curriculum and contribution to Western European universities concludes this chapter.

36. William of Tournai Prescribes Proper Education for Children

James A. Corbett

The text opens with a preface in the form of a letter in which the author says he wrote the treatise at the request of many of the friars. He intends to explain how to teach boys faith and good morals, and relies on Scripture,

From The "De Instructione puerorum" of William of Tournai, O.P. by James A. Corbett, pp. 7-9, in Texts and Studies in the History of Mediaeval Education, No. 3, A. L. Gabriel and J. N. Garvin, eds. (Notre Dame, Ind.: The Mediaeval Institute, University of Notre Dame, 1955).
[7]The rector's directives against the stealing or catching of citizens' dogs (1396), the practice of fencing or attending fencing schools (1415), frequenting brothels and public gaming houses, and dancing or wearing masks during Lent (1442) are translated by Lynn Thorndike, University Records and Life in the Middle Ages, pp. 260, 211, 332-323.

the saints, and the great authorities to supply him with supporting texts. His would be a simple and practical work, which is preferable to one of subtle things. . . .

Starting with the text: "Feed my sheep" he justifies the usefulness of teaching children morals and salutary knowledge. This he proves from Scripture, by reason and examples. The first reason is that youth is especially prone to evil; he quotes, besides Scripture, the *Glossa ordinaria* and Gratian's *Decretum* to prove it. A second reason is that it is easier to teach them while they are young, before they have become hardened in vice. The third is that they can be trained in the good while young because they retain to the end most firmly what they receive as youths. As examples of this he refers to Abraham, David, Tobias, Suzanna, the mothers of St. Bernard and St. Augustine. Parents, godparents, and teachers are morally obliged, then, to teach their children or students.

Children are to be corrected by word, example, and the rod. He emphasizes the need for discipline. Children should be asked and warned to live rightly; but they must be taught by example: the father should live in such a way that the son will know how to live. If this fails, one should remember the text of Proverbs: "Who spares the rod spoils the child." Fathers, according to St. Augustine, train their horses, and animals their young; children, then, should be disciplined with the switch if necessary.

He quotes again St. Augustine to show the obligation of godparents to warn their godchildren to remain chaste, love justice, and have charity. They must above all know the *Credo* and the *Pater noster*. They must not become usurers, dishonest merchants, robbers, etc. Godparents should warn their godchildren to love God, to go to church frequently and learn from sermons there, to pray and follow the example of the good.

Finally, the teachers, who take the place of parents, should lead exemplary lives. The greedy teacher thinks more of how he can gain money than how he can teach the children. The greed of teachers and students destroys schools and prevents the progress of the students.

But what are the children to be taught?—faith, morals and knowledge *(scientia)*. The need for faith is supported by quotations from St. Augustine and a directive to the reader to find other quotations in the *Summa de virtutibus* of William Peraldus. He explains the need for the *Credo,* and why it was composed, by many quotations from the *Vita sancti Eligii* of Audoenus which he ascribes to St. Augustine. The same work is used to explain what a good Christian is.

William had little difficulty finding quotations to justify his teaching that children should have all the virtues. These should be taught to girls as well as to boys.

The knowledge to be imparted was that which leads to salvation. This wisdom should be acquired because it is, as Hugh of St. Victor called it, the great solace of life. And as Lactantius expressed it; "There is no sweeter food for the soul than a knowledge of truth." This is attained by reading and meditation. Wisdom is acquired by prayer, instruction, and investigation. He ends this part of the treatise by stating that students need three things: 1) to understand readily and to retain well the precepts given, 2) to work diligently, 3) to form good habits and a conscience through discipline.

In the following chapter William points out that the serfs and maids of the household should be taught, as well as the sons and daughters, because the head of the household, as St. Augustine said, was responsible to God for those under him. The quotation refers primarily to moral education.

In the last chapter William warns that if one is obliged to care for the bodily well-being of the poor, one has an even greater obligation to their spiritual well-being. They should be urged to go to church frequently for spiritual nourishment. He divides the poor who are evil into seven categories: the proud, the greedy, the gluttonous, the lazy, the liars, those impatient in adversity, and the calumniators. There are also the poor who are good: those who, like the apostles, do not have or wish for temporal goods. This kind of poverty opens the gates of Paradise and hence is to be loved.

37. Schools Run by Secular Clergy

J. J. Bagley

The secular or non-monastic clergy took chief responsibility for education. The fourth Lateran council, summoned by Innocent III in 1215, confirmed that it was part of a bishop's duty to appoint one of his senior canons to be chancellor, or *magister scholarum,* master of the schools, and that the chancellor should teach in the cathedral school and license all other schools in the diocese. This had been the practice both before and after the Norman Conquest, but the twelfth-century enthusiasm for monasteries tended to shift the control of schools from the bishop to the abbot or prior of the local monastery. The peculiar English custom of combining cathedrals and monasteries confused still further this division of authority. At Canterbury, Durham, and eight other diocesan centres, the canons of the cathedral chapter lived a monastic life, and were either Benedictine monks or, at Carlisle only, Augustinian canons; contrarily, the abbots and

Reprinted by permission of G. P. Putnam's Sons from *Life in Medieval England* by J. J. Bagley, pp. 90-94. Copyright © 1960 by J. J. Bagley.

priors of other monasteries often employed secular clergy to teach those of their pupils who were not postulants for admission to the monastic order. Several old schools, such as those at Huntingdon, Gloucester, and Reading, passed from the control of secular clergy into monastic hands during the twelfth century, and in remoter areas of England, monasteries occasionally provided a teacher for the sons of their richer tenants. But the higher ecclesiastical authorities did not approve of monastic schools. On the other hand they encouraged collegiate churches to open schools for local boys. Early established at Derby, Pontefract, Shrewsbury, and elsewhere, and later to become popular and widespread, collegiate churches were the headquarters of secular canons, who lived a communal life, but whose principal work was to teach and preach to the laity. . . .

Until the nineteenth century the Church paid little attention to primary education, and left parents to make what provision they could for teaching children their letters, and guiding them in the first stages of reading and writing. In the Middle Ages most children learned this necessary groundwork from irregular and casual instruction given by busy parents, elder brothers and sisters, or a friendly priest. The only schools which taught at so elementary a stage were the song schools. Their chief purpose was to train choir boys to sing and chant, but since of necessity they had to teach their future choristers to read as well as sing, they were often asked to take young children, girls as well as boys, whose parents had no intention of putting them into the cathedral or church choir. In her story to the Canterbury pilgrims, the Prioress describes such a school, and tells how Christian children

> . . . lerned in that scole yeer by yere
> Swich maner doctrine as men used there,
> That is to seyn, to singen and to rede,
> As smale children doon in hir childhede.

Before they left the song school the most intelligent or regularly-attending pupils were capable of pronouncing and writing single words, reciting the Lord's Prayer and Creed, and chanting canticles and psalms. They could mouth Latin words and understand the purport of the main prayers and canticles, but usually they could not construe the simplest sentence. To acquire a knowledge of Latin, the next necessary stage in their education, the boys had to move to a school which taught grammar.

Medieval Latin was a living language, in which educated people from all over Europe regularly conversed, scholars wrote and taught, priests conducted services, and merchants and lawyers transacted their business. Just as modern English uses phrases and idioms which Shakespeare never knew, so medieval Latin used words and constructions unknown to Cicero.

At best, it was a homogeneous language still virile though past its greatest vitality; at worst, it was merely a Latinised form of Norman French or English, with no constructions of its own and using numerous borrowed words lightly disguised with a Latin suffix. The students' first stage in its conquest was to master the basic grammar. The teacher dictated section after section of Donatus's *Ars Minor* or Priscian's *Grammar,* and the boys learned each section by heart. A good memory served the medieval school-boy well, for he had no reference or text books. He could gradually build up a collection of notes, but hand-written books were too scarce for general possession, and dictionaries did not exist. From basic grammar he graduated through easy texts like Aesop's *Fables* to selected passages from Virgil, Ovid, Horace, the *Vulgate,* and the writings of the early Fathers of the Church. But ability to read Latin was not enough. It was necessary to write Latin prose and verse, and to converse and discuss in the language. To encourage this side of the work many schoolmasters forbade their senior pupils to speak anything but Latin on school premises. Boys of twelve, thirteen, and fourteen years managed to do this with varying degrees of accuracy, and once they began to study rhetoric and logic as well as grammar, they were regularly called upon to make speeches and to debate in Latin. The pride of a medieval schoolmaster was a pupil, fourteen years old at most, who could dispute in Latin nice points of grammar and logic before admiring parents and friends.

Grammar, rhetoric, and logic constituted the *trivium,* the first major stage in medieval education. In Norman times, instruction in these subjects was offered by the cathedral schools, the few collegiate churches of those days, and other schools licensed by the bishops, but none of them necessarily restricted themselves to the *trivium.* If they had capable teachers and ambitious pupils, they would teach one or more of the advanced subjects of the *quadrivium*—arithmetic, music, geometry, and astronomy. A few, especially the cathedral schools, had usually an advanced pupil or two studying theology or canon law. Some twelfth-century schools achieved reputations which attracted advanced students from all over England and even from across the Channel, and they soon tended to leave to lesser schools the teaching of basic grammar, logic, and rhetoric, and to close their own doors to pupils who were not already proficient Latin scholars. This specialisation eventually produced, on the one hand, the universities to offer the advanced teaching, and, on the other, the grammar schools to feed the universities with suitable students and to teach those boys who did not wish to do more than learn Latin. Some grammar schools remained under the direct control of a cathedral chancellor, the head of a monastery, or the warden of a collegiate church. Others were endowed by trade gilds or financed by chantry bequests, and, in the fourteenth and fifteenth centuries, a large number were founded by merchants and landowners, who wished to provide grammar education in the town or village in which they were particularly interested. By the end of the Middle Ages there could have been few towns and large villages without a grammar school.... But medieval grammar schools were very small. Most of them were housed in a single room or part of a church, and pupils rarely numbered more than twenty-five or thirty. In many grammar schools they could be counted on the fingers of one hand.... One master only was appointed to most grammar schools, and he had to teach all pupils, at whatever midway stage they were between an elementary knowledge of reading and an ability to speak and write Latin. He would count himself fortunate if he had an usher or pupil-teacher, who could relieve him of some of the elementary teaching and share the maintenance of discipline.

38. Bishop of Exeter's Mandate: Improve Religious Instruction in Grammar Schools.

John de Grandisson

We ourselves have learned and learn daily, not without frequent wonder and inward compassion of mind, that among masters or teachers of boys and illiterate folk in our diocese, who instruct them in Grammar, there prevails a preposterous and unprofitable method and order of teaching, nay, a superstitious fashion, rather heathen than christian; for these masters,—after their scholars have learned to read or repeat, even imperfectly, the Lord's Prayer, the Ave Maria, the Creed, and the Mattins and Hours of the Blessed Virgin, and other such things pertaining to faith and their soul's health, without knowing or understanding how to construe anything of the aforesaid, or decline the words or parse them—then, I say, these masters make them pass on prematurely to learn other advanced [*magistrales*] books of poetry or metre. Whence it cometh to pass that, grown to man's estate, they understand not the things which they daily read or say: moreover (what is more damnable) through lack of understanding they discern not the Catholic Faith. We, therefore, willing to eradicate so horrible and foolish an abuse, already too deeprooted in our diocese, by all means and methods in our power, do now commit and depute to each of you the duty of warning and enjoining all masters and instructors what-

From *Life in the Middle Ages* by George Gordon Coulton (Cambridge: Cambridge University Press, 1967), Part II, pp. 113-14. Reprinted by permission.

soever that preside over Grammar Schools within the limits of his arch-
deaconry, (as, by these letters present, we ourselves strictly command,
enjoin, and warn them), that they should not, as hitherto, teach the boys
whom they receive as Grammar pupils only to read or learn by heart; but
rather that, postponing all else, they should make them construe and
understand the Lord's Prayer, the Ave Maria, the Creed, the Mattins
and Hours of the Blessed Virgin, and decline and parse the words therein,
before permitting them to pass on to other books. Moreover we proclaim
that we purpose to confer clerical orders henceforth on no boys but upon
such as may be found to have learnt after this method. . . .

39. Schoolboy Competition: Physical and Intellectual

L. F. Salzman

Though there were no organized games as in modern schools, there were
plenty of games of one kind and another. Ball games, resembling (more or
less) hockey, fives, tennis, and rounders, were played, the walls of churches
being often chosen as fivescourts, to the considerable injury of the windows.
Football was also a favourite game, and the three schools of London—
those of St. Paul's, St. Mary-le-Bow, and St. Martin-le-Grand—used to
assemble on the open ground of Smithfield to play football in the afternoon
on Shrove Tuesday. The morning of Shrove Tuesday was given up to cock-
fighting, the boys bringing their game-cocks to school and matching them
against one another; this amusement, sufficiently barbarous in itself, degenerated in later times into the practice of tying a cock to a post and
throwing sticks at it until the unfortunate bird was killed, and such Shrove
Tuesday cock-throwing was practised, with the encouragement of the
masters, down to Puritan days. But if medieval boys indulged in brutality
for which a modern boy would be deservedly kicked by his companions,
they also indulged in an intellectual form of amusement, for which, one
cannot help thinking, a modern boy would run some risk of being unde-
servedly kicked; this was the practice of assembling in some public place,
in the streets, on a holiday, to dispute in Latin with rival scholars on points
of grammar or of logic.

This intellectual keenness was due to the fact that the schools taught not

From *English Life in the Middle Ages* by L. F. Salzman (Oxford: The Clarendon Press,
1926), pp. 146, 148. Reprinted by permission.

only grammar but also logic (the art of arguing) and rhetoric (the art of public speaking). These three subjects formed the *Trivium,* or threefold path of learning, with which most educated people were content; but scholars, who despised such "trivial" learning, would go on to the fourfold *Quadrivium* of arithmetic, geometry, music, and astronomy. It may seem strange that arithmetic should be regarded as one of the more advanced and less necessary subjects of education, but it must be remembered that it was not until the fourteenth century that Arabic numerals began to come into use, and the processes of arithmetic with Roman numerals were far from simple. The learned Bishop Aldhelm, when he took up mathematics, wrote: "The despair of doing sums oppressed my mind so that all the previous labour spent on learning seemed nothing. At last, by the help of God's grace, I grasped, after incessant study, that which lies at the base of reckoning:—what they call fractions."

40. Logic Consists of Grammar and Argument

Hugh of St. Victor

CHAPTER TWENTY-EIGHT: CONCERNING LOGIC, WHICH IS THE FOURTH PART OF PHILOSOPHY

Logic is separated into grammar and the theory of argument. The Greek word *gramma* means letter, and from it grammar takes its name as the science of letters. Properly speaking, the letter is a written figure, while the term "element" is reserved for a pronounced sound; here, however, "letter" is to be taken in a larger sense as meaning both the spoken and the written symbol, for they both belong to grammar.

There are those who say that grammar is not a part of philosophy, but, so to say, an appendage and an instrument in the service of philosophy. But concerning the theory of argument, Boethius declares that it can be at once a part and an instrument in the service of philosophy, just as the foot, hand, tongue, eyes, etc., are at once the body's parts and its instruments.

Grammar, simply taken, treats of words, with their origin formation, combination, inflection, pronunciation, and all things else pertaining directly to utterance alone. The theory of argument is concerned with the conceptual content of words.

From *The "Didascalicon" of Hugh of St. Victor, A Medieval Guide to the Arts* by Jerome Taylor (New York: Columbia University Press, 1961), pp. 79-82. Reprinted by permission.

CHAPTER TWENTY-NINE: CONCERNING GRAMMAR

Grammar is divided into the letter, the syllable, the phrase, and the clause. Or, according to another division, between letters or written signs, and vocables or spoken signs. Yet again, by another division, among the noun, the verb, the participle, the pronoun, the adverb, the preposition, the conjunction, the interjection, the articulate word, the letter, the syllable, metric feet, accents, pointing, punctuating, spelling, analogy, etymology, glosses, differences, the barbarism, the solecism, errors, metaplasm, schemata, tropes, prose composition, verse composition, fables, histories. But of all these I shall omit further explanation, both because I should otherwise be more lengthy than the brevity of my plan would warrant, and because in this little work I have designed to inquire only into the divisions and the names of things, so that the reader might thereby be established in some beginning of knowledge merely. Let him who desires to inform himself concerning these things read Donatus, Servius, Priscian *Concerning Accents,* Priscian *Concerning the Twelve Verses of Vergil, The Barbarism,* and Isidore's *Etymologies.*

CHAPTER THIRTY: CONCERNING THE THEORY OF ARGUMENT

Invention and judgment are integral parts running through the whole theory of argument, whereas demonstration, probable argument, and sophistic are its divisive parts, that is, mark distinct and separate subdivisions of it. Demonstration consists of necessary arguments and belongs to philosophers; probable argument belongs to dialecticians and rhetoricians; sophistic to sophists and quibblers. Probable argument is divided into dialectic and rhetoric, both of which contain invention and judgment as integral parts: for since invention and judgment integrally constitute the whole genus, that is, of argumentative logic, they are necessarily found in all of its species at once. Invention teaches the discovery of arguments and the drawing up of lines of argumentation. The science of judgment teaches the judging of such arguments and lines of argumentation.

Now it may be asked whether invention and judgment are contained in philosophy. They do not seem to be contained under the theoretical sciences, or under the practical, or under the mechanical, or even under the logical, where one would most expect them to be. They are not contained under the logical because they are not branches either of grammar or of argumentative logic. They are not branches of argumentative logic because they comprise it integrally, and nothing can at the same time constitute an integral and a divisive part of the same genus. Philosophy, therefore, seems not to contain all knowledge.

But what we should realize is that the word "knowledge" is customarily used in two senses, namely, for one of the disciplines, as when I say that dialectic *is* knowledge, meaning an art or discipline; and for any act of cognition, as when I say that a person who knows something *has* knowledge. Thus, for example, if I know dialectic I have knowledge; if I know how to swim I have knowledge; if I know that Socrates was the son of Sophroniscus I have knowledge—and so in every instance, anyone who knows anything may be said to have knowledge. But it is one thing when I say that dialectic is knowledge, that is an art or discipline, and another when I say that to know that Socrates was the son of Sophroniscus is knowledge, that is, an act of cognition. It is always true to say that any knowledge which is an art or discipline is a distinct branch of philosophy; but it cannot always be said that all knowledge which is an act of cognition is a distinct branch of philosophy: and yet it is certainly true that all knowledge, whether it be a discipline or any act of cognition whatever, is somehow contained in philosophy—either as an integral part, or as a divisive part or branch.

A discipline, moreover, is a branch of knowledge which has a defined scope within the range of which the objective of some art is perfectly unfolded; but this is not true of the knowledge of invention or of judgment, because neither of these stands independently in itself, and therefore they cannot be called disciplines but are integral parts of a discipline—namely, of argumentative logic.

Furthermore, the question is raised whether invention and judgment are the same thing in dialectic that they are in rhetoric. It seems they are not, since then two opposed genera would be constituted of identical parts. It can be said, consequently, that these two words, "invention" and "judgment," are equivocally used for the parts of dialectic and rhetoric; or better, perhaps, let us say that invention and judgment are properly parts of argumentative logic, and as such are univocally signified by these words, but that in the subdivisions of this particular genus they are differentiated from one another by certain properties—the differentiations are not revealed through the terms "invention" and "judgment" because these names, far from designating invention and judgment as separate species, designate them only as generic parts.

Grammar is the knowledge of how to speak without error; dialectic is clear-sighted argument which separates the true from the false; rhetoric is the discipline of persuading to every suitable thing.

41. Harshly Disciplined Boys Sought Release in Rowdy Play

J. J. Bagley

The medieval schoolboy had no reason to like school, and many reasons for hating it. Day after day he learned nothing but Latin, except a little rhetoric and logic if he stayed at school long enough to qualify for such lessons. The master's method of teaching never varied, and the boy was required to sit or stand in the classroom for eight or nine hours a day, learning by heart, and often without understanding, grammar rules or Latin passages dictated to him. Games were usually forbidden, holidays largely restricted to Church feast days, and severe corporal punishment automatically inflicted for both misbehaviour and single mistakes in repetition or translation.... Nor did medieval schoolboys find any sympathy at home. It was a universally held maxim that sparing the rod spoiled the child, and parents were as ready as schoolmasters to "trewly belassch hym tyl he wyll amend," as Agnes Paston advised her son's teacher to do, adding significantly, "and so ded the last maystr and the best that ever he had att Caumbrege." Another fifteenth-century mother advised her daughter not to curse her children if they rebelled and would

not bow them low,
But take a smart rod and beat them in a row,
Till they cry mercy and their guilt well know.

In *Piers Ploughman's Vision,* Reason charged the merchants to chasten their children, and not pamper them with soft living conditions and the thirteenth-century rules at Westminster School were full of instructions concerning prompt and severe chastisement.

Such hard and sustained suppression naturally built up a pressure which periodically exploded into violence and hooliganism. Some schools acknowledged certain days for letting off steam. William fitz Stephen, describing twelfth-century London, told of schoolboys arranging cock fights on Shrove Tuesday, tournaments in Lent, a water carnival at Easter, archery in the summer, and skating and bull baiting in the winter. Later in the Middle Ages school authorities usually permitted and even encouraged boys to practise archery, but they set their face against football, which inevitably developed into an unorganised rough-and-tumble dangerous to life and limb. Several cathedral schools indulged in traditional tomfoolery on St. Nicholas's Day, 6 December, and the Feast of the Innocents after Christmas. On 6 December the boys elected one of their leaders as bishop,

Reprinted by permission of G. P. Putnam's Sons from *Life in Medieval England* by J. J. Bagley, pp. 94-96. Copyright ©1960 by J. J. Bagley.

and he in turn appointed his dean and canons from among his school friends. Together on the Feast of the Innocents, commonly known as Childermas, these temporary dignitaries conducted a topsy-turvy service, and were afterwards entertained in state by the senior clergy. The ceremony originated from a desire to mark the feast with a practical demonstration of putting down the mighty and exalting the humble and meek, but it degenerated into an unholy, sacrilegious romp and a parody of church services. Despite periodic condemnation by ecclesiastical authorities, the practice persisted in several schools throughout the Middle Ages. Even the saintly Henry VI made provision for it in the statutes of Eton, and Colet, reformer though he was, ordered the boys of St. Paul's School to attend church on Childermas Day in order to hear the boy-bishop's sermon.

42. Hugh of St. Victor Recalls His Own Education

Hugh of St. Victor

"Once grounded in things small, you may safely strive for all." I dare to affirm before you that I myself never looked down on anything which had to do with education, but that I often learned many things which seemed to others to be a sort of joke or just nonsense. I recall that when I was still a schoolboy I worked hard to know the names of all things that my eyes fell upon or that came into my use, frankly concluding that a man cannot come to know the natures of things if he is still ignorant of their names. How many times each day would I make myself pay out the debt of my little bits of wisdom, which, thanks to their shortness, I had noted down in one or two words on a page, so that I might keep a mindful hold on the solutions, and even the number, of practically all the thoughts, questions, and objections which I had learned. Often I proposed cases and, when the opposing contentions were lined up against one another, I diligently distinguished what would be the business of the rhetorician, what of the orator, what of the sophist. I laid out pebbles for numbers, and I marked the pavement with black coals and, by a model placed right before my eyes, I plainly showed what difference there is between an obtuse-angled, a right-angled, and an acute-angled triangle. Whether or not an equilateral parallelogram would yield the same area as a square when two of its sides were multiplied together, I learned by walking both figures and measuring

From The "Didascalicon" of Hugh of St. Victor, A Medieval Guide to the Arts by Jerome Taylor (New York: Columbia University Press, 1961), pp. 136-37. Reprinted by permission.

them with my feet. Often I kept watch outdoors through the winter nights like one of the fixed stars by which we measure time. Often I used to bring out my strings, stretched to their number on the wooden frame, both that I might note with my ear the difference among the tones and that I might at the same time delight my soul with the sweetness of the sound. These were boyish pursuits, to be sure, yet not without their utility for me, nor does my present knowledge of them lie heavy upon my stomach. But I do not reveal these things to you in order to parade my knowledge, which is either nothing at all or very little, but in order to show you that the man who moves along step by step is the one who moves along best, not like some who fall head over heels when they wish to make a great leap ahead.

43. The Clerk of Oxford

Geoffrey Chaucer

> There was an *Oxford Cleric* too, a student,
> Long given to Logic, longer than was prudent;
> The horse he had was leaner than a rake,
> And he was not too fat, I undertake,
> But had a hollow look, a sober air;
> The thread upon his overcoat was bare.
> He had found no preferment in the church
> And he was too unworldly to make search.
> He thought far more of having by his bed
> His twenty books all bound in black and red,
> Of Aristotle and philosophy
> Than of gay music, fiddles or finery.
> Though a philosopher, as I have told.
> He had not found the stone for making gold.
> Whatever money from his friends he took
> He spent on learning or another book
> And prayed for them most earnestly, returning
> Thanks to them thus for paying for his learning.
> His only care was study, and indeed
> He never spoke a word more than was need,
> Formal at that, respectful in the extreme,

From Geoffrey Chaucer, *The Prologue to The Canterbury Tales*, translated into Modern English by Nevil Coghill (Baltimore: Penguin Books, 1952), p. 33. Reprinted by permission.

Short, to the point, and lofty in his theme.
The thought of moral virtue filled his speech
And he would gladly learn, and gladly teach.

44. Students Have Difficulty Travelling to School, But Are Not Eager to Leave

Charles H. Haskins

The student's journey and arrival were not always so prosperous, and the famous Bolognese *dictator* Buoncompagno devotes a chapter of his collection to the accidents that may befall one on the way to the university. Attacks from robbers seem to have been the chief danger: the scholar was hastening to Bologna, for the love of letters, but in crossing the Alps he was attacked by highwaymen, who took away his books, horses, clothing, and money, so that he has been obliged to remain in a neighbouring monastery till help can reach him. So a Northern student on his way to Paris is stripped and left bound by four youths in clerical habit with whom he had fallen in upon the road. In other instances the robbery, of fifteen marks of silver and grey furs, takes place in the forest of Bologna, or in the highway near Aosta. Sometimes advantage was taken of the greater security of forwarding by Italian merchants visiting the fairs of Champagne, or Italian pilgrims to Santiago de Compostela. Even a journey home from Bologna to Florence was not without its dangers, unless undertaken with a considerable armed company.

Once safely arrived at a centre of learning, medieval students were slow to quit academic life. Again and again they ask permission to have their term of study extended; war might break out, parents or brothers die, an inheritance have to be divided, but the student pleads always for delay. He desires to "serve longer in the camp of Pallas": in any event he cannot leave before Easter, as his masters have just begun important courses of lectures. A scholar is called home from Siena to marry a lady of many attractions; he answers that he deems it foolish to desert the cause of learning for the sake of a woman, "for one may always get a wife, but science once lost can never be recovered." In a similar case another student holds

From *Studies in Medieval Culture* by Charles Homer Haskins (Oxford: Clarendon Press, 1929; New York: Frederick Ungar Publishing Co., 1958). This selection is from pages 18-21 in the 1958 edition.

out against the charms of a proposed wife, who, "though she is dark, is clever and of placid demeanour and distinguished bearing, wise and noble, and moreover has a considerable dower and belongs to an influential family." A married student is reminded that he has remained in the schools longer than the stipulated two years; his wife is sure he has been studying in some other *Code,* and proposes to read a little in the *Digest* on her own account! Sometimes, however, the student is taken ill and writes for money and an easy-going horse to take him home, while occasionally he discovers his inability to learn and asks to enter the army or some other more congenial occupation. One father promises the delights of manual labour to a son who complains that the Scriptures are too hard for him to understand and desires to do "some more useful work which leads to temporal gain."

45. Student Housing

Urban T. Holmes

They dwell in a poor house with an old woman who cooks only vegetables and never prepares a sheep save on feast-days. A dirty fellow waits on the table and just such a person buys the wine in the city. After the meal the student sits on a rickety chair and uses a light, doubtless a candle which goes out continually and disturbs the ideas. So he sits all night long and learns the seven liberal arts. Often he falls asleep at his work and is troubled by bad dreams until Aurora announces the day and he must hasten to the college and stand before the teacher. And he wins in no way the mighty with his knowledge. But through the grace of Nature and Fortune he wins a bride at the end of the poem. [*Jehan de Hauteville*]

. . .

I eat sparingly in my little room, not high up in a castle. I have no silver money, nor do the Fates give me estates. Beets, beans, and peas are here looked upon as fine dishes and we joke about meat, which is not in our menu for a very good reason. The size of the wine skin on the table depends on the purse, which is never large. [*John of Garland*]

. . .

From Urban Tigner Holmes, *Daily Living in the Twelfth Century* (Madison: The University of Wisconsin Press; ©1952 by the Regents of the University of Wisconsin). Reprinted by permission. This selection is from pages 81-82 in the 1964 paperback edition.

From passages such as these it is possible to form a picture of how the twelfth-century student must have lodged. Someone, perhaps an old woman, would rent her two or three upstairs rooms to students. One of these rooms would be the main front room, or *salle,* which contained a fireplace. Beds would be set up there at night, and during the day it would serve as dining room and lounging room for all the students in the house. Surely a scribe's chair was to be found there, by the fire, which they all took turns in using. Twice a day the old woman, or other proprietor, cooked the food which they could pay for, and a man-servant ran errands and bought the wine. The proprietress doubtless slept in the kitchen, or, if she had a husband, it is possible that they reserved for themselves a bed somewhere on an upper floor. We suspect that each student had to provide his own bed, which with sheets, pillow, and coverlet, was worth some twenty sous, or about ten of our dollars. This price is furnished us in a document of the Hotel-Dieu, from the year 1168, which required each canon of the cathedral to bequeath his bed or the equivalent to the Hotel-Dieu.

46. Student Letters Reflect Student Problems

Charles H. Haskins

By far the largest element in the correspondence of mediaeval students consists of requests for money—"a student's first song is a demand for money," says a weary father in an Italian letter-writer, "and there will never be a letter which does not ask for cash." How to secure this fundamental necessity of student life was doubtless one of the most important problems that confronted the mediaeval scholar, and many were the models which the *dictatores* placed before him in proof of the practical advantages of their art. The letters are generally addressed to parents, sometimes to brothers, uncles, or ecclesiastical patrons—a much copied exercise contained twenty-two different methods of approaching an archdeacon on this ever delicate subject. Commonly the student announces that he is at such and such a centre of learning, well and happy but in desperate need of money for books and other necessary expenses. Here is a specimen from Oxford, somewhat more individual than the average and written in uncommonly bad Latin:

From *Studies in Medieval Culture* by Charles Homer Haskins (Oxford: Clarendon Press, 1929; New York: Frederick Ungar Publishing Co., 1958). This selection is from pages 7-14 and 27-28 in the 1958 edition.

B. to his venerable master A., greeting. This is to inform you that I am studying at Oxford with the greatest diligence, but the matter of money stands greatly in the way of my promotion, as it is now two months since I spent the last of what you sent me. The city is expensive and makes many demands; I have to rent lodgings, buy necessaries, and provide for many other things which I cannot now specify. Wherefore I respectfully beg your paternity that by the promptings of divine pity you may assist me, so that I may be able to complete what I have well begun. For you must know that without Ceres and Bacchus Apollo grows cold. . . .

A more permanent provision is suggested by a Paris student, who wants to receive from Saint-Victor's ten loaves of bread a week, besides a mattress and sixpence. Sometimes the supplies needed—books and parchment, clothing, linen, bedding, etc.—are sought directly from home. In an interesting set of letters written from Chartres at the beginning of the twelfth century and quite unspoiled by the phrases of the rhetoricians, we find two brothers asking their mother for thick lambskins for winter clothing, parchment for making a psalter, their father's great boots, and some chalk, good chalk, since theirs is worth nothing. A canon of Rouen sends his nephews ten sous, ten ells of linen cloth, a split ham, and a measure of white peas. A Vienna student who writes to his father N., citizen of Klosterneuburg, that he has spent his money for books and other things that pertain to learning, receives in reply "by this present messenger ten Rhenish gulden, seven ells of cloth for a cloak, and one pair of hose."

If the father was close-fisted, there were special reasons to be urged: the town was dear—as university towns always are!—the price of living was exceptionally high owing to a hard winter, a threatened siege, a failure of crops, or an unusual number of scholars; the last messenger had been robbed or had absconded with the money; the son could borrow no more of his fellows or of the Jews; he has been ill with the cold, and tempted to run away; the cold is so great that he cannot study at night; and so on. The student's woes are depicted in moving language, with many appeals to paternal vanity and affection. At Bologna we hear of the terrible mud through which the youth must beg his way from door to door, crying, "O good masters," and receiving nothing save a few scraps of refuse from the townsfolk and a "God go with you!" from his fellow students. Another student blows on his frosty fingers while he remarks that it is two years since he has tasted wine, washed his face, or trimmed his beard. In an Austrian formulary a scholar writes from the lowest depths of prison, where the bread is hard and mouldy, the drinking-water mixed with tears, the darkness so dense that it can actually be felt. Another lies on straw with no covering, goes without shoes or shirt, and eats he will not say what —a tale designed to be addressed to a sister and to bring in response a hundred sous *tournois,* two pairs of sheets, and ten ells of fine cloth, all sent without her husband's knowledge. In another form of appeal to the sister's mercy the student asks for the loan of twenty sous from her, since he has been so short a time at school that he dare not make the demand of his parents, "lest perchance the amount of his expenses displease them." ...

Letters from all parts of Europe testify to the expense attendant upon securing a degree. Thus a student at Paris asks a friend to explain to his father, "since the simplicity of the lay mind does not understand such things," how at length after much study nothing but lack of money for the inception banquet stands in the way of his graduation. From Orleans D. Boterel writes to his dear relatives at Tours that he is labouring over his last volume of law and on its completion will be able to pass to his licentiate provided they send him a hundred livres for the necessary expenses. A student of medicine at Montpellier asks for "more than the usual amount of money" in view of his promotion. A successful inception at Bologna is thus described by Buoncompagno:

> Sing unto the Lord a new song, praise him with stringed instruments and organs, rejoice upon the high-sounding cymbals, for your son has held a glorious disputation, which was attended by a great number of teachers and scholars. He answered all questions without a mistake, and no one could get the better of him or prevail against his arguments. Moreover he celebrated a famous banquet, at which both rich and poor were honoured as never before, and he has duly begun to give lectures which are already so popular that others' classrooms are deserted and his own are filled.

Buoncompagno also tells of an unsuccessful candidate who could do nothing in the disputation but sat in the chair like a goat while the spectators in derision called him rabbi; his guests had such eating that they had no will to drink, and he must needs hire students to attend his classes.

If we were to judge them by their own accounts, mediaeval students were models of industry and diligence, hearing in some instances at least three lectures a day and expecting soon to excel their professors as well as their fellows.

47. Advice to Students on Writing Materials

Alexander Neckham

Let him have a razor or knife for scraping pages of parchment or skin; let him have a "biting" pumice for cleaning the sheets, and a little scraper for making equal the surface of the skin. He should have a piece of lead and a ruler with which he may rule the margins on both sides—on the back and on the side from which the flesh has been removed.

There should be a fold of four sheets (a quaternion). I do not use the word *quaternio* because that means "a squad in the army." Let these leaves be held together at top and bottom by a strip (of parchment threaded through). The scribe should have a bookmark cord and a pointed tool about which he can say, "I have pricked *(punxi)* not pinked *(pupigi)* my quaternion." Let him sit in a chair with both arms high, reinforcing the back rest, and with a stool at the feet. Let the writer have a heating basin covered with a cap; he should have a knife with which he can shape a quill pen; let this be prepared for writing with the inside fuzzy scale scraped out, and let there be a boar's or goat's tooth for polishing the parchment, so that the ink of a letter may not run (I do not say a whole alphabet); he should have something with which letters can be canceled. Let him have an indicator *(speculum)* or line marker *(cavilla)* in order that he may not make a costly delay from error. There should be hot coals in the heating container so that the ink may dry more quickly on the parchment in foggy or wet weather.

48. Advice on the Proper Care of Books, 1345

Richard de Bury

In the first place, there should be a natural decorum in the opening and closing of books, so that they are not unclasped in too great a hurry, or, after they have been looked at, put away not properly clasped. For we ought to take much better care of a book than of a shoe. But scholars as a class are commonly not well brought up, and unless they are held in check

From Urban Tigner Holmes, *Daily Living in the Twelfth Century* (Madison: The University of Wisconsin Press; ©1952 by the Regents of the University of Wisconsin). Reprinted by permission. This selection is from pages 69-71 in the 1964 paperback edition.

From *The Philobiblon of Richard de Bury*, Vol. I, 113-116, reprinted in *Chaucer's World* by Edith Rickert (New York: Columbia University Press, 1948). This selection is from pages 119-24 in the 1962 paperback edition.

by the rules of their elders, are puffed up with all sorts of nonsense. They act on impulse, swell with impudence, and lay down the law on one point after another, when, as a matter of fact, they are inexperienced in everything.

You may see, perhaps, a headstrong youth sitting lazily over his studies. Because it is winter, and he is chilly, his nose runs, and he does not even bother to wipe it with his kerchief until it has soiled his book. Such a fellow should have, instead of a book, a shoemaker's apron.

He has long fingernails, black as jet, with which he marks passages that he likes. He puts innumerable straws in various parts of the book, so that their stems may help him to find again what his memory cannot retain. These straws, which are never removed, the book cannot digest, and so becomes distended until it bursts its clasps; and there the straws remain, carelessly forgotten until they rot.

Such a fellow does not hesitate to eat fruit or cheese over his open book, or negligently to set his cup here and there on it; and having no alms bag at hand, he leaves the scraps and crumbs in the book. He never stops barking at his fellows with endless chatter, and while he produces an infinitude of reasons void of all sense, he also sprinkles the open book in his lap with sputtering saliva.

What is worse still, he lies on his book with folded arms, supplementing his brief study with a long nap; and by way of smoothing out the wrinkles, he doubles up the pages of the book, to its no small detriment.

When the rain is past and gone and flowers appear on the earth, this so-called scholar will stuff his book with violets, primroses, roses, and even four-leaved clover. Sometimes he paws it over with wet or sweaty hands; or, again, he handles the white parchment with dusty gloves and hunts for his page, line by line, with a forefinger covered with an old piece of skin. And at the prick of a biting flea, he throws aside his previous volume so that it may not be closed again for a month; and by that time it will be so full of dust that it cannot be clasped at all.

It is especially important to keep from contact with our books those impudent boys who, as soon as they have learned to form the letters of the alphabet, immediately become incongruous annotators of the fairest volumes that come their way, and either ornament with a hideous alphabet every wider margin that they find to the text or make free to write with ungoverned pen whatever nonsense comes into their heads. In one place a Latinist, in another a philosopher, or, perhaps, some ignorant scribe tries out his pen—a trick which we have very often seen damage the fairest books in both their utility and their value.

There are also thieves who mutilate books shamefully, cutting off the side margins even into the very letters of the text, to get materials for their own correspondence, or for various uses and abuses steal the fly-leaves which are put there to protect the book.

Again, it is only decent that we scholars, when we return to study after meals, should wash our hands before we begin to read; no greasy finger should turn the leaves or even touch the clasp. No crying child should be allowed to admire the illuminated capitals, lest he defile the parchment with his wet hands, for a child touches whatever he looks at.

Furthermore, the illiterate, who view a book with the same interest whether it is upside down or rightside up, are not at all suitable persons to meddle with books. And let the clerk see to it that no sooty scullion reeking from his unwashed pots touch the leaves of books; but let him who has the care of the precious volumes be always spotlessly clean. . . .

49. Humility is the Student's Chief Virtue

Hugh of St. Victor

The good student, then, ought to be humble and docile, free alike from vain cares and from sensual indulgences, diligent and zealous to learn willingly from all, to presume never upon his own knowledge, to shun the authors of perverse doctrine as if they were poison, to consider a matter thoroughly and at length before judging of it, to seek to *be* learned rather than merely to seem so, to love such words of the wise as he has grasped, and ever to hold those words before his gaze as the very mirror of his countenance. And if some things, by chance rather obscure, have not allowed him to understand them, let him not at once break out in angry condemnation and think that nothing is good but what he himself can understand. This is the humility proper to a student's discipline.

50. Rules of the University of Paris

Robert, Cardinal Legate

Robert, servant of the cross of Christ by divine pity, cardinal priest of the title, St. Stephen in Mons Caelius, legate of the apostolic see, to all the masters and scholars of Paris, eternal greeting in the Lord. Let all know

From *The "Didascalicon" of Hugh of St. Victor, A Medieval Guide to the Arts* by Jerome Taylor (New York: Columbia University Press, 1961), p. 97. Reprinted by permission.

From *Chartulary of the University of Paris* translated by Lynn Thorndike in *University Records and Life in the Middle Ages* (New York: Columbia University Press, 1944), pp. 27-30. Reprinted by permission.

that, since we have had a special mandate from the pope to take effective measures to reform the state of the Parisian scholars for the better, wishing with the counsel of good men to provide for the tranquility of the scholars in the future, we have decreed and ordained in this wise:

No one shall lecture in the arts at Paris before he is twenty-one years of age, and he shall have heard lectures for at least six years before he begins to lecture, and he shall promise to lecture for at least two years, unless a reasonable cause prevents, which he ought to prove publicly or before examiners. He shall not be stained by any infamy, and when he is ready to lecture, he shall be examined according to the form which is contained in the writing of the lord bishop of Paris . . . And they shall lecture on the books of Aristotle on dialectic old and new in the schools ordinarily and not *ad cursum*. They shall also lecture on both Priscians ordinarily, or at least on one. They shall not lecture on feast days except on philosophers and rhetoric and the quadrivium and *Barbarismus* and ethics, if it please them, and the fourth book of the *Topics*. They shall not lecture on the books of Aristotle on metaphysics and natural philosophy or on summaries of them or concerning the doctrine of Master David of Dinant or the heretic Amaury or Mauritius of Spain.

In the *principia* and meetings of the masters and in the responsions or oppositions of the boys and youths there shall be no drinking. They may summon some friends or associates, but only a few. Donations of clothing or other things as has been customary, or more, we urge should be made, especially to the poor. None of the masters lecturing in arts shall have a cope except one round, black, and reaching to the ankles, at least while it is new. Use of the pallium is permitted. No one shall wear with the round cope shoes that are ornamented or with elongated pointed toes. If any scholar in arts or theology dies, half of the masters of arts shall attend the funeral at one time, the other half the next time, and no one shall leave until the sepulture is finished, unless he has reasonable cause. . . .

Each master shall have jurisdiction over his scholar. No one shall occupy a classroom or house without asking the consent of the tenant, provided one has a chance to ask it. No one shall receive the licentiate from the chancellor or another for money given or promise made or other condition agreed upon. Also, the masters and scholars can make both between themselves and with other persons obligations and constitutions supported by faith or penalty or oath in these cases: namely, the murder or mutilation of a scholar or atrocious injury done a scholar, if justice should not be forthcoming, arranging the prices of lodgings, costume, burial, lectures and disputations, so, however, that the university be not thereby dissolved or destroyed.

As to the status of the theologians, we decree that no one shall lecture at Paris before his thirty-fifth year and unless he has studied for eight years at least, and has heard the books faithfully and in classrooms, and has attended lectures in theology for five years before he gives lectures himself publicly. And none of these shall lecture before the third hour on days when masters lecture. No one shall be admitted at Paris to formal lectures or to preachings unless he shall be of approved life and science. No one shall be a scholar at Paris who has no definite master.

Moreover, that these decrees may be observed inviolate, we by virtue of our legatine authority have bound by the knot of excommunication all who shall contumaciously presume to go against these our statutes, unless within fifteen days after the offense they have taken care to emend their presumption before the university of masters and scholars or other persons constituted by the university. Done in the year of Grace 1215, the month of August.

51. Lecture Method Prescribed at Paris, December 10, 1355

Chartulary of the University of Paris

In the name of the Lord, amen. Two methods of lecturing on books in the liberal arts having been tried, the former masters of philosophy uttering their words rapidly so that the mind of the hearer can take them in but the hand cannot keep up with them, the latter speaking slowly until their listeners can catch up with them with the pen; having compared these by diligent examination, the former method is found the better. Wherefore, the consensus of opinion warns us that we imitate it in our lectures. We, therefore, all and each, masters of the faculty of arts, teaching and not teaching, convoked for this specially by the venerable man, master Albert of Bohemia, then rector of the university, at St. Julien le Pauvre, have decreed in this wise, that all lecturers, whether masters or scholars of the same faculty, whenever and wherever they chance to lecture on any text ordinarily or cursorily in the same faculty, or to dispute any question concerning it, or anything else by way of exposition, shall observe the former method of lecturing to the best of their ability, so speaking forsooth as if no one was taking notes before them, in the way that sermons and recommendations are made in the university and which the lectures in other

From *Chartulary of the University of Paris* translated by Lynn Thorndike in *University Records and Life in the Middle Ages* (New York: Columbia University Press, 1944), p. 237. Reprinted by permission.

faculties follow. Moreover, transgressors of this statute, if the lecturers are masters or scholars, we now deprive henceforth for a year from lecturing, honors, offices and other advantages of our faculty. Which if anyone violates, for the first relapse we double the penalty, for the second we quadruple it, and so on. Moreover, listeners who oppose the execution of this our statute by clamor, hissing, noise, throwing stones by themselves or by their servants and accomplices, or in any other way, we deprive of and cut off from our society for a year, and for each relapse we increase the penalty double and quadruple as above. . . .

52. University Methods of Study

Frank Pierrepont Greaves

The training of a mediaeval student consisted not only in acquiring the subjects mentioned, but in learning to debate upon them. The acquisition of the subject matter was accomplished through lectures, which consisted in reading and explaining the textbook under consideration. This was rendered necessary by the scarcity of manuscripts, which had to be used until the invention of printing, and the difficulty in purchasing or renting copies of them. Each work consisted of a text and commentaries upon it. The glosses, which had often grown to such proportions as completely to overshadow the original, consisted of explanatory notes, summaries, cross-references, and objections to the author's statements. To these the teacher might add a commentary of his own as he read. Odofredus, the jurist, thus describes his procedure at Bologna: —

> First, I shall give you summaries of each chapter before I proceed to the text; secondly, I shall give you as clear and explicit a statement as I can of the purport of each Law (included in the chapter); thirdly, I shall read the text with a view to correcting it; fourthly, I shall briefly repeat the contents of the Law; fifthly, I shall solve apparent contradictions, adding any general principles of Law (to be extracted from the passage), and any distinctions or subtle and useful problems arising out of the Law with their solutions.

The master must often have had to read the passage repeatedly, in order that all might grasp it, and he ordinarily read slowly enough for the student to treat his commentary as a dictation. There was always considerable

From *A History of Education During the Middle Ages* by Frank Pierrepont Greaves (New York: The Macmillan Co., 1919), pp. 90-92. Reprinted by permission.

objection to rapid reading, and even university regulations were made against a master's lecturing so fast as not to permit of full notes. Naturally, such a method afforded little freedom in thinking. There could be no real investigation, but simply a slavish following of the text and lecture. The whole exercise was carried on in Latin, which had to be learned by the student before coming to the university.

The training in debate was furnished by means of formal disputations, in which one student, or group of students, was pitted against another. In these contests, which also were conducted in Latin, not only were authorities cited, but the debaters might add arguments of their own. Sometimes a single person might exercise himself by arguing both sides of the question and coming to a judgment for one side or the other. This debating had been instituted to afford some acuteness and vigor of intellect, and, compared with the memorizing of lectures, it served its purpose well, but by the close of the fifteenth century it had gone to such an extreme as to be no longer reputable. The aim came to be to win and to secure applause without regard to truth or consistency.

53. The Scholastic Method of Inquiry and Dispute

St. Thomas Aquinas

Fifth Article
WHETHER SACRED DOCTRINE IS NOBLER THAN
OTHER SCIENCES?

We proceed thus to the Fifth Article:—

Objection 1. It seems that sacred doctrine is not nobler than other sciences, for the nobility of a science depends on its certitude. But other sciences, the principles of which cannot be doubted, seem to be more certain than sacred doctrine; for its principles—namely, articles of faith—can be doubted. Therefore other sciences seem to be nobler.

Objection 2. Further, it is the part of a lower science to draw upon a higher; as music draws upon arithmetic. But sacred doctrine does draw upon the philosophical sciences; for Jerome observes, in his Epistle to Magnus, that *the ancient doctors so enriched their books with the doctrines and thoughts of the philosophers, that thou knowest not what more to*

From *Introduction to St. Thomas Aquinas,* Anton C. Pegis, ed. (New York: Random House, Modern Library, 1948), pp. 8-10, "The Summa Theologica, Question I, Article 5." Copyright, 1945, 1948, by Random House, Inc. Reprinted by permission of the publisher.

admire in them, their profane erudition or their scriptural learning. Therefore sacred doctrine is inferior to other sciences.

On the contrary, Other sciences are called the handmaidens of this one: *Wisdom sent her maids to invite to the tower (Prov.* ix. 3).

I answer that, Since this science is partly speculative and partly practical, it transcends all other sciences, speculative and practical. Now one speculative science is said to be nobler than another either by reason of its greater certitude, or by reason of the higher dignity of its subject-matter. In both these respects this science surpasses other speculative sciences: in point of greater certitude, because other sciences derive their certitude from the natural light of human reason, which can err, whereas this derives its certitude from the light of the divine knowledge, which cannot err; in point of the higher dignity of its subject-matter, because this science treats chiefly of those things which by their sublimity transcend human reason, while other sciences consider only those things which are within reason's grasp. Of the practical sciences, that one is nobler which is ordained to a more final end, as political science is nobler than military science; for the good of the army is directed to the good of the state. But the purpose of this science, in so far as it is practical, is eternal beatitude, to which as to an ultimate end the ends of all the practical sciences are directed. Hence it is clear that from every standpoint it is nobler than other sciences.

Reply Objection. 1. It may well happen that what is in itself the more certain may seem to us the less certain because of the weakness of our intellect, *which is dazzled by the clearest objects of nature; as the owl is dazzled by the light of the sun.* Hence the fact that some happen to doubt about the articles of faith is not due to the uncertain nature of the truths, but to the weakness of the human intellect; yet the slenderest knowledge that may be obtained of the highest things is more desirable than the most certain knowledge obtained of the lowest things, as is said in *De Animalibus* xi.

Reply Objection 2. This science can draw upon the philosophical sciences, not as though it stood in need of them, but only in order to make its teaching clearer. For it accepts its principles, not from the other sciences, but immediately from God, by revelation. Therefore it does not draw upon the other sciences as upon its superiors, but uses them as its inferiors and handmaidens: even so the master sciences make use of subordinate sciences, as political science of military science. That it thus uses them is not due to its own defect or insufficiency, but to the defect of our intellect, which is more easily led by what is known through natural reason (from which proceed the other sciences), to that which is above reason, such as are the teachings of this science.

54. Ignorance, Permissiveness, Vanity: Sins of the University Teachers

Charles H. Haskins

For the faults of the masters the preachers show little indulgence. Many begin to teach before they have studied long enough in the schools, an abuse which prevails in all faculties but particularly in that of arts. Such masters, says Jacques de Vitry, draw their lectures from books and closets, not from well stored minds, but they succeed in securing students none the less, by personal solicitation and friendship and even by hiring them to come. The number of their scholars is the masters' pride, wherefore their class-rooms should be large and easily accessible; to crowd their class-rooms they preach new and strange doctrines, and for money they will lecture even on Sundays and holy days. Masters there are, too, who make life easy for the scholars who live with them, letting them sleep late in the morning and roam about and amuse themselves freely, and even conniving at their vices. The great aim of the master is not to instruct his pupils but to appear learned and be called rabbi; many speak obscurely in order to appear more profound and even pay the beadles to magnify them and cover up their ignorance. Their quarrels are like cock-fights and they are so jealous that they seek to draw away one another's scholars and, even when detained by illness, will not suffer their pupils to hear lectures from another.

55. Requirements for the Bachelor's Degree, 1340

Item, it was ordained that no one after this year should be licensed to take a degree in arts.... unless he first swears that he has read cursorily two books of logic at least, one of the old logic, and the other of the new, or both of the new; and one of the books of physics: namely, the four books "Coeli et mundi" (Of Heaven and Earth), or three books "De anima" (On the Soul), or the four books "Meteororum" (Of Meteors), or the two books "De generatione et corruptione" (Of Birth and Decay), or the books "De sensu et sensation" (Of Feeling and What Is Felt), with the books "De

From *Studies in Medieval Culture* by Charles Homer Haskins (Oxford: The Clarendon Press, 1929; New York: Frederick Ungar Publishing Co., 1958). This selection is from pages 54-56 in the 1958 edition.

From *Munimenta academica*, Anstey, ed., Vol. I, pp. 142-43, reprinted in *Chaucer's World* by Edith Rickert (New York: Columbia University Press, 1948). This selection appears on page 133 in the 1962 paperback edition.

memoria et reminiscentia" (Of Memory and Recollection), and "De somno et vigilia" (Of Sleep and Waking), or the book "De motu animalium" (Of the Movement of Animals), with two books "De minutis natural ibus" (Of Minor Points in Natural History), and this correctly and rightly according to the form prescribed above.

56. College Statutes Governing Student Living

Robert de Sorbonne

I wish that the custom which was instituted from the beginning in this house by the counsel of good men may be kept, and if anyone ever has transgressed it, that henceforth he shall not presume to do so.

No one therefore shall eat meat in the house on Advent, nor on Monday or Tuesday of Lent, nor from Ascension Day to Pentecost.

Also, I will that the community be not charged for meals taken in rooms. If there cannot be equality, it is better that the fellow eating in his room be charged than the entire community.

Also, no one shall eat in his room except for cause. If anyone has a guest, he shall eat in hall. If, moreover, it shall not seem expedient to the fellow to bring that guest to hall, let him eat in his room and he shall have the usual portion for himself, not for the guest. If, moreover, he wants more for himself or his guest, he should pay for it himself. . . .

Also, the fellows should be warned by the bearer of the roll that those eating in private rooms conduct themselves quietly and abstain from too much noise, lest those passing through the court and street be scandalized and lest the fellows in rooms adjoining be hindered in their studies.

Also, those eating in private rooms shall provide themselves with what they need in season as best they can, so that the service of the community may be disturbed as little as possible. But if there are any infringers of this statute who are accustomed to eat in private rooms without cause, they shall be warned by the bearer of the roll to desist, which if they will not do, he shall report it to the master. If, moreover, other reasons arise for which anyone can eat in a private room, it shall be left to the discretion of the roll-bearer and proctors until otherwise ordered.

Also, the rule does not apply to the sick. If anyone eats in a private room because of sickness, he may have a fellow with him, if he wishes, to entertain

From *Chartulary of the University of Paris* translated by Lynn Thorndike in *University Records and Life in the Middle Ages* (New York: Columbia University Press, 1944), pp. 88-92. Reprinted by permission.

and wait on him, who also shall have his due portion. What shall be the portion of a fellow shall be left to the discretion of the dispenser. If a fellow shall come late to lunch, if he comes from classes or a sermon or business of the community, he shall have his full portion, but if from his own affairs, he shall have bread only....

Also, all shall wear closed outer garments, nor shall they have trimmings of vair or grise or of red or green silk on the outer garment or hood.

Also, no one shall have loud shoes or clothing by which scandal might be generated in any way.

Also, no one shall be received in the house unless he shall be willing to leave off such and to observe the aforesaid rules.

Also, no one shall be received in the house unless he pledges faith that, if he happens to receive books from the common store, he will treat them carefully as if his own and on no condition remove or lend them out of the house, and return them in good condition whenever required or whenever he leaves town.

Also, let every fellow have his own mark on his clothes and one only and different from the others. And let all the marks be written on a schedule and over each mark the name of whose it is. And let that schedule be given to the servant so that he may learn to recognize the mark of each one. And the servant shall not receive clothes from any fellow unless he sees the mark. And then the servant can return his clothes to each fellow....

Also, for peace and utility we propound that no secular person living in town—scribe, corrector, or anyone else—unless for great cause eat, sleep in a room, or remain with the fellows when they eat, or have frequent conversation in the gardens or hall or other parts of the house, lest the secrets of the house and the remarks of the fellows be spread abroad.

Also, no outsider shall come to accountings or the special meetings of the fellows, and he whose guest he is shall see to this.   .

Also, no fellow shall bring in outsiders frequently to drink at commons, and if he does, he shall pay according to the estimate of the dispenser.

Also, no fellow shall have a key to the kitchen.

Also, no fellow shall presume to sleep outside the house in town, and if he did so for reason, he shall take pains to submit his excuse to the bearer of the roll....

Also, no women of any sort shall eat in the private rooms. If anyone violates this rule, he shall pay the assessed penalty, namely, sixpence....

Also, no one shall form the habit of talking too loudly at table. Whoever after he has been warned about this by the prior shall have offended by speaking too loudly, provided this is established afterwards by testimony of several fellows to the prior, shall be held to the usual house penalty, namely two quarts of wine.

The penalty for transgression of statutes which do not fall under an oath is twopence, if the offenders are not reported by someone, or if they were, the penalty becomes sixpence in the case of fines. I understand "not reported" to mean that, if before the matter has come to the attention of the prior, the offender accuses himself to the prior or has told the clerk to write down twopence against him for such an offence, for it is not enough to say to the fellows, "I accuse myself."

57. Preachers Decry Riotous Life of Paris Students

Charles H. Haskins

When we turn from studies and teachers to the students themselves, we find the material contained in the sermons fuller and more satisfactory. The ideal scholar of the pulpits was a rather colourless personage, obedient, respectful, eager to learn, and keeping very much to himself. In order to win the favour of the master and his personal instruction, one should be assiduous at lectures, quick at learning, and bold in debate, and should also attract other pupils to the master. When, in the Lenten season, a master in theology takes the chair and proposes a question, to which one of the bystanders replies, it is a mark of deference and honour to the respondent if the master determines the question in accordance with his reply. Robert de Sorbon lays down six rules for successful study: a fixed time for each subject, concentrated attention, memorizing specific things, note-taking, conference with others, and finally prayer, "which availeth much for learning." The good student should imitate Christ among the doctors, hearing many masters, always seeking good teachers without regard to their fame or place of birth, and listening as well as asking questions—unlike those who will not wait for the end of a question but cry out, "I know what you mean." Even when he goes to walk by the Seine in the evening, the good student ought to ponder or repeat his lesson.

It need scarcely be said that the students of mediaeval Paris did not as a rule spend their time in such studious promenades; indeed if further evidence were needed to dispel the illusion that a mediaeval university was an institution devoted to biblical study and religious nurture, the preachers of the period would offer sufficient proof. We have already seen how the

From *Studies in Medieval Culture* by Charles Homer Haskins (Oxford: The Clarendon Press, 1929; New York: Frederick Ungar Publishing Co., 1958). This selection is from pages 56-59 in the 1958 edition.

theological faculty, the only one dealing directly with religious subject-matter, was suffering from the competition of the canon law and other "lucrative" subjects, and it is on every hand apparent that the morals of at least a considerable portion of the student body were as profane as their studies. Students, we are told, care nothing for sermons, and for most of them holy days are only an occasion for idleness; they remain outside during mass, and like their masses short and their lectures and disputations long. If their voice is in the choir, their mind is without, in the street, in bed, or at the table — as the rhyme ran,

> Vox in choro, mens in foro
> Vel in mensa vel in thoro.

Confession they likewise neglect; instead of seeking to have his soul cleansed by confession on his arrival at Paris, the student hastens to the laundress. Dominicans like Etienne de Bourbon attend vespers, at Notre-Dame or elsewhere, but a miracle or special providence is often needed in order to bring students or masters into this order, and one subprior complains that parents are more anxious to keep their sons away from the friars than from the brothel or the tavern. "The student's heart is in the mire," says another Dominican, "fixed on prebends and things temporal and how to satisfy his desires." "He is ashamed to sin against the rules of Donatus, but not to violate the law of Christ." He is much more familiar, says Robert de Sorbon, with the text of the dice, which he recognizes at once, no matter how rapidly they are thrown, than with the text of the Old Logic — yet the gloss of the dice he forgets, which is, Swear, steal, and be hanged. "This very week within two leagues of Paris a priest hanged himself after gambling away ten livres and his horse. Such is the fate of gamesters." Many students come to Paris like the prodigal to a far country, and indulge in practices they would not even think of at home, wasting in riotous living not only their own portion but the substance of their churches.

What the forms of riotous living were which prevailed among students the preachers do not hesitate to specify, sometimes with more particularity than modern taste permits. Gambling is mentioned, even on the altars of churches, and feasting and free indulgence in the wine-cup, as well as wild carouses in the streets and the visiting of disreputable resorts, which were often found in close proximity to the class-rooms. Many of the students led a life that was by no means celibate, and there are allusions to the darkest of monastic vices.

58. Town /Gown Controversy in Rome, Early Fourteenth Century

The Senators of Rome

To the most holy Father, etc.

The detestable infamy of crimes which are continually committed by certain sons of iniquity, who claim only in word the distinction of the clerical character, being themselves utter strangers to all honesty of morals and knowledge of letters, hath moved us to write to the feet of your Holiness. Know indeed, most Holy Father, that many in the city, furnished only with the shield and privilege conferred by the first tonsure, strive not in honesty of manners, but rather are ordinarily guided by the rule of horrible misdeeds; wandering armed from tavern to tavern and other unhonest places; sometimes going on to quarrel or fight in arms with laymen; committing manslaughter, thefts, robberies and very many other things that are far from honesty. For which things no safeguard or remedy is applied by the ecclesiastical judges holding the place of your most Holy See; but rather, when [these evildoers] are accused of the aforesaid misdeeds in our courts, they compel us to release them from our examination, saying that they themselves will see to the infliction of a fine upon them; and thus, under the cloke of such assertions, these so nefarious and most criminal men, hateful both to God and to man, pass unpunished; which is known to redound no little to the dishonour of the Holy See and to the damage of the Romans. Moreover, this is imputed to our official negligence, when misdeeds so enormous are not quelled by the rigour of our justice; and a most horrible and detestable belief haunts the minds of the Romans, who will say at times, in our presence or elsewhere: "Alas! these miscreants who call themselves clerics and yet comport themselves as layfolk, wherefore are they not punished out of their evil courses? In this the Senators do ill; for in the past, when our lord Boniface of blessed memory sat on the papal chair, the Senate made complaint to him concerning like matters, and he not only commanded their punishment but was as it were troubled in mind against them, for those who had gone scot-free; so likewise, if our present Lord learned the truth, he also would be displeased at their impunity." Wherefore we most piously beseech your Holiness, with all humility and devotion,

From *Life in the Middle Ages* by George Gordon Coulton (Cambridge: Cambridge University Press, 1967), Vol. I, Part 2, pp. 87-89. Reprinted by permission.

Author's Note: The University of Rome was founded by Boniface VIII in 1303. The removal of Boniface's successors to Avignon, and the long-standing lawlessness of the city, no doubt reacted unfavourably on the discipline of the Roman scholars. The petition from the Senators to the absentee Pontiff is printed by F. Novati in *Giorn. Storico d. Lett. Italiana,* vol. II, p. 138, from a fourteenth-century manuscript: it belongs almost certainly to the first quarter of that century.

that if it should so befall that our rigour should go so far as to punish them in virtue of our office as judges, then you would vouchsafe (if it so please you) to permit this unto us and to support us in future with the authority of your Holiness. For let not your clemency believe that we are on this account minded to go so far as to touch clerics in possession of church benefices, whom we are purposed and ready to treat with all due reverence, since we are unwilling to do anything derogatory to ecclesiastical liberties. For, most Holy Father, we fear lest, if the aforesaid impious fellows are not controlled to some extent by the secular arm, then the people of Rome will grow to such horror of these their misdeeds as to rise up in wrath and fury not only against these, but even against the aforesaid clerics who are zealous for the orthodox faith. Meanwhile we are ready from the bottom of our heart to carry out cheerfully whatsoever may' conduce to the honour of the Papal See.

59. The Battling Welsh Students at Oxford (1388-1389): Two Accounts

Adam of Usk

In these days there happened at Oxford a grave misfortune. For, during two whole years there was great strife between the men of the south and the men of Wales on the one side and the northerners on the other, whence arose broils, quarrels, and ofttimes loss of life. In the first year the northerners were driven clean away from the university. And they laid their expulsion chiefly to my charge. But in the second year, in an evil hour, coming back to Oxford, they gathered by night, and denying us passage from our quarters by force of arms, for two days they strove sorely against us, breaking and plundering some of the halls of our side and slaying certain of our men. Howbeit, on the third day our party, bravely strengthened by the help of Merton Hall, forced our adversaries shamefully to fly from the public streets, which for the two days they had held as a camp, and to take refuge in their own quarters. In short, we could not be quieted before many of our number had been indicted for felonious riot; and amongst them I, who am now writing, was indicted, as the chief leader and abettor of the Welsh, and perhaps not unrighteously. And so indicted we were hardly acquitted, being tried by jury before the King's judge. From that

From Adam of Usk, *Chronicon*, reprinted in *Chaucer's World* by Edith Rickert (New York: Columbia Press, 1948). Reprinted by permission. This selection is from pages 131-32 in the 1962 paperback edition.

day forth I feared the King, hitherto unknown to me in his power, and his laws, and I put hooks into my jaws.

* * *

Henrici Knighton

In Lent there arose a painful conflict in Oxford; the trouble of the preceding year had not been entirely allayed, but still kept irritating the parties. The scholars from Wales, always restless, rose, along with the scholars from the south, who stood by them against the northern scholars, and many evils and even deaths resulted. This disagreement increased to such an extent that a day for an open battle in the field was fixed between the parties. But God intervened, and Thomas of Woodstock, duke of Gloucester, came in and arranged matters with slight loss; many of the students of Wales were banished from the University of Oxford. They were compelled to this by some of the scholars from the north, who were prepared for this when they came to the gates to offer reconciliation.

60.   Student Poleaxed To Death at Cambridge: Coroner's Inquest

E. P. Cheyney

Pleas of the crown held in the presence of Stephen Morys and Edmund Listere, coroners of the liberty of Cambridge, from the Monday after the feast of St. Mary Magdalen, in the forty-third year of the reign of King Edward the Third, even to the feast of St. Luke the Evangelist, in the fourth year of the reign of King Richard the Second.

On the Sabbath day, in the vigil of Pentecost, in the forty-eighth year of the reign of King Edward the Third, it happened at Cambridge that a certain Roger Kebbel was found dead, bearing a wound on the right side of his head four inches in length and two in depth. Inquiry concerning the death was made of William de Cumberton, William Hyndercle, John Colvile, skinner, John de Norfolk, John Coupere, Robert de Holm, Richard Bowyer, Andreas Breustere, Richard Ferrour, John Albyn, John Hosyere, and Thomas Maydenston. These men declared on oath that on

From *Chronicon Henrici Knighton* reprinted in *Readings in English History Drawn from the Original Sources* by E. P. Cheyney (Boston: Ginn & Co., 1908), p. 191.

From *Readings in English History Drawn from the Original Sources* by Edward P. Cheyney (Boston: Ginn & Co., 1908), p. 192.

Wednesday, on the feast of St. Mark the Evangelist, in the year above mentioned, just before midnight, a certain quarrel arose in Cambridge near the corner of St. Benedict, between Master Robert Utesle and John de Stowe, John Saunford, and other clerks, who began to fight among themselves. When this was announced to the friends of the said John Saunford, clerks came from the different inns and from the castle to the said corner to aid the said John, among whom came the above-mentioned Roger Kebbel. One Richard Reyner came with a poleax and dealt the said Roger the above-mentioned blow, from which he died, after lingering from the said feast of St. Mark even to the vigil of Pentecost. Immediately after this wicked deed the said Richard fled. They say that the said Richard has no lands, dwellings, goods, or chattels which can be valued or appraised.

61. Many Study; Few Find Knowledge

Hugh of St. Victor

We must say why it is that from such a throng of students, of whom many are both strong in natural talent and energetic in applying themselves, so few, easily counted, are found who manage to reach knowledge. And, leaving out of our consideration those who are naturally dull and slow in understanding things, it seems especially important and worthwhile to ask why it is that two persons who have equal talent and exert equal effort and who are intent upon the same study, nevertheless do not attain a similar result in their understanding of it. The one penetrates it quickly, quickly seizes upon what he is looking for. The other labors long and makes little progress. But what one should know is that in every business, no matter what it is, two things are necessary, namely work and a method for that work, and these two are so connected that one without the other is either useless or less effective. And yet, as it is said, "Wisdom is better than strength," for sometimes even weights which we cannot budge by force, we raise through cleverness. Thus it is, to be sure, in all our study. He who works along without discretion works, it is true, but he does not make progress, and just as if he were beating the air, he pours out his strength upon wind. Consider two men both traveling through a wood, one of them struggling around in bypaths but the other picking the short cuts of a direct route: they move along their ways with the same amount of motion, but they do not reach

From *The "Didascalicon" of Hugh of St. Victor, A Medieval Guide to the Arts* by Jerome Taylor (New York: Columbia University Press, 1961), pp. 126-27. Reprinted by permission.

the goal at the same time. But what shall I call Scripture if not a wood? Its thoughts, like so many sweetest fruits, we pick as we read and chew as we consider them. Therefore, whoever does not keep to an order and a method in the reading of so great a collection of books wanders as it were into the very thick of the forest and loses the path of the direct route; he is, as it is said, "always learning yet never reaching knowledge." For discretion is of such importance that without it every rest from work is disgraceful and work itself is useless. May we all draw our own conclusion!

There are three things above all which ordinarily provide obstacles for the studies of students: carelessness, imprudence, and bad luck *(fortuna)*. Carelessness arises when we simply omit, or when we learn less carefully, those things which are there to be learned. Imprudence arises when we do not keep to a suitable order and method in the things we are learning. Bad luck shows up in a development, a chance happening, or a natural occurrence, when we are kept back from our objective either by poverty, or by illness, or by some non-natural slowness, or even by a scarcity of professors, because either none can be found to teach us, or none can be found to teach us well. But as to these three matters, in the first of them—carelessness, that is—the student needs to be admonished; in the second—imprudence, that is —he needs to be instructed; while in the third—bad luck, that is—he needs to be assisted.

62. Muslim Colleges Founded Before Christian Universities

Bayard Dodge

It proved to be so inconvenient to hold lectures and lively discussions in the mosques, where pious worshippers were trying to pray and to memorize the Qur'ān, that the Muslim educators developed a new type of institution called in Arabic "al-madrasah," referred to in English as the "college." This form of school did not bring to an end the educational work in the mosques, but existed side by side with the mosque classes.

Although the term "al-madrasah" was used during the ninth century, the first institution really deserving the name was probably built at Naysā-būr in North-Eastern Persia during the first quarter of the eleventh century. Then in 1067 Nizām al-Mulk erected at Baghdad the great college, which

From *Muslim Education in Medieval Times* by Bayard Dodge (Washington, D. C.: The Middle East Institute, 1962), pp. 19-22. Reprinted by permission.

became a model for orthodox Islam and was named after its founder "al-Nizamīyah," the Caliph himself presiding over its dedication.

The building was a quadrangle located near the Tigris, probably with colonnades or half open vaulted halls surrounding a central courtyard. On the side facing Makkah there was undoubtedly a prayer niche, with a pulpit standing near it, and somewhere in the building there was a library of considerable importance. Either on upper floors or in adjoining loggias there must have been sleeping quarters for the students, while in the basements there were store rooms, lavatories and a kitchen. Most of the classes probably met in the porches or colonnades, although it is possible that there were a number of individual classrooms. As the building was completely destroyed, it is impossible to know exactly what it was like.

The teacher followed the old custom of sitting on a low chair, with his students on the ground around him. When a lecture was given, it began with prayer, followed by the recital of some verses from the Qur'ān and an appeal for Allāh to bless the Prophet.

Nizām al-Mulk provided large enough endowments to assure generous salaries for the teachers as well as board, lodging, clothing, furnishings and heat for the students. The professors, who wore academic robes of black and marine blue, were so highly regarded that they were frequently chosen to perform diplomatic missions. Whenever a professor gave his first lecture it attracted many important persons, who attended a banquet as soon as the class was ended.

The honorary head of the college was a high official, with a deputy or vice-chancellor to conduct the administration. As a rule each professor had at least one assistant and in addition to the members of the teaching staff there were numerous clerks and servants as well as the librarian, prayer leader and registrar.

The assistant repeated the words of the professor in a loud voice, so that the students could write them down from dictation. He also answered questions, explained the lessons and helped the students to correct their notes. In case an assistant took the place of an absent professor, he showed proper respect by holding his master's manuscript in his hand and praying for his safe return.

After removing his shoes a student sat on the ground, often using his knees to serve as a desk. He held his paper in his left hand, while with his right hand he wrote from right to left, dipping his reed pen in an inkstand, which was as a rule a small brass container inserted in a wooden pen box fixed to his girdle. The notes, which the student took down from dictation and memorized, served as his textbook.

There was no regular schedule, the student being free to continue his studies as long as he himself and his teachers felt it wise for him to do so.

Time was not an important factor, the principal aim of the system being thoroughness. The professor started his course by giving an outline of the material to be studied, followed by a general explanation of the subject and the ways in which the authorities differed about it. Finally there was an exhaustive study of every aspect of the material. In order to avoid confusion the student was advised to study one subject at a time and to refrain from using too many sources. He was also encouraged to learn logic and rhetoric, so as to know how to avoid ambiguity of language and thought. As, however, the bright students were too ambitious to limit their efforts to studying only one course at a time, it was not long before it became the custom for them to study a number of subjects every day.

Most of the teachers were true scholars and men of good character, sincerely interested in their students. Many of them were known for their piety, frugality, industry, kindness and sense of humor. They had, however, certain shortcomings, one of which was the tendency to imitate rather than to create. They were also accused of being vain and envious. Competition to have large classes, jealousy at time of failure and self-satisfaction when there was success, were frailties which gave a human touch to these men of religion and learning.

The famous traveller ibn-Jubayr visited al-Nizāmīyah about 1184 and was much impressed by a lecture, which he attended one Friday afternoon. The gathering must have been of a special nature, as classes did not as a rule meet on Fridays. After several reciters had intoned passages of the Qur'ān, a religious leader delivered an address from the top step of the pulpit, commenting on the Qur'ān and the traditions of the Prophet. After he had finished his discourse, questions in written form were showered on him from all sides. He answered them in a patient way, throwing away the paper on which each question was written, after the answer had been given.

Nizām al-Mulk established colleges like al-Nizāmīyah at al-Basrah and al-Mawsil in 'Irāq, at Isfahan and Naysābūr in Persia, and Balkh and Harat further to the east.

A century later, Saladin founded five colleges in Cairo, to take the place of the heretical classes, which had existed there during the Fātimid régime. As the members of his dynasty added twenty-six other colleges and the Mamlūk Sultāns added many more, there were forty-five colleges in the older parts of Cairo and seventy in the newer quarter of al-Qahirah during the first half of the fifteenth century.

63. Curriculum of Muslim Colleges and Mosque-colleges

Bayard Dodge

THE MEDIEVAL CURRICULUM

A. The Revealed Sciences and Sciences of the Arabic Language.

The Arabic Language	*al-lughah*
Grammar	*al-nahw*
Rhetoric	*al-balāghah*
Literature	*al-adab*
Readings (Qur'anic)	*al-qirā'āt*
Exegesis (Commentary)	*al-tafsīr*
Traditions (of the Prophet)	*al-hadīth*
Law	*al-fiqh*
Sources or Principles of the Law	*usūl al-fiqh*
Theology	*al-tawhīd, al-kalām* or *usūl al-dīn*

B. The Rational Sciences.

Mathematics	*al-riyādiyāt*
Division of Inheritance	*al-farā'id*
Logic	*al-mantiq*

The Rational Sciences were regarded as supplementary to the other stud-·ies. As a rule mathematics was taught in connection with the fixing of the times of prayer, fasting and religious feasts, or else with the division of inheritance. Logic was included, because ever since the time of the theologian al-Ash'arī it was regarded as useful for the defense of orthodox doctrines.

Many individual scholars studied philosophy, astrology, astronomy, geometry, medicine, pharmacy and certain aspects of the natural sciences, as well as alchemy; but these subjects were as a rule taught by private teachers in their homes or else in the hospitals. The basic curriculum of medieval times did not include secular subjects, but was devoted to studies explaining the revelations of the Qur'an and their application to everyday life.

From *Muslim Education in Medieval Times* by Bayard Dodge (Washington, D. C.: The Middle East Institute, 1962), pp. 29-30). Reprinted by permission.

64. Contributions of Medieval Muslim Education: An Appraisal

Mehdi Nakosteen

1. Throughout the twelfth and part of the thirteenth centuries, Muslim works on science, philosophy, and other fields were translated into Latin, particularly from Spain, and enriched the curriculum of the West, especially in northwestern Europe.

2. The Muslims passed on the experimental method of science, however imperfect, to the West.

3. The system of Arabic notation and decimals was introduced to the West.

4. Their translated works, particularly those of men such as Avicenna in medicine, were used as texts in classes of higher education far into the middle of the seventeenth century.

5. They stimulated European thought, reacquainted it with the Greek and other classical cultures and thus helped bring about the Renaissance.

6. They were the forerunners of European universities, having established hundreds of colleges in advance of Europe.

7. They preserved Greco-Persian thought when Europe was intolerant of pagan cultures.

8. European students in Muslim universities carried back new methods of teaching.

9. They contributed knowledge of hospitals, sanitation, and food to Europe.

The strength of the Muslim educational system lay in the following areas: It produced great scholars in almost every field. It developed literacy on a universal scale when illiteracy was the rule in Europe. It transmitted the best features of classical cultures to the West. It led the way in the development of libraries and universities. Its higher education in its creative centuries was open to rich and poor alike, the only requirements being ability and ambition. It held teachers and books in reverence, particularly on higher levels of instruction. The teacher, the book, the lecture, the debate—these were the nerve centers of its educational system.

The curriculum, which was in the early centuries balanced between sectarian and secular studies, became in the later centuries scholastic, making all or practically all secular studies subject to religious and theological approval. The curriculum became formal, fixed, traditional, religious, dogmatic, backward-looking. It encouraged static minds and conformity. It became authoritarian and essentialist.

From *History of Islamic Origins of Western Education, A. D. 800-1350* by Mehdi Nakosteen (Boulder, Col.: University of Colorado Press, 1964), pp. 62-63, 173-74. Reprinted by permission.

Whereas in its early centuries Muslim education encouraged debates, experimentation, and individualism, in its later stages it encouraged formal methods, memorization, and recitation. A system which was in its early stages rather spontaneous and free, encouraging individuals to pursue learning and inspire others to enlightenment, lost in the later stages this sense of intellectual adventure and its direction became superimposed from the top (the state and church) rather than inspired by the people. This led in time to an elite and aristocratic concept of education, replacing its early democratic educational spirit. Muslim education did not, and with its scholastic disciplines could not, take advantage of the tools of science and experimentation which it had inherited and improved upon. Rather, it passed on these tools to European men of science, who utilized them effectively after the Renaissance and thus initiated and developed the modern world of science.

The eighth and ninth centuries, particularly the period between 750 and 900, saw the introduction of classical learning, education, and refinement into the Islamic culture and schools. This epoch may be characterized by the initial organization, consolidation, adaptation, and assimilation of these classical elements. The tenth and eleventh centuries—the golden age of Islamic scholarship—were centuries of interpretation of classical thought (chiefly neo-Platonic and Aristotelian life and world views), criticism and further adaptations of these, and to some extent the adaptation of Persian and Hindu thought to Muslim theology and philosophy. Hellenistic, Persian, and Hindu sciences (mathematics, astronomy, trigonometry, algebra, technology, medicine and its associated disciplines), and other practical skills were introduced into Muslim schools. The application of these to the needs and interests of the Muslim world challenged the genius of many Muslim scholars. Finally, successful modifications of, and new and significant additions to, important areas of this classical cultural heritage were achieved—mainly in the fields of medicine, mathematical sciences, philosophical systems, and the social disciplines, such as geography, history, and educational theory.

The twelfth and thirteenth centuries were centuries of translation. They were marked on the one hand by the gradual and visible decline of Muslim creative scholarship and, on the other, by a steady flow of the results of Hellenistic-Hindu-Persian-Muslim learning in scientific, philosophic (and to some extent theological), technical, geographic, historical, esthetic, and other fields into the Hebrew and Latin Christian schools through the steady and systematic translations of the writings of the most eminent (even some lesser) Muslim thinkers and scholars from the Arabic (occasionally Persian) into Hebrew and Latin.

The decline of Muslim scholarship and creativity coincided, therefore, with the early phases of the European intellectual awakening, which was largely stimulated by the introduction of Muslim science, philosophy, and art into European society and educational institutions. The process had reversed itself, for the renaissance of Muslim learning had coincided during the earlier centuries of Islam with a period of relative intellectual inactivity and non-creativity in Latin Christianity brought about, in part, by the rejection of Hellenistic traditions of science and philosophy, more precisely, the Ionian experimental and inquiring spirit.

It is probable that as early as 1200, Islam had exhausted itself as a great world force; intellectual courage and innovation had sagged; orthodox scholasticism, sustained by al-Ghazzali, had largely taken over and written off the fate of independent research.

As Islam was declining in scholarship and Europe was absorbing the fruits of Islam's three and a half centuries of creative productivity, signs of Latin Christian awakening were obvious throughout the European continent. These forerunners of what developed after the thirteenth century into a full-fledged European all-inclusive renaissance were such educators and scholars as (1) the French Roscelin of Campiegne, Odo of Meung, Gerald of Besancon, Franco of Liege, and Marbode of Augers; (2) the German Lambert of Hersfeld, Theophilus, Hermann of Reichenau, Adam of Bremen, Wilhelm of Hirsan, and Frutolf of Bemberg; (3) the Greek Christians, Paullus, Simeon Seth, Scylitzes, Atha-Liates, Xephilinus, and Theophylactus; (4) the Irish Marianus Scottas; (5) the Tunisian Jew al-Fasiq, the French Jew Raslu, and the Italian Jews Nathan ben Jehiel and Ahimaaz; (6) the Italian St. Anselm; (7) Constantine of Carthage; (8) the English Honorius Inclusus; (9) and others, as Papias the Lombard and Joannes Plalearius the Younger.

The twelfth century was one of intensified traffic of Muslim learning to the Western Latin and Hebrew worlds, which in itself helped Europe seize the initiative from Islam, when political conditions in Islam brought about indications of an intellectual decline in Muslim scholarship. By 1300, when all that was worthwhile in Muslim scientific-philosophic-social learning had been transmitted to European schoolmen through Latin translations, European scholars stood once again on the solid ground of Hellenistic thought, enriched or modified through Muslim efforts, and they were ready to pick up and continue the Greek spirit of inquiry which they had abandoned for centuries but which had been preserved and promoted, fortunately, during the early Christian centuries in the Syrian schools (Antioch, Nisibis, and Edessa) and in the Persian Sassanian Academy of Jundi-Shapur and, after the seventh century Islamic conquests, by Muslim scholarship.

PART VI

Medical Education

CONTEMPORARY men are disposed to regard the practice of medicine during the Middle Ages rather like a chamber of horrors in which only the fortunate survived the diagnoses and treatments of their physicians. Accounts of exotic cures prepared with the root of the mandrake, milk from nursing ewes, ground frog bones, and leaves of myrtle only serve to confirm the impression that the pharmacology of those earlier days was truly "medieval." Such a view of medical practice, however, tends to overexaggerate the reliance upon superstition and folk-wisdom in the treatment of disease. There is ample evidence to claim that the study of medicine was advanced during the Middle Ages and that medical practice had improved over classical times.

Isidore of Seville, that Bishop so interested in preparing an adequate library to aid monks in their studies and so intrigued with the notion of cataloging human knowledge by creating a compendium of wisdom from both pagan and Christian sources, prepared a discussion of medical science as portions of his *Etymologiae*. According to Dr. William Sharpe, who translated Isidore's medical writings for the American Philosophical Society, Isidore's discussion of medicine was not novel, but rather reflected part of the early Christian and early medieval interest in Medicine.

> ... Both in ancient Rome and in the west during the early Middle Ages, bona fide medical training extended to three fairly distinct groups: medical craftsmen who learned their profession by a practical apprenticeship, and who provided most general medical care; a small but extremely influential group of master physicians who learned their profession through formal study of classical Greco-Roman medical texts with another physician; and, finally, a group of well educated laymen and clerics who did not formally practice medicine, as physicians, but for whom the study of medical literature was part of a general education. It is apparently for this group, and not for physicians as such, that Isidore intended the medical and anatomical portions of his *Etymologiae*.[1]

Having discussed man's dualistic nature as being both corporal and spiritual, Isidore used a head-to-foot scheme to identify and describe the function of each of the various parts of human anatomy. According to Sharpe, such a sequence was typical of many other medical glosses used during the early history of medical writing. *De Medicina*, Isidore's fourth book of the *Etymologies*, is in the Galenic tradition of viewing medicine as the art to protect, preserve, or restore bodily health with essentially three varieties of treatment for disease: dietetic, pharmaceutical, and surgical. It is in *De Medicina* that Isidore discusses the four humors of the body; acute, chronic, and skin diseases; remedies and medications, as well as balsams and unguents; medical books; and the study of medicine as a discipline.

Materials included from Isidore's writings help to provide a partial understanding of the *theoretical* formulation of medical studies during the medieval period. Medicine was initially studied in the monasteries, as both Sharpe and Knowles illustrate below; later, medicine became one of the four faculties of the university, and it was the Italian universities, in particular, that were most successful in

---

[1]William D. Sharpe, M. D. *Isidore of Seville: The Medical Writings*, p. 11.

the teaching of medical theory. As A. C. Crombie[2] notes, there was considerable interest in expanding medical knowledge and improving medical practice through experimentation and through speculation. Cassiodorus, in the sixth century, had been concerned with instructing his monks in the study and use of herbs in medicine to be employed in the monastery informary; the tenth century saw the publication of Bald's *Leech Book* with its discussion of diseases and their treatments; Arabic scholars, such as Haly Abbas, Avicenna, and Rhazes not only brought translations of ancient Greek medical sources to Christian Europe in the tenth century, but added original observations of their own such as Rhazes' work on the diagnosis of smallpox and measles; Mondino of Luzzi, who spanned the end of the thirteenth and the beginning of the fourteenth century, wrote the textbook in anatomy which became the standard text when he was a professor of medicine at Bologna. Mondino conducted extensive dissections in preparing his text and did original work on the abdomen muscle, the pancreatic duct, and the production of urine by the kidneys as a consequence of their blood-filtration function. Henry of Mondeville prepared illustrated charts and models to use in his teaching of medicine at Montpelier; he made contributions to the study of tendons, ligaments, and the structure of the brain. As the study of medicine spread throughout the universities, advances were made not only in pharmacology, anatomy, and surgery, but also in the related medical sciences of ophthalmology, dentistry, and epidemiology.

From Hippocrates on, medical practitioners have been viewed as having a special moral relationship with their patients; and patients have also been acutely aware that the physician-patient relationship is financial as well as moral. As medical practice grew during the later Middle Ages, it became very lucrative—so much so, in fact, that the Church ultimately forbade members of the clergy to study or practice medicine. Practical advice to the physician on the conduct of his practice—in both its moral and financial dimensions, as well as its more purely "medical" nature—was not lacking. Pro-

[2]A. C. Crombie, *Medieval and Early Modern Science*, Vol. I. Garden City N. Y.: Doubleday & Co., 1959.

fessor Power has edited and translated the *Treatises of Fistula in Ano*, written around 1376 by the physician-surgeon, John Arderne. This material contains a description of the ethical relations between patient and physician, as well as advice to the practitioner in diagnnosing, operating, and using local anesthetics in the treatment of fistula.

The importance of uroscopy and urinalysis in medieval medical practice is indicated not only by the numerous illuminations showing the physician holding a flask of urine to the light, but also by the advice which Peter of Blois sent to a colleague after having examined an ailing knight, Geldowin, while traveling near Amboise near the River Loire in 1170.

Isidore had argued that the study of medicine involved each of the liberal arts in its attempt to embrace all knowledge about the body; later developments in the study of medicine pointed to the need for an empirically based science of medicine, rather than the heavy reliance upon the deductive application of theory about human nature which had been found in Isidore's writings. The study of medicine improved as the university movement grew; however, during most of the medieval period, the practice of medicine tended to be somewhat haphazard. As Urban Tigner Holmes argues, in discussing the twelfth century's medical practice, there were some very sound medical practices employed at the same time that bizarre treatments were used.

65. The Learned Doctor

Geoffrey Chaucer

> A *Doctor* too emerged as we proceeded;
> No one alive could talk as well as he did
> On points of medicine and of surgery,
> For, being grounded in astronomy,

From Geoffrey Chaucer, *The Prologue to The Canterbury Tales*, translated into Modern English by Nevil Coghill (Baltimore: Penguin Books, 1952), pp. 36-37. Reprinted by permission.

He watched his patient's favorable star
And, by his Natural Magic, knew what are
The lucky hours and planetary degrees
For making charms and magic effigies.
The cause of every malady you'd got
He knew, and whether dry, cold, moist or hot;
He knew their seat, their humor and condition.
He was a perfect practicing physician.
These causes being known for what they were.
He gave the man his medicine then and there.
All his apothecaries in a tribe
Were ready with the drugs he would prescribe,
And each made money from the other's guile;
They had been friendly for a goodish while.
He was well-versed in Esculapius too
And what Hippocrates and Rufus knew
And Dioscorides, now dead and gone,
Galen and Rhazes, Hali, Serapion,
Averroes, Avicenna, Constantine,
Scotch Bernard, John of Gaddesden, Gilbertine.
In his own diet he observed some measure;
There were no superfluities for pleasure,
Only digestives, nutritives and such.
He did not read the Bible very much.
In blood-red garments, slashed with bluish-gray
And lined with taffeta, he rode his way;
Yet he was rather close as to expenses
And kept the gold he won in pestilences.
Gold stimulates the heart, or so we're told.
He therefore had a special love of gold.

66. English Monastic Interest in Medicine

Dom David Knowles

During the early Middle Ages the monasteries were the only seats of what
medical learning had survived in western Europe from the ancient world.

From *The Monastic Order in England* by Dom David Knowles (London: Cambridge University Press, 1963), pp. 516-18. Reprinted by permission.

In England, however, more than in southern France and Italy, almost all traces of the Greco-Roman medicine had disappeared, and its place was taken by a mixture of traditional practice, herbal knowledge and popular magic. Neither Cluny nor Fleury was interested in medical science, and there is no evidence that in this department the revival under Dunstan brought new life into this country. The Norman monasticism, however, had inherited the traditions of William of Dijon, who, himself an Italian, had established first at his monastery in Dijon and later in many of his other foundations something like a serious study of physic deriving from the south Italian tradition which had already begun to break into new life at Salerno. Consequently, from the first arrival of Norman monks in England until the end of our period there is a succession of monk-physicians, at first trained within the cloister, but later themselves graduates of Salerno or other medical universities.

The first of these was Baldwin, originally a monk of St. Denis at Paris, who came to the court of Edward the Confessor as the king's physician. Rewarded with the abbacy of Bury he continued his good offices with the Conqueror and was recognized as the leading consultant of the realm. He was Lanfranc's physician, and the archbishop sent him other patients; among those who consulted him was Arfast, bishop of Thetford, who had been seriously injured in the eye by the branch of a tree. Baldwin died in 1097; his place at the head of the faculty was almost immediately taken by another abbot, the great Faricius of Abingdon (1100-17). Faricius was an Italian from Arezzo, and it is quite possible that he had studied at Salerno; in any case his reputation was very great. He became the trusted physician of both Henry I and his queen Matilda, whom he assisted in her first confinement, and the numerous royal charters of gifts and confirmations in his favour, often attested by his colleague Grimbald, presumably a secular clerk or layman, are evidence of his assiduity in attendance upon the king and of the success of his ministrations. In addition to his activities at court, Faricius also acted as consultant to a number of the great families of England, and the Abingdon cartulary contains a number of charters of gifts bestowed in recompense for professional services, in particular from the families of de Vere, fitz Haymon and Crispin; indeed, when there was talk of his succeeding to Canterbury, his practice of medicine was one of the disabilities alleged against him by those who opposed his candidature.

Faricius was not the only well-known monastic physician of his time. Hugh, a monk of St. Swithun's at Winchester and afterwards abbot of Chertsey (1107-28), was a distinguished practitioner, and William of Malmesbury tells of a monk of his abbey, named Gregory, possibly a pupil of Faricius, who had been cellarer there; he also was a noted consultant. Later in the century occurs the family group of distinguished physicians at St.

Albans, all trained at Salerno, at whose head was Warin, sometime prior and later abbot (1183-95). Warin's successor, John, was likewise a skilled physician, and had among his monks at least one other trained in medicine, by name William, later prior of Worcester. Indeed, it would seem probable that a number of the greater monasteries counted a physician among their members; then as now a celebrated consultant could command a great price, and we hear of at least two such at the end of the twelfth century who materially assisted their community. Walter, almoner of Bury *c.* 1190, constructed the almonry from fees received, and Thomas of Northwick, a monk of Evesham and a physician with a wide reputation, assisted in building the tower of the abbey church *c.* 1200. The lucrative nature of the profession, and the contact with the world that its practice implied, caused it to be banned to monks by conciliar legislation, but the prohibition, at least as regards England, was inoperative; circumstances combined to make the great monasteries almost the only places in the kingdom where medical books, traditions of treatment, and constant need for a physician's skill were present in combination, and even if those with a reputation could have resisted the desire for fame or gain, it would have been difficult to resist the claims of those in real need of healing. But though the monasteries, and especially the black monk monasteries, housed the ablest physicians all through the century and no doubt established for themselves a fairly efficient tradition of clinical treatment, it cannot be claimed that they did anything to forward the study of medical science for Europe in general. In so far as this can be said to have been accomplished by any teaching body in the twelfth century, it was the work of such universitites as Salerno and Montpellier.

67. Man's Nature and Anatomy

Isidore of Seville

6. Man is, however, double: interior and exterior. The interior man is the soul (and) the exterior man is the body.

7. The soul, *anima*, was so called by the pagans because they took it to be wind. Whence also "wind" is ANEMOS in Greek, because we seem to live

From *Isidore of Seville: The Medical Writings* by William D. Sharpe (Philadelphia: Transactions of the American Philosophical Society, Vol. 54, Pt. 2, 1964), pp. 38-39, 42, 48. These selections are from Sharpe's translation of Isidore's "De Homine et Portentis," Book 11 of the *Etymologiae*. Reprinted by permission.

by taking in air with our mouths, but this is most clearly false since the soul arises long before air can be taken in by the mouth, and is already alive in its mother's womb.

8. The soul, therefore, is not air as some who were not able to comprehend its incorporeal nature have thought.

9. The "vital spirit," *spiritus*, is the same as the soul of which the Evangelist speaks, saying (John 10: 18): *Potestatem habeo ponendi animam meam, et rursus potestatem habeo sumendi eam*, "I have the power to lay down my spirit, and again I have the power of picking it up." Likewise, it is of this very soul of Our Lord that the aforesaid Evangelist speaks at the time of His passion, when he says (John 19: 30): *Et inclinato capite emisit spiritum*, "And bowing His head he gave up His spirit." For what is it to give up the spirit if not to lay down (one's) soul?

10. But the soul is so named because it lives; the spirit is named either because of its spiritual nature, or because it imparts breath in the body.

11. Likewise, the mind, *animus*, is the same as the soul, but the soul pertains to life, the mind to deliberation. For this reason, philosophers say that life remains even without the mind, and the soul persists without the intellect: whence also the "mindless." For it is called the intellect that it may know; the mind, that it may will.

12. The intellect, *mens*, is named because it is eminent in the soul, or because it remembers, *memini*, Whence also the forgetful are "mindless." Nor is it the soul but what is most excellent in the soul, as though its head or eye, which is called the mind. Whence also man himself is said to be an image of God because of his mind. However, all these (faculties) are joined to the soul so that it is a single thing, but diverse names are applied to the soul according to its different functions.

13. The memory, *memoria*, is also the intellect and for this reason those who are forgetful are "mindless." When it gives life to the body, it is the soul, *anima*; when it wills, it is the mind, *animus*; when it knows, it is the intellect, *mens*; when it remembers, it is the memory; when it judges correctly, it is the reason, *ratio*; when it breathes, it is the vital spirit, *spiritus*; when it perceives anything, it is called sensation, *sensus*. For the mind is called "sense" after the things which it senses, and "sentiment," *sententia*, is similarly derived.

14. The body, *corpus*, is named because, being corruptible, it perishes; for it is soluble and mortal, and some time will be dissolved.

15. But flesh, *caro*, is named from "creation," *creare*. There is power of increase in the male's semen from which the bodies of animals and men are conceived. Hence also, parents are called "creators."

16. The flesh, however, is composed of four elements: earth is in the fleshy parts, air in the breath, water in the blood, fire in the vital heat. For

the elements each have in us a proper proportion, of which something is lacking when the conjunction is dissolved.

.   .   .

54. The gums, *gingivae*, are named because they grow teeth: they were created to adorn the teeth, lest bare they might seem more of a horror than an ornament.

.   .   .

70. The digits are named either because there are ten, *decem*, of them, or because they are thought to be so properly, *decenter*, put together, constituting in themselves a perfect number and the most elegant order. The first is called the thumb, *pollex*, because it surpasses, *pollere*, the others in strength and power. The second is the *index* and greeting or demonstratory finger, because we generally greet and point out with it.

71. The third is the lewd finger, *impudicus*, since very often derision at unchaste conduct is manifested by it. The fourth is the ring finger, *anularis*, since the ring is worn on it: it is also the medicinal finger, *medicinalis*, since physicians apply salve with it. The fifth is the *auricular* finger, for we scratch our ears with it.

.   .   .

139. Seed, *semen*, is that which once sown, is taken up either by the earth or by the womb for the generation of fruit or fetus. It is a liquid made through a decoction of food and of the body and spread through the veins and spinal cord whence, sweated out in the manner of bilge-water, it condenses in the kidneys. Ejaculated during coitus and taken up in the woman's womb, it is shaped in the body of a certain visceral heat and the humidity of the menstrual blood.

140. The menstrual flow is a woman's superfluous blood: it is termed "menstrual," *menstrua*, because of the phase of the light of the moon by which this flow comes about. The moon is called MENE in Greek. These are also called the "womanlies," *muliebria*, for woman is the only menstrual animal.

141. On contact with this gore, crops do not germinate, wine goes sour, grasses die, trees lose their fruit, iron is corrupted by rust, copper is blackened. Should dogs eat any of it, they go mad. Even vituminous glue, which is dissolved neither by iron nor by (strong) waters, polluted by this gore, falls apart by itself.

142. After many menstrual days, however, the semen is no longer germinable because there is no menstrual blood by which the ejaculate can be irrigated. Thin semen does not adhere to the female parts; lacking this power

to adhere, it is lost. Likewise, thick semen also lacks the power of growth, being unable to mix with the female blood because of its own excessive thickness. This is why men or women become sterile: from excessive thickness of semen or blood, or from excessive thinness.

143. They say that the human heart is the first part of the body to be formed, because in it is all life and wisdom; then, by the fortieth day, the whole task is made up. This has been learned, they say, from abortions. Others say that the fetus begins to develop at the head, whence also we see in eggs that the eyes are the first parts to be formed in the fetus of birds.

144. The fetus, *foetus*, is named since it is still nourished, *fovere*, in the womb; its afterbirth, *secundae*, is called the "sac," *folliculus*, which is born at the same time as the infant and which encloses him: it is so called because when he comes forth, it also follows.

145. They say that children resemble their fathers if the paternal seed be stronger; the mother if the maternal seed be the stronger. This is the reason faces are formed to resemble others; those with the likeness of both parents were conceived from an equal admixture of paternal and maternal semen. Those resembling their grandparents and great-grandparents do so since, just as there are many seeds hidden in the soil, seeds also lie hidden in us which will give back the figures of our ancestors. Girls are born from the paternal semen and boys from the maternal, because every birth consists of two seeds. When its greater part prevails, it produces a similarity of sex.

68. A Doctor's Code of Professional Ethics, Ca. 1376

John Arderne

In the first place, a doctor who wishes to succeed in his profession should always remember God in all his works and should always meekly pray with heart and mouth for his help; and he should from time to time give of his earnings to the poor that they by their prayers may get him grace of the Holy Ghost.

He must not be rash or boastful in speech or in deed. He had better not talk much, especially among great men. And he should answer cannily to all questions so that he may not be tripped up by his own words. If his results do not carry out his words and his promises, he will be looked down upon, and his reputation will suffer....

From Arderne, *Treatises of Fistula in Ano*, edited and translated by E. Power, reprinted in *Chaucer's World* by Edith Rickert (New York: Columbia University Press, 1948). Reprinted by permission. This selection is from pp. 174-76 of the 1962 paperback edition.

A doctor should also be careful not to laugh and joke too much; and, as far as he can, he should avoid the company of knaves and dishonest persons.

Let him keep always busy with matters that belong to his profession—reading or writing or studying or praying. The use of books is creditable to a doctor because they both keep him occupied and teach him something. Above all, it is important that he be found always sober; for drunkenness spoils every good thing. . . .

If anyone talks to him about another doctor, he should neither make light of him nor praise or commend him too much, but he may say with all courtesy, "I have no real knowledge of him, but I have heard nothing about him but what is good and to his credit.". . .

A doctor should not look too boldly at the lady of the house or her daughters or other fair women in great men's houses, or offer to kiss them, or touch them with his hands, lest he move to indignation the lord or some one of his household.

So far as he can, he should avoid giving offence to servants, but should try to get their love and good will.

Let him refrain from vice, as well in word as in deed, for if he be given to secret vice, some time he will be found out and dishonored for his evil practices. . . .

When sick men or their friends come to consult him, let him be neither too haughty nor too familiar, but adapt his manner to the status of the persons: to some respectful, to others friendly. For wise men say that familiarity breeds contempt.

It is a good thing for him to make up excuses that he cannot do anything for them safely or without causing the indignation of some great person, or because he is too busy. Or he might pretend to be hurt or ill if he wants to get out of undertaking a case. And if he does take up a case, let him make terms for his work and take the money in advance.

He should be careful not to pronounce upon a case until he has seen it and observed what it is. When he has made an examination, even though he may think that the patient can be cured, in his prognosis he should warn him of the danger of deferring treatment. And if he sees that the patient is eager for the cure, let him boldly adjust his fee to the man's position in life. But let him never ask too little; for this is bad for both the market and the patient. For a case of fistula, when it is curable, he may safely ask of an important man a hundred marks or forty pounds with robes and fees amounting to a hundred shillings a year for his life. Of less important men, he might ask forty pounds, or forty marks without fees. But let him never take less than a hundred shillings. For never in my life have I taken less than that sum for the cure of this disease. But every man should, of course, do as he thinks best and most expedient.

If the patients or their friends or servants ask how soon a cure may be expected, the doctor should always say twice as long as he really thinks... For it is better to indicate too long a time than to have the cure drag on. This discourages the patient at a time when faith in the doctor is one of the greatest aids to recovery. If the patient later asks why the doctor was able to cure him in half the time he mentioned, he may answer that it was because the patient was strong and bore well the severe treatment, and that he was of good complexion, and that his flesh healed quickly, and other things that would please the patient. For patients are, with this kind of talk, made proud and glad.

Furthermore, a doctor should always be well dressed and neat in appearance, not gay like a minstrel but sober like a clerk, because any discreet man dressed like a clerk may sit at a gentleman's table. A doctor should also have clean hands and well-shaped nails, thoroughly cleaned. He should always be courteous at lords' tables and not displease the other guests, either by his words or his manner. He should listen well but say little... And when he does speak, his words should be brief, agreeable, full of sense, and free of oaths. And he should never lie; for if he be found truthful in his speech, few or none will lack confidence in what he does.

A young doctor should also learn good proverbs suited to his profession to comfort his patients... Moreover, he should comfort his patient by admonishing him to be of strong heart. For greatness of heart makes men strong and hardy to suffer sharp and grievous pain....

It is also useful for a doctor to have a stock of good and amusing stories to make the patient laugh, both from the Bible and from other tragedies, and any others that are not objectionable which may make the patient more cheerful.

A doctor should be careful never to betray the secrets of his patients, either men or women, or belittle some to others... for if a man knows that other men's secrets are well kept, he will be the readier to trust you with his own.

69. Using and Preparing Local Anesthetics

John Arderne

A sleeping ointment, with which if any man be anointed, he shall be able to bear cutting in any part of the body without sensation or pain. Take juice

From Arderne, *Treatises of Fistula in Ano*, edited and translated by E. Power, reprinted in *Chaucer's World* by Edith Rickert (New York: Columbia University Press, 1948). Reprinted by permission. This selection is from pp. 178-79 of the 1962 paperback edition.)

of henbane, mandragora, water hemlock, lettuce, poppy, both white and black, and the seeds of all the aforesaid herbs if they can be had, in equal parts; Thebian opium and meconium, one or two drams each; fresh swine's grease as needed. Crush all these well and strongly together in a mortar, and afterward boil them hard and then cool them. And if it be not thick enough, put in a little bee-bread, that is, white wax; and keep it for thy use.

And when thou will use thereof, anoint his pulses, his temples, his armpits, and the palms of his hands and the soles of his feet, and very soon he shall sleep so that he shall feel no cutting.

This is also useful if a man cannot sleep for some other cause, as in fevers or something of the sort, for this ointment either shall give him remedy or the patient shall die. Also one grain of Thebian opium to the quantity of half a dram, mixed with a pint of wine or more according to the strength of him that shall drink it, shall make a person sleep. Also the seed of white henbane alone given in wine makes the drinker sleep very soon, so that he shall not feel whatsoever is done to him. And this I myself proved for certain.

And know that it helps to draw him that sleeps by the nose and by the cheeks and by the beard that the spirits be quickened so that he sleep not overrestfully. Also the doctor should beware of giving opium without crocus to drink, for crocus and cassia lignea are the bridles of opium.

To wake a man that sleeps thus, put to his nose gray bread toasted and wet in strong vinegar; or put vinegar and mustard in his nose; or wash his head in strong vinegar; or anoint his temples with the juice of rhubarb. And give him some other things to make him sneeze, and soon he shall wake. And know that it is good to give him afterward castoreum, for it is the cure of henbane and opium and other such things, whether it is given in the mouth, or in drink, or is put in the nose. For castoreum heats and comforts most effectively the sinews that are chilled and loosens the rigidity. And also give him what comforts the brain, for example castoreum, nutmeg, roses, water-lily, myrtle, and sumac.

70.   Urinalysis: An Important Aid to Medical Diagnoses

Peter of Blois

...Experience is untrustworthy according to the testimony of Hippocrates. Sometimes the Lord reveals to one what He hides from others. Do

From "Peter of Blois as a Physician" by Urban T. Holmes, Jr., and Frederick R. Weedon. Reprinted, by permission, from *Speculum*, XXXVII (April 1962), published by the Mediaeval Academy of America, pp. 252-56.

not be annoyed to hear the manner of this illness and the aids which are to be used. It is a common fault among physicians to differ always about maladies. Wherefore if three or four visit a patient they are never in agreement over the cause or the treatment. Since you and I are in agreement in our wishes it seems proper that we should conform in our doings and observations. I was present in the early stages of this case which, I am certain, will be easily cured if some one continues the treatment with care. You will observe that the patient is surely suffering from a medium tertian ague [malaria of a bilious remittent type]: he is in much distress since the fever is suffered continuously from one period to another. You know that if this were simple malaria the patient would never thrice repeat his vomitings when he has putrefied matter generated from the phlegm in and outside his vessels. If, on the other hand, this were a major ague [blackwater fever and other malignant types] the patient would suffer non-remittent prostration because of the putrefaction of the black bile, inside and outside, in the movement of the interior matter; and his teeth would chatter. All these things occur to a minimum degree in this present case; it is obviously a medium ague due to the bile which has been putrefacted in the vessels and the stomach. If it were putrefaction in the liver, which sometimes can happen, the reddish thin urine would burn and would tend to a smoky color; because this has not happened you will see that the matter still resides in the vessels and stomach. When I arrived on the very day that the fever set in I had the hepatic vein opened. Because while the disease is on the increase (which is evident here because the urine is reddish and thin) a purgative should not yet be used, I have employed repellents and have placed violet oil on the heart, liver, and forehead. It remains then, when thicker urine announces the time of more complete digestion, for you to give the patient a refrigerant of scammony ash, which is safer than an oxymel [vineger and honey syrup] or anything else, for in it all the harm of the scammony has disappeared through decoction. Best of all for him would be a decoction of cassia fistula, of *Terminalia citrina* [*myrobalani citrini*] with maidenhair fern, and the seeds of watermelon, gourd, and melon, if you should see that the strength of the patient is sufficient for this. The diet, as you know, must be very thin: a ptisan and a piece of bread dipped three or four times in water. Fomentations [hot applications] of mallow, violets, and poppy seed should not be neglected for the feet; for there heat does a great deal of good. If a great heat should afflict the top of the head, as is customary, let the head be shaved and the head, forehead, and temples may be soothed with cloths dipped into rose water, atropine juice, everlasting orpine [*sedum*], wormwood, and plantain. If there is an increase of thirstiness let the tongue be washed, as you know, with parsley, and be scraped with wood. For sleeplessness let there be applied a decoction of black poppy, mallow, violet, and henbane to the feet, which decocted herbs are for the head also.

For stubborness of the belly a suppository or clyster should be applied— [not a purge]. I write you these things, not that you need to be taught, but in order that the medicine may be safer for you and more acceptable to the patient, since it proceeds from our common deliberation. For frequently from the skill of a tactful doctor and from a certain confidence which the patient has in him a patient gets well without help from Nature. You must be rigorously circumspect around this man from whose healing a reputation of considerable honor will come and the usefulness of this will respond to your wishes.

71. Medical Education: A Specialty at Bishop Fulbert's School of Chartres

Loren C. MacKinney

Among the specialized sciences, medicine was outstanding. Here, . . . Fulbert appears to have been an active leader, teacher, and also practicioner. As in the field of music, however, he had eminent predecessors, notably Heribrand, whom he may have known at Gerbert's school in Rheims, and by whom (along with Herbert) he is thought to have been persuaded to go to Chartres. It is certain that Heribrand proselyted another of Gerbert's students, the monk Richer. The detailed account appears in Richer's own *Historia*: how Heribrand sent a messenger to Rheims with a letter urging him to come to Chartres "to read the Aphorisms [of Hippocrates] with him"; inasmuch as Richer in his eagerness for "studying the logical [medicine] of Hippocrates of Cos, had thought much and often of liberal studies", and since his friend Heribrand was "a person of great liberality and learning . . . most expert in the art [of medicine] and not ignorant of pharmacology, pharmacy, botany, and surgery", he left immediately for Chartres; and there (he related) "I studied zealously in the Aphorisms of Hippocrates . . . [and] when I had learned of the prognostics of diseases therefrom, a simple recognition of ailments being insufficient for my desires, I asked for a reading of his book entitled *De Concordia Yppocratis, Galieni et Su-*

From *Bishop Fulbert and Education at the School of Chartres* by Loren C. MacKinney, pp. 31-34, in *Texts and Studies in the History of Medieval Education*, No. 3, A. L. Gabriel and J. N. Garvin, eds. (Notre Dame, Ind.: The Mediaeval Institute, University of Notre Dame). Reprinted by permission.

rani.'' The effectiveness of Richer's training is shown by the numerous technical descriptions of ailments that appear in his *Historia.*

Fulbert, also, may have studied medicine with Heribrand, but of this there is no certainty. Strangely enough, the name of Heribrand, founder of the reputation of Chartres as a medical center, appears in no extant record save that of Richer. Heribrand was undeniably the most eminent teacher of medicine at Chartres, but even in his case existing evidence suggests an informal type of instruction, the individual student *reading* Hippocrates under the direction of an expert in the subject. There is no hint of a formal school with professorial lectures. All of which fits into the picture of Fulbert's school as a religious community devoted to the training of young clergymen in the varied practical functions of the priesthood.

With regard to medicine and Fulbert's relations thereto, it is certain that as a young cleric he compounded medicines and that after becoming bishop he discontinued the practice, and that thereafter he depended for his pharmaceutical supplies on professional medics (*medici*) and for his practice on assistants such as Hildegar who took over many of the duties of the busy, elderly bishop. Hildegar may have learned medicine from Fulbert in the same informal fashion in which Richer learned it from Heribrand. There is, however, a marked difference. Richer was an expert theorist; Hildegar merely an amateur practicioner. Richer read classical treatises intensively and wrote detailed analyses of ailments; Hildegar may have been well versed in "the art of Hippocrates" (as his friend Adelman wrote), but our only evidence of his medical ability is a letter of detailed instruction that he sent along with a portion which had doubtless been compounded at Fulbert's orders. . . .

There is no doubt that Fulbert knew considerable about the practical aspects of pharmacy, but his general comprehension of medical science, and especially of classical writings on the subject, was decidedly inferior to that of Gerbert, Heribrand, and Richer. It may be that he knew more than they about practical medicine. He had a stock of compound medicines (including three Galen potions, three diatessaron theriacs, and laxative pills). He knew the difference between emetics and purgatives, both gentle and violent, and was familiar with handbooks of recipes called *antidotaria.* . . . But if Fulbert was acquainted with the classical medical works, of which there are extant tenth- and eleventh-century copies from Chartres, he did not reveal the fact in his writings. The medicine that he learned, practiced, and taught at Chartres was, we believe, the simple home-remedy type of healing that clergymen were supposed to know and use in an amateur fashion.

In the realm of classical medicine, Fulbert knew only vaguely about Esculapius and Hippocrates, both of whom he considered less important than Christ in the art of healing. He stressed the healing power of religion in his verses in honor of St. Pantaleon, patron saint of medicine. He also wrote a jingle concerning the dangers of overeating, which reflects more ignorance than knowledge of the science of diet. All in all, he seems to have picked up the rudiments of practical medicine and to have passed them on to his assistants in an empirical rather than academic manner.

72. On Medicine

Hugh of St. Victor

"Medicine is divided into two parts"—"occasions" and operations. "The 'occasions' are six: air, motion and quiet, emptiness and satiety, food and drink, sleep and wakefulness, and the reactions of the soul. These are called 'occasions' because, when tempered, they occasion and preserve health," or, when untempered, ill-health. The reactions of the soul are called occasions of health or ill-health because now and again they either "raise one's temperature, whether violently as does wrath or gently as do pleasures; or they withdraw and lower the temperature, again whether violently as do terror and fear, or gently as does worry. And among them are some which, like grief, produce their natural effects both internally and externally."

Every medicinal operation is either interior or exterior. "The interior are those which are introduced through the mouth, nostrils, ears, or anus, such as potions, emetics, and powders, which are taken by drinking, chewing, or sucking in. The exterior are, for example, lotions, plasters, poultices, and surgery, which is twofold: that performed on the flesh, like cutting, sewing, burning, and that performed on the bone, like setting and joining."

Let no one be disturbed that among the means employed by medicine I count food and drink, which earlier I attributed to hunting. For these belong to both under different aspects. For instance, wine in the grape is the business of agriculture; in the barrel, of the cellarer, and in its consumption, of the doctor. Similarly, the preparing of food belongs to the mill, the slaughterhouse, and the kitchen, but the strength given by its consumption, to medicine.

From *The "Didascalicon" of Hugh of St. Victor, A Medieval Guide to the Arts* by Jerome Taylor (New York: Columbia University Press, 1961), pp. 78-79. Reprinted by permission.

73. Muslim Medieval Medical Education

Mehdi Nakosteen

The medical profession and medical education in the early centuries of Islam followed the pattern and standards of the Greeks, particularly as they were maintained and improved upon at the medical school of the Academy of Jundi-Shapur. The Greek educational influences through this medical school in Iran may be traced beyond the Sassanian period to the Achaemenians. The standards and traditions of the school of medicine of the Academy of Jundi-Shapur were transferred and developed further in Baghdad under the Abbasside caliphs, and many of the teacher-physicians of the school of Jundi-Shapur, mostly Nestorian Christians and Jews, carried the tradition to the Muslim hospitals in Baghdad where the foundations of Muslim medical education were laid.

Medical education began early in a student's academic career, usually between his fifteenth and seventeenth years, although ibn Sina began at eleven, and Hunain ibn Is'haq had already completed his basic medical education at Jundi-Shapur when he was seventeen.

Studies in music, astronomy, and geometry were among optional pre-medical courses: Music to develop appreciation for the "subtleties of the human pulse; astronomy to determine lucky and unlucky times; geometry to determine the shape of wounds, for round wounds heal with ease."

Students learned medical theory and practices interdependently in small classes and, as a rule, under a senior practitioner. The most basic aspect of training was clinical instruction in hospitals, including attendance at operations "and of those things that are incumbent upon the profession." In addition to observation and internship, students attended lectures given by senior practitioners in their homes or in public places. Students questioned their masters on minute medical and surgical points with complete freedom, even to pointing out any fallacies in the master's theory. When so cornered, the teacher was often forced to revise his outlook or write treatises proving his position against objections. One such treatise, the *Cure Within an Hour*, was written by Barr'-al-Sa'at after being challenged by hecklers in his class for stating that "it was possible to disperse the *materies morbi* of certain diseases within one hour." The methodology of instruction and learning stated here regarding medical students was, with some modifications, the methodology of higher education in all branches of study in Islamic colleges and universities.

In lecture rooms, in the practitioner's home, or at the mosque, students

From *History of Islamic Origin of Western Education, A. D. 800-1350* by Mehdi Nakosteen (Boulder, Colo.: University of Colorado Press, 1964), pp. 54-56, 162-64. Reprinted by permission.

took their seats according to academic seniority, the advanced students being seated together and closer to the lecturer. These lectures were always based on some written medical document and were immediately open to questions for clarification of obscure points, or definition of medical terms used during the lecture and indication of their correct pronunciation. Lectures were held sometimes during the evening hours, particularly during the *Ramadhan*, the month of fasting. Students gathered around famed lecturers from all over the Muslim world, with complete freedom to go from center to center to listen to other important lecturers, or to move to another teacher when the first one's professional "lemon was squeezed dry," or seemed dehydrated from the outset. Some of these international gatherings of students were quite large; usually the more famous a professor, the larger his classes.

The most frequently used medical texts and references were the following: *Aphorisms*, Hippocrates; *Questions*, Hunain ibn Is'haq; *Guide*, Razes; also his book of al-Mansuri, *Continens*; *Commentaries*, Abu Sahl al-Nile; *Treasury*, Thabit ibn-Qurra; *Aims*, al-Jurjani; *Hidaya (Guide)*, Ajwini; *Kifaya (Sufficiency)*, ibn Faraj; *Treatises*, Galen; *Liber Regius*, Haly Abbas; *Hundred Chapters*, Abu Sahl; *Canon*, ibn Sina; *Thesaurus*, al-Jurjani. It should be noted here that the bulk of this list, when translated into Latin during the twelfth to fourteenth centuries, constituted the basis for the medicial curricula of European medical schools, such as that of the University of Paris.

.   .   .

Medicine. During the golden age of Muslim learning, the preeminence of Persian scholars in the assimilation and further development of Islamic medicine was obvious. Medical scholarship passed from the hands of the Christians and Sabians into the possession of Muslim scholars, mostly Persians.

The greatest of these medical writers was al-Razi, better known as Rhazes (865-925), a Persian-Muslim scholar born at Rayy. Rhazes studied in Baghdad under the medical tradition of Hunain ibn Is'haq and mastered Greek, Persian, and Indian medicine. This all-embracing education is evidenced by his remarkable output of scientific works, totaling some two hundred, half of which dealt with medicine. Of these, the best kown is *Al-Hawi* in thirty volumes, *Al-A'sah (The Nerves)*, and *Al Jami (The Universal)*. Some of his works were translated into Latin and later into other European languages, including English. Some of them were printed as many as forty times between 1498 and 1866. In addition to his works on medicine, Rhazes also wrote on philosophy, theology, mathematics, astronomy and the natural sciences. Unfortunately, most of his writings have been lost.

Next to Rhazes is the Persian-Muslim physician ibn Sina, or Avicenna, of whom we have already spoken as a philosopher (980-1037). As a physician, his influence on European medical education was overwhelming. Avicenna developed upon the science of Hippocrates and Galen, as well as the philosophies of Aristotle and Plato, exercising an influence on the best brains of both the East and the West, not only during his lifetime but for many centuries after his death. He handed over many ideas which became part of the stream of philosophical-educational thought in the West. Among these the most famous was his notion of the intelligibles, *intentio*, which was taken over by Albertus Magnus and became part of the scholastic tradition. But it is in medicine that Europe and the Muslim world owe him an incalculable debt as the greatest clinical observer in Islam. The first translations of his works were made in Latin between 1130 and 1150 by Archdeacon Dominic Gundisalvus and John Avendeath of Seville, at the order of Raymond, the Archbishop of Toledo. His *Canon of Medicine*, an encyclopedia of medical knowledge, was translated into Latin by Gerard of Cremona in the twelfth century and was reprinted fifteen times in the last decades of the fifteenth and twenty times in the sixteenth century. Besides his medical works, he wrote more than a hundred treatises on theology, philology, philosophy, and astronomy, and made special studies in music far ahead of Latin works and in the philosophy of mathematics along neo-Platonic lines. The tomb of Avicenna at Hamadan in western Iran is visited today by natives and foreign visitors with pious veneration.

It is interesting to note that this was taking place in the Muslim world at a period when Saint Anselm was laying the foundations of Christian scholasticism in Europe at the School of Bec in Normandy and arguing his realist position on universals with Rocelin, the nominalist, and at a time when there was a neo-Platonic revival in Byzantine Constantinople under Psello, a forerunner of the revival of Platonism in Florence four hundred years later.

Haly Abbas (994) was another Persian-Muslim physician well known among the Latins. His excellent and compact encyclopaedia on *The Whole Medical Art*, known in the Latin as *Liber Regius*, was twice translated into that language.

Muwaffaq (ibn Mansur) was another famous Persian-Muslim writer on medicine (975). His most famous medical work is *The Foundations of the True Properties of Remedies*, in which the author describes some 585 drugs. It is a compact of Persian, Syrian, Greek, Arabic, and Indian knowledge.

74. Muslim Contributions to Medical Scholarship

Mehdi Nakosteen

Medicine. Muslim commentaries on ibn Sina's *Qanun (Canons)* by Muwaffaq al-Din, the Samaritan, ibn al-Quffi, ibn al-Sa'ati, ibn al-Nafis, and Qutb al-Din al-Shirazi appeared during this period under consideration. Also, creative commentaries were written on Galen and Hippocrates by ibn al-Nafis, Yusuf ibn Hasda'i, ibn al-Quffi, and David ben Solomon. The *Zorihaguf* of Nathan ben Joel Falaquera, in Hebrew, containing medical extracts from Muslim and Hellenistic authors, and similar ones in Latin by William Corvi *(Aggregator Brixiensis)* and John of Saint Amands' *Revocativum Memoriose* were in popular use. Numerous commentaries on Muslim medicine, including commentaries on Arabic translations of Greek works, were published by Taddeo Alderotti, Arnold of Villanova, and Peter of Spain.

"By the middle or end of the thirteenth century the same medical classics reached the libraries of Paris, Montpellier, Bologna, Salerno, Granada, Cairo, Damascus, or Baghdad." By the end of the century, Greco-Muslim medical knowledge and art had reached and stabilized Latin and Hebrew medical skills and schools. Latin medical education for another two centuries or more remained predominantly Muslim—more accurately Greco-Zoroastrian-Hindu-Syrian—in theory and practice, save in surgery, in which Europe advanced upon Muslim practices.

Important among the Muslim medical scholars of the twelfth and thirteenth centuries were the following:

Sa'id ibn Hibat Allah al-Baghdadi, who wrote *Mughni fi Tadhir al-Amradh (A Discourse on Cure of Diseases);* Adnan al-Ainzarbi, who wrote *Kafi fi ilm al-Tibb (Sufficient Complete Discourse in the Science of Medicine);* ibn Hubal, author of *Mukhtar fi'l-Tibb (Authority on Medicine);* ibn al-Jawzi, author of the *Lughat al-Manafi fi'l-Tibb (Words of Advantages in Medicine);* Isma'il al-Jurjani, author of *Zakhira ye-Khwarizmshahi (A Storehouse Treasure of Khwarizmshahi),* a medical work dedicated to Khwarizm-Shah; Fakhr al-Din al-Razi, who wrote an encyclopedia, including essays in medicine; Najib al-Din of Samarkand, who wrote *Kitab al-Asbab wa'l-Alamat* (the *Book of Causes and Symptoms of Disease);* ibn Jami and his son, Abu Tahir Isma'il, both Egyptian Jewish medical scholars, who wrote *Irshad al-Masalif al-Anfas wa'l-Ajsad (Instruction [Direction] for the Benefits of Souls and Bodies [Body and Mind]);* Maimonides,

From *History of Islamic Origins of Western Education, A. D. 800-1350* by Mehdi Nakosteen (Boulder, Colo.; University of Colorado Press, 1964), pp. 171-73. Reprinted by permission.

author of *Fusul fi'l-Tibb (Discourses [Chapters] on Medicine);* al-Kuhin al-Attar, an Egyptian Jew, author of *Minhaj al-Dukkan (The Manners [Ways] of Shops);* Solomon Cohen, an Egyptian Jew, author of *Al-Muntakhab (The Selected Works);* Abu al-Ala al-Zuhr, author of *Kitab al-Nukat al-Tibbiyya (The Book of Medical Subtleties [Minute Points];* Abu Marwan ibn Zuhr, "the Medieval Avenzoar," author of the *Taisir;* and ibn Rushd, the *Kulliyat (Complete Work).*

Muslim medical works and their Latin translations included lists (tables) of diseases and cures; anatomy, as in ibn Sina's *Qanun,* and the Egyptian Adb al-Latif's work; surgery; pulse and urine, as discussed in Is'haq al-Isra'il's *Kitab al-Baul* (the *Book of Urine*) translated into Latin by Constantine the African; blood-letting, the practice of which went back to the Greeks and Persians; midwifery; children's diseases; diseases of the eye, ophthalmology, as in *Nur-al-Uyun (Light of Eyes),* by the Persian Zarrin Dast, 1087; and the works of Ali ibn Rabban al-Tabari, Razi, ibn Masawaih, Khalaf al-Tuluni and Hunain ibn Is'haq (ninth century); Ali ibn Isa's *Tadhkirat al-Kahhalin (On Blindness),* Ammar ibn Ali al-Mawsili's *Muntakhab fi Ilaj Amradh al-Ain (The Cure of the Diseases of the Eye)* (eleventh century); Khalifa ibn Abi-al-Mahasin's *Al-Kafi fi'l-Kuhl (Book of Blindness)* and Salah al-Din's *Nur al-Uyun (Light of Eyes)* (thirteen century); psychotherapy, as in the works of ibn Sina and Hebat Allah ibn Malka; hygiene; veterinary medicine; clinical-experimental medicine, as in the works of Abu al-Ala al-Zuhr, ibn Tilmidh and others, who wrote *Mujarrabats (Experimentations);* hospitals and bathing.

75. Twelfth Century Medical Practice

Urban T. Holmes

Practitioners in the twelfth century were continually hoping to simplify the practice of medicine. They had "wonder salves"—a green salve, a red salve, and so on—which they claimed could be applied with sure results. Many formulas for such salves are found in the *materiae medicae.* They had many regimes for improving one's general health. They advised resting after meals to aid the digestion. Bathing in mineral springs, such as those at Bath, was thought to be efficacious against cold humors. This bathing

From Urban Tigner Holmes, *Daily Living in the Twelfth Century* (Madison: The University of Wisconsin Press; ©1952 by the Regents of the University of Wisconsin), Reprinted by permission. This selection is from pages 137-40 in the 1964 paperback edition.

was most helpful, therefore, in old age. Jewish physicians taught that it was better to drink water at mealtimes because water is heavier than wine and therefore better for the digestion. Wine should be taken an hour after eating to augment the natural heat. Hard foods were not good for the kidneys. People were advised to let blood on general principles four times a year. Special strengthening drinks were prescribed. Some sickly folk, like the fictitious Uther, father of King Arthur, drank only cold water. Foods such as cheese, garlic, and pepper were forbidden. Women were brought out of a faint by sprinkling with water.

The art of surgery was still not separated from medicine. Those who had studied their art out of books had three problems with which they were constantly engaged. The phlegm, blood, bile, and black bile—were cold and moist. These qualities were the complexions of the humors. All drugs of the pharmacopoeia were classified according to their degrees of moisture, dryness, heat, and cold, and they were prescribed so as to maintain the proper balance of the humors within the body. The physician "discovered" how these were out of balance by examining visually the urine, sometimes the stool, and by feeling the pulse of the right wrist. He would count up to a hundred beats. This routine did not take long, so a physician could make a phenomenal number of calls in a morning.

The second problem was that of treating fevers. These were classified roughly into tertian, quartan, daily, and hectic. Sometimes pestilential fever was given separately. Among these the modern observer will recognize malaria, tuberculosis, nervous tension, influenza, and, under the heading hectic, the terrible diseases such as typhoid, scarlet fever, and typhus. These classifications were according to the intervals at which the fever recurred —every third day, every fourth—or according to the severity of the onset.

A third problem, which the twelfth-century *mire* could cope with more satisfactorily, was that of healing wounds, visible sores, and skin diseases. These were very common indeed. The physician, and the victim himself, knew the need for bandaging with strips of linen, often torn from a shirt. No idea of asepsis was held, but empirically some use was made of alcohol (in wine) and of white of egg (which is sterile when broken immediately before use). Counterirritants and plasters were popular. Bad tissue was cut away and the exposed area was doused in white of egg and drains were inserted to draw off the bad humors. Pus was usually encouraged to provide healing by second intention. A deep wound, such as that made by an arrow, was kept open with a paraffin tent—a finger of paraffin set into the hollow— and a drain was added. In gynecology a tent of cloth was inserted with some medication at the tip. There was very little cutting on the part of orthodox physicians, except for cataract, abscesses, and trepanning. It was considered sinful to cut into a living body so that lithotomists were not in good repute. Some of them were remarkable surgeons for their time. Certain Italian families, like the Preciani, wandered about practicing this art. When they arrived in a community, various physicians contrived to notify sufferers who were willing to take the risk. The operation was a daring one. The "staff," a rod invented later to prevent the operator from cutting too far, was not yet devised. The ulcers and skin diseases were very many. Usamah gives us a "frankish remedy" for scrofula: "Take uncrushed leaves of glasswort, burn them, then soak the ashes in olive oil and sharp vinegar. Treat the scrofula with them until the spot on which it is growing is eaten up. Then take burnt lead, soak it in ghee butter and treat him with it. That will cure him." One Bernard, treasurer of Fulk of Anjou, King of Jerusalem, had a compound fracture of the leg, in fourteen places. The Frankish physician washed the wounded limb frequently in strong vinegar alcohol. By this treatment all cuts were healed. Bad wounds were always sewed up with thread (probably silk when it was available). A wound in the *vuit buc*, probably the side at the waistline, was not greatly dreaded. Cendal, a silk material, was preferred for bandages.

All births were attended by midwives; men were forbidden to be present on pain of death. However, as Marie demonstrates in her Milon, infant care was rather good, once the child had been brought safely into the world. If such care had not been sensible, few of us would be here today. The baby was kept wrapped in swaddling bands, which are loose linen or wool wrappings with broad cloth bands, wrapped in crisscross fashion, holding the material firmly around him. The child was lifted, bathed, and changed every three hours. It was nursed on those occasions by wet nurses, as nothing but human milk could be given a suckling.

PART VII

Education of Women

FEW women were formally instructed[1], either in school, convent, or private tutorial, during the medieval period—but all were educated. The major responsibilities of women centered around religious, occupational, marital, and familial tasks. Peasant women found plenty of hard physical chores to occupy their time in addition to the tasks of raising children, cooking, making clothes, and keeping house. Most of these responsibilities, however, have been discussed, particularly by Eileen Power and Lord Ernle, in an earlier chapter. The duties of the child nurse as outlined by the English Franciscan, Bartholomew Anglicus, not only provides insight into a

---

[1]Urban T. Holmes argues that daughters of upper-class families often learned to read and write: "Guernes of Pont-Sainte-Maxence says, 'All those other romances which have been made about the Martyr, written by clerks or laymen, monks or ladies, I have heard many of them lie.' Some girls went even further and received some advanced instruction in Latin literature. Marie de France was one of these; Giraldus writes a poem to a 'learned lady'; Baudri de Bourgueil addressed the learned Emma. Examples of just plain reading ability can be multiplied. Gaimar says that Dame Custance read the *Life of Henry of England* in her private chamber. In the *Yvain* a young girl reads from a romance to her father and mother." (Urban Tigner Holmes, *Daily Living in the Twelfth Century*, p. 229.)

nurse's responsibilities towards children in the late thirteenth century but also describes the infant-raising practices followed by those women who were not in a position to hire nurses. Some women living in town or city helped their husbands sell goods at the market and fairs, as did the fishmongers' wives, while others helped to run shops as did the wives of cordwainers and pastycooks; indeed, some women were trained to specialize in certain crafts themselves, notably spinning, embroidery, and ale brewing. (Sylvia Thrupp's account here is helpful in understanding the extent to which women did work at such tasks; she argues that minimal reading, writing, and computational skills were needed by women so engaged in business.)

Eileen Power's translation of *The Goodman of Paris*[2] offers considerable insight into the tasks bourgeois women were obliged to perform in running their enlarged households, with their staffs of servants, as well as the attitudes and behaviors their husbands expected of them. Apparently an elderly husband, aged sixty or so, had married a young bride, still in her teens, and, as he was a well-to-do Parisian with a large household which required careful supervision by the lady of the house, he set about writing a book of instructions for his bride on her marital responsibilities and household management. The book, written around 1393, is divided into three parts. The first section outlines his advice to his wife on her obligations to God in order to win her soul's salvation as well as her responsibility for being obedient to her husband and lovingly concerned for his comfort and well-being. (Edith Rickert's translation of the section concerned with providing for the husband's comfort is included below.) The second part deals with household management including tips on dealing with servants, advice on gardening, a large section on menu planning and cooking (see recipes and advice on selecting foodstuffs), as well as some advice on other domestic problems such as removing grease spots, cleaning furs, and catching fleas from the chambers (the latter advice is also reproduced below). The third section remains uncompleted, except for a treatise on hawking, but according to its author was supposed also to deal with parlour games and riddles for the indoor amusement of ladies so that his wife

---

[2]*Le Ménagier de Paris*, edited in 1848 by Jerome Pichon.

could be accomplished as a hostess. Professor Power has created a day in the life of such a woman, based upon *Le Menagier de Paris*, and a portion is reproduced below.

Other careers open to women but requiring very different training were those of the whore and the nun. Prostitution thrived in the Middle Ages, despite the Christian church's opposition to adultery and unchaste women; in fact, the church, according to Richard Lewinsohn, whose work is quoted below, frequently profited from the houses of easy virtue. While little survives as far as explicit instruction to the young "fille" in training for this oldest of professions, one can little doubt that certain arts of seduction, cosmetics, and song were taught by the medieval equivalent of Doll Tearsheet to neophytes in the arts of love.

Finally the religious life was a vocation for some girls and an absolute necessity for others if they were orphaned or consecrated to nunneries by fathers unwilling or unable to pay doweries and marry them off. Chaucer's portrait of Madame Eglentyne served Eileen Power well, in addition to her own study of English nunneries,[3] as she created her portrait of the prioress's life in *Medieval People*. Although girls learned a smattering of Latin, French, and needlework in convents, these institutions were not renowned intellectual centers.[4] Moreover, convents were not great centers of pious womanhood, according to Professor Power; they tended, particularly during the later Middle Ages, to be places where the performance of religious obligations was perfunctory, where spiteful wrangling between nuns led to some unhappy hours, where drinking and gossiping (particularly as visiting women came to spend some months' seclusion from the world if their husbands were dead or away on lengthy business trips or wars) became cause for alarm to the bishops charged with visiting and supervising the convents; and where nuns longed to leave—on almost any pretext—to partake of some of the frivolity of secular life.

[3]Eileen Power. *Medieval English Nunneries*, Cambridge: The University Press, 1922.
[4]Clearly the case of Heloise, the cloistered wife of the ill-fated Abelard, is a striking exception to the typical lack of intellectuality found amongst nuns; but even Heloise did not receive her instruction in the convent (but through loving tutorials with Abelard prior to their marriage) and her letters to him make clear that devotion to love, and not religious piety, remained at the core of her cloistered life.

76. · The Child Nurse

Bartholomew Anglicus

A nurse hath that name of nourishing, for she is ordained to nourish and to feed the child, and therefore like as the mother, the nurse is glad if the child be glad, and heavy, if the child be sorry, and taketh the child up if it fall, and giveth it suck: if it weep she kisseth and lulleth it still, and gathereth the limbs, and bindeth them together, and doth cleanse and wash it when it is defiled. And for it cannot speak, the nurse lispeth and soundeth the same words to teach more easily the child that can not speak. And she useth medicines to bring the child to convenable estate if it be sick, and lifteth it up now on her shoulders, now on her hands, now on her knees and lap, and lifteth it up if it cry or weep. And she cheweth meat in her mouth, and maketh it ready to the toothless child, that it may the easilier swallow that meat, and so she feedeth the child when it is an hungered, and pleaseth the child with whispering and songs when it shall sleep, and swatheth it in sweet clothes, and righteth and stretcheth out its limbs, and bindeth them together with cradlebands, to keep and save the child that it have no miscrooked limbs. She batheth and anointeth it with good anointments.

77. The Businesswoman

Sylvia L. Thrupp

In the merchant class married women's business activities were less often an economic necessity than an outlet for surplus energy or a means of earning additional money to spend. Margery Kempe was the wife of one of the wealthiest merchants at Lynne, yet she took up first brewing and then "a new huswyfre," the grinding of corn in a horsemill, because she had time on her hands and because, in her own words, she was envious that any other woman in Lynne "schuld be arrayd so wel as sche." In London a fishmonger's heiress who was four times married went in both for tailoring

From *Medieval Lore*, Bartholomew Anglicus, edited by Robert Steele (London: Elliot Stock, 1893), p. 46.

From *The Merchant Class of Medieval London* by Sylvia L. Thrupp (Chicago: University of Chicago Press, 1948). Copyright ©1948 by The University of Michigan. Reprinted by permission. This selection is from pages 170-72 in the 1962 paperback edition (Ann Arbor: University of Michigan Press).

and for brewing. A fishmonger's widow bequeathed a male apprentice all the "anavildes & Slegges" of some kind of metal-working shop that she had directed. Dame Elizabeth Stokton had cloth manufactured for export to Italy. The favorite trades were embroidery, the "garnishing" of cloth and wearing apparel with jewelry, and the manufacture of silk; this last was managed almost entirely by merchants' wives, some of them having their raw silk imported by their husbands.

Illiteracy would have hampered a woman's efficiency in business matters. It followed that girls were recognized as in need of at least some elementary education for the same mixed reasons, economic and religious, as their brothers. They were admitted to the elementary schools, though not to grammar schools. Pecock advocated the sending of "femawlis" to school in order that they should be able to read treatises such as his own, which were written in English; liberal though he was, he did not urge that girls be taught Latin. Yet they could learn a little Latin in an elementary school and get more by private tuition. The story of Rahere tells of a twelfth-century priest in the suburbs with a daughter "whome he lovynge with fadirly affeccionn /yn yonge age put her to lernynge /." In 1390 there is a note of 25s. spent on school fees for a chandler's daughter, the ward of a broiderer, between her eighth year and her thirteenth, when she was married; and a century later a mercer gave instructions for his daughter to be sent to school for the same length of time as her brothers, four years. A woman could become a teacher, a wealthy grocer in 1408 leaving the sum of 20s. to E. Scolemaysteresse. One of the earliest London deeds found bearing a signature as well as a seal was drawn between two women, in 1478, signed by a wool merchant's widow. Bequests of devotional primers, which contained parts of the liturgy in Latin together with prayers in English, were made to women as well as to men. This evidence is not enough to show whether education was actually as general among the women as it was among the men of the merchant class, but one may infer that it was quite commonly within their reach.

In the silk industry and sometimes in other trades, women trained their assistants through a formal apprenticeship. Terms ran from seven to fifteen years, and up to L5 was paid as premium. If the mistress was a married woman, the indentures were made out in her husband's name as well as in her own, but they would specify that it was her trade, not his, that was to be taught. It was expected that a girl apprentice would receive more consideration than a boy, for the indentures might include an agreement to treat her "pulcrior' modo."

78. A Parisian's Idea of the Model Wife

Le Ménagier de Paris

Take pains to cherish the person of your husband, and I beg of you to keep him in clean linen, for that is your business; and since men have the trouble and pains of outside matters, so must a husband take pains to go and come and to run from one place to another, through rain, through winds, through snow and through hail, wet one day, dry the next, sweating one day, shivering the next, ill-fed, ill-lodged, ill-warmed, ill-bedded. Yet no real harm is done him, because he is consoled by his confidence in the care which his wife will take of him upon his return, and in the ease, the joys, and the pleasures which she will give him, or cause to be given him in her presence: to have his hose taken off before a good fire, to have his feet washed, and fresh hose and shoes, to be well fed and given good drink, to be well served and cared for, to be put to sleep in clean sheets and clean nightcaps, to be well covered with good furs and solaced with other joys and entertainment, privities, loves and secrets, about which I do not speak. And the next day, fresh underlinen and garments ... Therefore I advise you to prepare such comforts for your husband whenever he comes and stays, and to persevere therein; and also to keep peace with him and remember the country folks' proverb that three things drive a goodman out of his home: a leaky roof, a smoking chimney, and a scolding wife.

79. Recipes and Cooking Tips

Le Ménagier de Paris

To MAKE SAUSAGES. When you have killed your pig, take the flesh of the ribs ... and the best fat, as much of the one as of the other, in such quantity as you would make sausages; and cause it to be minced and hashed up very small by a pastrycook. Then bray fennel and a little fine salt, and afterwards take your brayed fennel and mix it very well with a quarter as much of fine [spice] powder; then mix thoroughly your meat, your spices and

From *Le Ménagier de Paris*, ed. Pichon, I, pp. 168-69, reprinted in *Chaucer's World* by Edith Rickert (New York: Columbia University Press, 1948). This selection is from pages 71-72 in the 1962 paperback edition.

From *The Goodman of Paris* by Eileen E. Power (New York: Harcourt, Brace & Co., 1928), pp. 308-9. Reprinted by permission from Routledge & Kegan Paul Ltd., London.

your fennel and afterwards fill the intestines, to wit the small ones. (And know that the intestines of an old pig be better for this, than those of a young one, because they be larger). And afterwards put them in the smoke for four days or more and when you would eat them, put them in hot water and boil them once and then put them on the grill.

To take Salt out of Butter, put it in a bowl on the fire to melt and the salt will precipitate at the bottom of the bowl, and salt thus precipitated is good for pottage; and the rest of the butter remaineth sweet. Otherwise put your salt butter in fresh sweet water and rub and knead it with your hands therein and the salt will remain in the water.

(Item, note that flies will never swarm on a horse that is greased with butter or with old salt grease.)

Magpies, Crows, Jackdaws. These be slain with the arrows of a crossbow, the which are blunt; and with weak crossbows you may shoot at those crows that be on the branches, but those that be in their nests must be shot at with stronger bolts to bring down nest and all. They should be skinned, then parboiled with bacon and then cut up into pieces and fried with eggs, like shredded meat (*charpies*).

Rique-menger. Take two apples as big as two eggs or a little bigger and peel them and take out the pips, then cut them up into little slices and set them to boil in an iron pot, then pour away the water and set the rique-manger to dry. Then fry butter and while you are frying it break two eggs into it and stir them up; and when it is fried sift a fine |spice| powder onto it and colour it with saffron and eat it on bread in the month of September.

80. Selecting Poultry and Fish

Le Ménagier de Paris

Item, you may tell young mallards from old ones, when they be the same size, from the quills of the feathers, which be tenderer in the young birds than in the old. *Item*, you may tell the river mallard, because they have sharp black nails and they have also red feet and the farmyard ducks have

From *The Goodman of Paris* by Eileen E. Power (New York: Harcourt, Brace & Co., 1928), pp. 224-225. Reprinted by permission from Routledge & Kegan Paul Ltd., London.

them yellow. *Item*, they have the crest or upper part of the beak green all along, and sometimes the males have a white mark across the nape of the neck, and they have the crest feathers very wavy.

Item, Ring doves be good in winter and you may tell the old ones for that the mid-feathers of their wings be all of a black hue, and the young ones of a year old have the mid-feathers ash coloured and the rest black.

Item, you may know the age of a hare from the number of holes that be beneath the tail, for so many holes, so many years.

Item, the partridges whose feathers be close set and well joined to the flesh, and be orderly and well joined, as are the feathers of a hawk, these be fresh killed; and those whose feathers be ruffled the wrong way and come easily out of the flesh and be out of place and ruffled disorderly this way and that, they be long killed. *Item*, you may feel it by pulling the feathers of the belly.

Item, the carp which hath white scales and neither yellow nor reddish, is from good water. That which hath big eyes standing forth from the head and palate and tongue joined, is fat. And *note* if you would carry a carp alive the whole day, wrap it up in damp hay and carry it belly upmost, and carry it without giving it air, in a cask or bag.

81. Getting Rid of Fleas

Le Ménagier de Paris

In summer take heed that there be no fleas in your chamber nor in your bed, which you may do in six ways, as I have heard tell. For I have heard from several persons that if the room be scattered with alder leaves the fleas will get caught therein. Item, I have heard tell that if you have at night one or two trenchers of bread covered with birdlime or turpentine and put about the room with a lighted candle set in the midst of each trencher, they will come and get stuck thereto. Another way which I have found and which is true: take a rough cloth and spread it about your room and over your bed and all the fleas who may hop on to it will be caught, so that you can carry them out with the cloth wheresoever you will. Item, sheepskins. Item, I have seen blankets placed on the straw and on the bed and when the black fleas jumped upon them they were the sooner found and killed

From *Medieval People* by Eileen Power (London: Methuen & Co., 1924; 10th edition, 1963). Reprinted by permission. This selection appears on page 112 of the 1968 paperback edition published by Barnes & Noble, New York.

upon the white. But the best way is to guard oneself against those which are within the coverlets and furs and the stuff of the dresses wherewith one is covered. For know that I have tried this, and when the coverlets, furs or dresses in which there be fleas are folded and shut tightly up, in a chest straitly bound with straps or in a bag well tied up and pressed, or otherwise compressed so that the said fleas are without light and air and kept imprisoned, then they will perish and die at once.

82. A Day in the Life of the Ménagier's Wife

Eileen Power

In the morning she rises, much earlier than ladies rise nowadays, though not so early as nuns, who must say matins, for that, her husband tells her, is not a fitting hour for married women to leave their beds. Then she washes, much less than ladies nowadays, hands and face only perchance, and says her orisons, and dresses very neatly, for she knows whose eye is upon her, and so goes with Dame Agnes the béguine to Mass, with eyes on the ground and hands folded over her painted primer. After Mass, and perhaps confession, back again to see if the servants are doing their work, and have swept and dusted the hall and the rooms, beaten the cushions and coverlets on the forms and tidied everything, and afterwards to interview Master John the steward and order dinner and supper. Then she sends Dame Agnes to see to the pet dogs and birds, "for they cannot speak and so you must speak and think for them if you have any." Then, if she be in her country house, she must take thought for the farm animals and Dame Agnes must superintend those who have charge of them, Robin the shepherd, Josson the oxherd, Arnoul the cowherd, Jehanneton the milkmaid, and Eudeline the farmer's wife who looks after the poultry yard. If she be in her town house she and her maids take out her dresses and furs from their great chests and spread them in the sun in the garden or courtyard to air, beating them with little rods, shaking them in the breeze, taking out spots and stains with one or other of the master's tried recipes, pouncing with lynx eyes upon the moth or sprightly flea.

After this comes dinner, the serious meal of the day, eaten by our ancestors about 10 a.m. What the Ménagier's wife gives to her lord and master

From *Medieval People* by Eileen Power (London: Methuen & Co., 1924; 10th edition, 1963). Reprinted by permission. This selection appears on pages 116-18 of the 1968 paperback edition published by Barnes & Noble, New York.

will depend upon the time of year and upon whether it be a meat or a fast day; but we know that she has no lack of menus from which to choose. After dinner she sees that the servants are set to dine, and then the busy housewife may become the lady of leisure and amuse herself. If in the country she may ride out hawking with a gay party of neighbours; if in town, on a winter's day, she may romp and play with other married ladies of her tender years, exchange riddles or tell stories round the fire. But what she most loves is to wander in her garden, weaving herself garlands of flowers, violets, gilly flowers, roses, thyme, or rosemary, gathering fruit in season (she likes raspberries and cherries), and passing on to the gardeners weighty advice about the planting of pumpkins ("in April water them courteously and transplant them"), to which the gardeners give as much attention as gardeners always have given, give still, and ever shall give, world without end, to the wishes of their employers. When she tries of this, the busy one gathers together Dame Agnes and her maids, and they sit under the carved beams of the hall mending his mastership's doublet, embroidering a vestment for the priest at his family chantry, or a tapestry hanging for the bedchamber. Or perhaps they simply spin (since, in the words of the Wife of Bath, God has given women three talents—deceit, weeping, and spinning!); and all the while she awes them with that tale of Griselda, her voice rising and falling to the steady hum of the wheels.

At last it is evening, and back comes the lord and master. What a bustle and a pother this home-coming meant we know well, since we know what he expected. Such a running and fetching of bowls of warm water to wash his feet, and comfortable shoes to ease him; such a hanging on his words and admiring of his labours. Then comes supper, with a bevy of guests, or themselves all alone in the westering sunlight, while he smacks connoisseur's lips over the roast crane and the blankmanger, and she nibbles her sweet wafers. Afterwards an hour of twilight, when she tells him how she has passed the day, and asks him what she shall do with the silly young housemaid, whom she caught talking to the tailor's 'prentice through that low window which looks upon the road. There is warm affection in the look she turns up to him, her round little face puckered with anxiety over the housemaid, dimpling into a smile when he commends her; and there is warm affection and pride too in the look the old man turns down upon her. So the night falls, and they go round the house together, locking all the doors and seeing that the servants are safe abed, for our ancestors were more sparing of candlelight than we. And so to bed.

83. Medieval Prostitution

Richard Lewinsohn

As in all ages, so in that of the cult of woman, the honest citizen naturally claimed the right to visit women who wore no chastity girdle. Prostitution flourished greatly throughout the whole Middle Ages. From time to time penal measures were enacted against prostitutes. One of the most energetic, certainly one of the most expert enemies of prostitution was the sixth-century Byzantine Empress Theodora, the Emperor Justinian's consort, whose own road to the throne had not been one of rigid virtue. Nevertheless, she dealt unkindly with the poor creatures whose careers had been less brilliant than her own. She sent five hundred prostitutes from the brothels of Constantinople to the other shore of the Bosphorus, there to spend their days and nights in cloistered seclusion. But the girls refused to enter the place of asylum. Many of them leapt into the water during the crossing and others took their own lives in their loneliness.

In the West, Charlemagne took up the campaign against prostitution. Adultery, whoring and prostitution figure together in his laws as the three sexual vices which are to be rooted out—how, the chronicles do not say. In any case, the effects of the Carolingian legislation in this field seem to have been short-lived. One of Charlemagne's successors on the Imperial throne laid down a barbarous procedure against prostitution: the woman was to be thrown naked into cold water, and passers-by were not to help her, but to mock and deride her. But prostitution survived even these aberrations of sex-jurisdiction, and the commoner methods of disgracing its practitioners—the pillory, shaving of the head, the stocks, flogging and whipping, were no more effectual. A few women may possibly have been converted by them to virtuous ways, but the institution went on—inevitably, for it is not there for women's satisfaction but for men's pleasure, and men always went unpunished, even if caught *in flagranti*.

The Crusades brought with them an extraordinary increase in prostitution. The pious warriors could face parting from their wives, painful as this was, but complete abstinence, perhaps for several years, seemed to them altogether too hard. The organizers of the Crusades fully understood the impossibility of getting and keeping an army together without women.

Abridged from pp. 144-47 and 148 (hardbound edition) in *A History of Sexual Customs* by Richard Lewinsohn, translated by Alexander Mayce. English translation copyright ©1958 by Longmans, Green & Co., Ltd. and Harper & Row, Publishers, Inc. Original edition in German ©1956 by Rowohlt Verlag GmbH, Hamburg, under the title *Eine Weltgeschichte der Sexualitat.* By permission of the publishers. This selection is from pages 134-38 of the 1964 paperback edition (Greenwich, Conn.: Fawcett Publications).

The ports of embarkation themselves swarmed with women offering themselves to the Crusaders, and many went on board the ships. A calculation by the Templars (the Order which kept the accounts of the Crusades) noted that in one year thirteen thousand prostitutes had to be provided for.

When the Crusades ended, the problem of keeping the prostitutes under control became more urgent still. Many new towns had been founded. Women who formerly tramped the highways now followed the trend of the age and were practising their trade inside the town walls, or outside the gates. The citizens, even if they patronized the women, were scandalized. The nuisance must be abated. The Church appreciated the position. It would be vain to attempt to eliminate prostitution altogether; this would do more harm than good. St. Augustine himself had said: "If you put down prostitution, licence and pleasure will corrupt society." After long consideration, the authorities reverted to the methods of antiquity: putting the prostitutes into public houses, under police supervision, seemed the lesser evil. In many places the Church itself took control of the problem. In the papal city of Avignon a public house of ill-fame was established under the name of "Abbaye," Abbey, and the official patronage of Queen Joanna of Naples. The women employed there were required to keep the hours of prayer punctually and not to miss any service, for, depraved as their trade was, they were to remain good Christians. The customers, too, were subject to a rule of religion: only Christans might enter the house; heathens and Jews were specifically excluded. The enterprise seems to have prospered so well that Pope Julius II afterwards founded a similar house in Rome.*
In other towns the Church refrained from active participation in the business, but brothels were not infrequently established in houses which were owned by priests or Mothers Superior of convents. One Archbishop of Mainz, a highly educated man, was said to have as many prostitutes in his houses as books in his library. An English cardinal bought a house in which a brothel was situated, with no intention of shutting it down.**

It was, of course, a great advantage for a brothel-keeper if he could carry on his business on such premises, for he was then safeguarded against any slanderous accusation of commerce with the devil. Even lacking such extraneous protection, however, the profession was not very dangerous. The inquisition paid small attention to brothels, unless for some special reason. It persecuted prostitutes who worked on their own account and at their own risk, for they might be witches; but women working as the employees of a brothel-keeper were obviously not consorting with the devil, but with honest citizens, and they could not be stopped from doing that. Brothel-

*Robert Briffault, *The Mothers* (London 1927), Vol. III, p. 216.
**George F. Fort, *History of Medical Economy during the Middle Ages* (1883), pp. 336-347 — Victor Robinson, *The story of Medicine* (New York, 1963), pp. 213-215.

keepers were forbidden only to employ renegade nuns, married women or girls suffering from dangerous contagious diseases—all prohibitions which were often difficult to enforce.

Virtuous citizens, however, did not rest content with placing the brothels under police supervision. They genuinely desired the welfare of these women, who were called "free" but in reality were half prisoners. When a sinner tired of her profession and wished to return to the paths of righteousness, the doors of civic society were not to be shut against her. The Church encouraged these endeavours; in 1198 Pope Innocent III recommended well-intentioned citizens to reclaim prostitutes by marrying them. They could not, of course, be taken at once into a respectable burgher's house, as maids or even something higher; first they had to go through a sort of purgatory, to reaccustom them to discipline and order. Nevertheless, the world wanted to make their path to repentance and reform as smooth as possible. To this end some places, while not closing down their brothels, established special "Magdalene Homes" for repentant sinners.

The Penitents' House at St. Jerome's in Vienna, known to the populace as the "Soul House," was a model of this kind of institution. It was founded at the beginning of the fourteenth century, on the private initiative of a few rich citizens, and was given a charter in 1384 by Duke Albrecht III as a recognized institution for "penitent women." From outside it looked like a convent, but no excessive asceticism was required of its inmates, who were not asked to vow themselves either to chastity, or to poverty. It received so many endowments that it soon became the richest institution in Vienna. The best of the vineyards outside the city walls were its property. The penitents were able to build themselves a magnificent church, and when they married they were given handsome portions. Not a few respected citizens chose their wives from among the former "pretty ladies" of the Soul House.

The educative method having yielded such good results, the Emperor Frederick III, in 1480, incautiously granted the penitent women a retail licence for the sale of produce of their vineyards. The foundation of St. Jerome now became witness of animated scenes. Many of the women reverted to their former way of life.

.   .   .

"WOMAN-HOUSES" AND BATHS

By the later Middle Ages every town had its *lupanar*, as in the old Roman Empire. Where German was spoken, the establishments were called *Frauenhäuser* ("Woman-houses") and this neutral, uncompromising name became usual in other countries also. The house was usually situated in a side street near the church. It bore no sign, but everyone knew where it was. The business was less often combined with the sale of liquor than in antiquity, but a new attraction had been invented. The public baths were not great mansions as in ancient Rome, but modest utilitarian establishments, often simply disguised brothels. The hub of such a place was not a drawing-room, but a basin with room for five or six people, not to swim, but to enjoy physical contact. The women presented themselves to the guests undressed, and welcomed them hospitably. Larger tubs were provided for more intimate enjoyment, unless the customers preferred to withdraw into a dry chamber to carry out the real purpose of their visit. Paris, whose population of two hundred thousand made it by far the largest city of Europe, had thirty such establishments at the beginning of the fifteenth century.

Every large town also contained many street-walkers, who gave the police endless trouble. It was the dress of these women that particularly occupied the authorities: the problem was not so much to check the prostitutes from displaying too much of their charms, as to prevent confusion between them and honest women. . . .

84. Madame Eglentyne: The Prioress

Eileen Power

The nuns had seven monastic offices to say every day. About 2 a.m. the night office was said; they all got out of bed when the bell rang, and went down in the cold and the dark to the church choir and said Matins, followed immediately by Lauds. Then they went back to bed, just as the dawn was breaking in the sky, and slept again for three hours, and then got up for good at six o'clock and said Prime. After that there followed Tierce, Sext, None, Vespers, and Compline, spread at intervals through the day. The last service, compline, was said at 7 p.m. in winter, and at 8 p.m. in summer, after which the nuns were supposed to go straight to bed in the dorter, in which connexion one Nun's Rule ordains that "None shall push up against another wilfully, nor spit upon the stairs going up and down, but if they tread it out forthwith"! They had in all about eight hours' sleep, broken in the middle by the night service. They had three meals, a light repast of bread and beer after prime in the morning, a solid dinner to the ac-

Abridged from *Medieval People* by Eileen Power (London: Methuen & Co., 1924; 10th ed. 1963). Reprinted by permission. This selection is from pages 79-86 of the 1968 paperback edition published by Barnes & Noble, New York.

companiment of reading aloud in the middle of the day, and a short supper immediately after vespers at 5 or 6 p.m.

From 12 to 5 p.m. in winter and from 1 to 6 p.m. in summer Eglentyne and her sisters were supposed to devote themselves to manual or brain work, interspersed with a certain amount of sober and godly recreation. She would spin, or embroider vestments with the crowned monogram M of the Blessed Virgin in blue and gold thread, or make little silken purses for her friends and finely sewn bands for them to bind round their arms after a bleeding. She would read too, in her psalter or in such saints' lives as the convent possessed, written in French or English; for her Latin was weak, though she could construe *Amor vincit omnia*. Perhaps her convent took in a few little schoolgirls to learn their letters and good manners with the nuns, and when she grew older she helped to teach them to read and sing; for though they were happy, they did not receive a very extensive education from the good sisters. In the summer Eglentyne was sometimes allowed to work in the convent garden, or even to go out haymaking with the other nuns; and came back round-eyed to confide in her confessor that she had seen the cellaress returning therefrom seated behind the chaplain on his nag, and had thought what fun it must be to jog behind stout Dan John.

Except for certain periods of relaxation strict silence was supposed to be observed in the convent for a large part of the day, and if Eglentyne desired to communicate with her sisters, she was urged to do so by means of signs. . . .

The nuns, of course, would not have been human if they had not some-times grown a little weary of all these services and this silence; for the religious life was not, nor was it intended to be, an easy one. It was not a mere means of escape from work and responsibility. In the early golden age of monasticism only men and women with a vocation, that is to say a real genius for monastic life, entered convents. Moreover, when there they worked very hard with hand and brain, as well as with soul, and so they got variety of occupation, which is as good as a holiday. The basis of wise St. Benedict's Rule was a nicely adjusted combination of variety with regularity; for he knew human nature. Thus monks and nuns did not find the services monotonous, and indeed regarded them as by far the best part of the day. But in the later Middle Ages, when Chaucer lived, young people had begun to enter monastic houses rather as a profession than as a vocation. Many truly spiritual men and women still took the vows, but with them came others who were little suited to monastic life, and who lowered its standard, because it was hard and uncongenial to them. Eglentyne became a nun because her father did not want the trouble and expense of finding her a husband, and because being a nun was about the only career for a well-born lady who did not marry. Moreover, by this time, monks and nuns had grown more lazy, and did little work with their hands and still less with their heads, particularly in nunneries, where the early tradition of learning had died out and where many nuns could hardly understand the Latin in which their services were written. . . .

Carelessness in the performance of the monastic hours was an exceedingly common fault during the later Middle Ages, though the monks were always worse about it than the nuns. Sometimes they "cut" the services. . . . Sometimes they came late to matins, in the small hours after midnight. This fault was common in nunneries, for the nuns always would insist on having private drinkings and gossipings in the evening after compline, instead of going straight to bed, as the rule demanded—a habit which did not conduce to wakefulness at 1 a.m. Consequently they were somewhat sleepy at matins. . . . At the nunnery of Stainfield in 1519 the bishop discovered that half an hour sometimes elapsed between the last stroke of the bell and the beginning of the service, and that some of the nuns did not sing, but dozed, partly because they had not enough candles, but chiefly because they went late to bed. . . . There was a tendency also among both monks and nuns to slip out before the end of the service on any good or bad excuse: they had to see after the dinner or the guest-house, their gardens needed weeding, or they did not feel well. But the most common fault of all was to gabble through the services as quickly as they could in order to get them over. They left out the syllables at the beginning and end of words, they omitted the dipsalma or pause between two verses, so that one side of the choir was beginning the second half before the other side had finished the first; they skipped sentences, they mumbled and slurred what should have been "entuned in their nose ful semely" and altogether they made a terrible mess of the stately plainsong.

But the monotony of convent life. . . . sometimes played havoc with their tempers. The nuns were not chosen for convent life because they were saints. They were no more immune from tantrums than was the Wife of Bath, who was out of all charity when other village wives went into church before her; and sometimes they got terribly on each others' nerves. . . . All prioresses were not "full pleasant and amiable of port," or stately in their manner. The records of monastic visitations show that bad temper and petty bickering sometimes broke the peace of convent life.

But we must be back at Eglentyne. She went on living for ten or twelve years as a simple nun, and she sang the services very nicely and had a sweet temper and pretty manners and was very popular. Moreover, she was of good birth; . . . even her personal beauty—straight nose, grey eyes, and little red mouth—conforms to the courtly standard. The convents were apt to be rather snobbish; ladies and rich burgesses, daughters got into them, but poor and low-born girls never. . . .

[As Prioress] At first it was very exciting, and Eglentyne liked being called "Mother " by nuns who were older than herself, and having a private room to sit in and all the visitors to entertain. But she soon found that it was not by any means all a bed of roses; for there was a great deal of business to be done by the head of a house—not only looking after the internal discipline of the convent, but also superintending money matters and giving orders to the bailiffs on her estates, and seeing that the farms were paying well, and the tithes coming in to the churches which belonged to the nunnery, and that the Italian merchants who came to buy the wool off her sheeps' backs gave a good price for it. In all this business she was supposed to take the advice of the nuns, meeting in the chapter-house, where all business was transacted. I am afraid that sometimes Eglentyne used to think that it was much better to do things by herself, and so she would seal documents with the convent seal without telling them. One should always distrust the head of an office or school or society who says, with a self-satisfied air, that it is much more satisfactory to do the thing herself than to depute it to the proper subordinates; it either means that she is an autocrat, or else that she cannot organize. Madame Eglentyne was rather an autocrat, in a good-natured sort of way, and besides she hated bother. So she did not always consult the nuns; and . . . she often tried to evade rendering an account of income and expenditure to them every year, as she was supposed to do.

The nuns, of course, objected to this; and the first time the bishop came on his rounds they complained about it to him. They said, too, that she was a bad business woman and got into debt; and that when she was short of money she used to sell woods belonging to the convent, and promise annual pensions to various people in return for lump sums down, and lease out farms for a long time at low rates, and do various other things by which the convent would lose in the long run. And besides, she had let the roof of the church get into such ill repair that rain came through the holes on to their heads when they were singing; and would my lord bishop please to look at the holes in their clothes and tell her to provide them with new ones? Other wicked prioresses used sometimes even to pawn the plate and jewels of the convent, to get money for their own private purposes. But Eglentyne was not at all wicked or dishonest, though she was a bad manager; the fact was that she had no head for figures. . . .

PART **VIII**

Jewish Education

JEWS in medieval Europe were alternately sought after to serve Christendom as artisans, merchants, moneylenders, and translators of Hebrew and Arabic books, including the Torah and many works of philosophy, and subjected to religious persecution when they would not forswear Judaism and become converted to Christianity.[1] Max I. Dimont has provided capsule accounts of both alternatives which are quoted below. The one method of religious persecution of Jews which is of particular interest to the historian of education is that of religious disputation in which Jewish scholars competed with Christian theologians with the price for losing set at mass conversion of the Jewish community to Christianity.

That Jews were scholars and were also respected as artisans, merchants, moneylenders, and translators sets the stage for any discussion of Jewish education. The respect for learning amongst the

---

[1]It is true that some Jews did so convert, particularly in Spain; but the vast majority of European Jews refused to renounce the religion of their fathers.

Jews was recognized by their Christian contemporaries (as Dimont's quotation from Abelard's pupil makes clear), although few Christians probably understood why Jews believed so strongly in education. Dimont argues that whether Jews dwelled in urban ghettoes or in rural *stetl* villages, learning was regarded as an avenue to esteemed status within the Jewish community.

European Jewish scholarship traced back to the entry of Jews into Italy, according to H. J. Zimmels. During the seventh, eighth, ninth, and tenth centuries, the major centers for talmudic scholarship were to be found in Italy; Venosa, Oria, Bari, Otranto, Siponto, Pavia, Rome, and Lucca all alternately played a part not only in retaining the connections between Palestinian and Babylonian Jewry, but also in helping to spread talmudic studies both to Northern Europe, via Germany, and to Spain, via North Africa.

One of the most illustrious scholars of Roman Jewry, R. Nathan ben Jehiel, born around 1035, wrote a lexicographical work, "Aru<u>k</u>", which spread not only to France and Germany, but also to Spain. (Zimmels's description of Nathan's work and his library are included below.)

The Talmud (characterized below by Dimont) consists of both Mishna and Gemara, a compilation of traditional laws (initially transmitted orally) and their explanations, expositions, and illustrative examples. The Talmud served as the central object of rabbinic study in Europe. I. A. Agus argues that Rhineland Jewish communities concentrated on the study of the Talmud not only as the major source of religious instruction, but also as a guide to all phases of community life, particularly during the ninth and tenth centuries. As with all studies of religious works, Jews needed teachers and students of the Talmud (and Torah) and they also required reinterpretation of Talmudic injunctions so as to be applicable to the changes of living experienced over the centuries. One of the luminaries of Rhineland Jewish scholarship was Rabbenau Gershom (ca. 950-1028) whose fame was spread from his Yeshiva at Mainz by his devoted students. Another beloved teacher and scholar of Northern Europe was Rabbi Shlomo Itzhaki, a French Jew, who became popularly known as Rashi. Rashi became famed for his sensitive re-interpretation of certain Talmudical complexities in a way that was both understandable and applicable to living conditions. (Agus's and Dimont's characterizations of Rashi and his method of study and teaching are included below.)

Jewish scholars faced two problems similar to those faced by Christian theologians. Just as Christian exegesis became highly torturous as the scholastic theologians attempted to reconcile growing church dogma with varying texts of the Old and New Testaments and writings of the Fathers, so, too, did Jewish study of the Torah and Talmud become more hair-splitting during the latter part of the Middle Ages. (Dimont characterizes this belabored study as the "bibliosclerosis" of the Talmud.[2]) The second problem hinged on the question of the literal truth of the Bible (a problem which St. Augustine had wrestled with, but not solved for all subsequent Christian scholars).

The most famed of Jewish scholars was Moses Maimonides, 1135-1204, whose philosophy shows clear connections to that of the Arabian, Averroes, who translated much of Aristotle's work. Maimonides' most famous treatise was *Guide to the Perplexed*. (An account of Maimonides, by Abram Leon Sachar, is included below.)

But it was not only by talmudic scholarship that Jews continued their contributions to learning. Moral education was provided to Jewish adults and children by a variety of tales, two of the best known being the twelfth century "fox fables"[3] of Rabbi Berechiah ben Natronai ha-Nakdan, a Frenchman, and the *Tales of Sendebar*[4] (whose precise author is unknown). The "fox fables" resemble the animal morality stories of Aesop as well as the Romance of Renart, the Fox, but include considerable biblical quotations and an emphasis upon the didactic moral of each fable. (Moses Hadas has translated these and one is selected as illustrative of the general trend.) The *Tales of Sendebar* show themselves to be of the genre in which the

---

[2] Max I. Dimont, *Jews, God, and History*, p. 172-181.
[3] *Mishle Shualim*
[4] *Mishle Sendebar*, translated by Morris Epstein.

Decameron and *Arabian Nights* are written. Here a series of tales are told, somewhat in contest fashion, about the wiles of women and the perfidy of evil sons.

In addition to formal talmudic study and moral education via fables, Jews provided for the education of their children through the observance of high holy days, particularly the Passover Feast, in which children used the Haggadah to ask the ritualistic questions about the flight of the Jews from Egypt.

The education of young Jews into the occupational roles of their parents paralleled that of Christian youth learning to become merchants and artisans; however, for a considerable number of years, Jews monopolized the money business because of the Christian Church's opposition to the practice of taking interest on loans (usury).[5] Here, Jewish youth had to learn complex conversion tables for money as there were many differing units of coinage in circulation in Europe.

85. Jews' Contributions to Christian Europe

Max I. Dimont

Because the Jew was not part of the feudal system, it did not tie him to any of its institutions, but allowed him to become a cosmopolitan in his life and a universalist in his thought. He spoke the languages of the world, and appreciated its cultures. Because he had no prejudices he could carry ideas and commodities from one nation to another. Because he was an outsider with an education, he could view societies objectively and assess their weaknesses and strengths. He became the social critic and the prophet for new social justice.

Popes and princes of the Middle Ages could have wiped out the Jews

---

[5]One should also note that the Church learned to change her opposition to the taking of interest on money lent as a money-economy developed in Europe. In fact, as Herbert J. Muller observes, the Church became one of the greatest moneylenders and money-borrowers once she redefined the sin of usury from the taking to any profit on money lent, to the taking of *excessive* profit on lent money. (Herbert J. Muller, *The Uses of the Past*.)

From *Jews, God and History* by Max I. Dimont (New York: Simon & Schuster, 1962), p. 283. Copyright ©1962 by Max Dimont. Reprinted by permission of Simon & Schuster, Inc.

completely had they wanted to, but they did not want to. They realized the Jews were indispensable to them. The Jews were their physicians, their ambassadors, their businessmen, their financiers, their men of learning in an age of darkness. But it would be an injustice to the spirit of the Middle Ages to leave the implication that if the Jews had not been useful they would have been exterminated. When, because of social, economic, or even religious pressures, the presence of the Jews became unwanted, they were banished, not killed. The Church endowed all human beings with a soul, and it took a man's life only to save his soul. It was only when religion lost its deterrent hold on man that modern society could entertain the idea of coolly murdering millions because it felt there was no room for them.

86. Persecution of Jews

Max I. Dimont

In no other phase of their history were the Jews subjected to such unremitting efforts to convert them to Christianity as in the Christian Middle Ages. In no other age had they been subjected to such unremitting persecution for rejecting conversion. The Babylonians, Assyrians, and Persians had only asked them to be nice tax-paying Jews. The Greeks and Romans had only asked them to throw a little incense at the feet of their gods as a mark of respect. No one cared whether the Jews converted to paganism or not. Jews had been slain, hanged, crucified, decimated, beheaded, tortured for all the reasons people have always been slain, hanged, crucified, decimated, beheaded, tortured—in anger, in justified indignation, in battle, for sheer pleasure, as an object lesson, as a punishment for rebellion, for not paying taxes—but never for not converting.

The Mohammedans may have looked down upon both Christians and Jews for their inability to perceive the superiority of Allah over Christ and Jehovah. But the Mohammedans never made it their mission in life to convert Christians and Jews to Mohammedanism. The Romans would have regarded the Christian effort as sheer lunacy. The Greeks would have been faintly amused. Other pagans would have been utterly bewildered. The Jews were all for leaving the Christians alone. The trouble was that the Christians would not leave the Jews alone....

From *Jews, God and History* by Max I. Dimont (New York: Simon & Schuster, 1962), pp. 232-36. Copyright ©1962 by Max Dimont. Reprinted by permission of Simon & Schuster, Inc.

The persecution of the Jews was rather desultory and of little historic consequence until the eleventh century, when the religious phase of Jewish persecutions began, with four main motifs standing out in the over-all design. These were ritual-murder accusations, Host-desecration libels, burnings of the Talmud, and religious disputations.

The ritual-murder charge stemmed from the superstitious belief that upon each Passover the Jews slew a Christian male child and used his blood to spray over their Passover *matzos* (the unleavened bread Jews eat during this holiday). It was easy for such a notion to take hold in the medieval mind, because the Old Testament was not translated into the languages of the people until the sixteenth century. Until then, the people received all their Bible stories secondhand, as digested legends. It was in such second-hand fashion they heard the story of Exodus and learned how the Lord had smitten the male children of Egypt in order to force Pharaoh to let the Israelites go. Was it not logical that now the Jews were similarly smiting Christian children? . . .

Closely resembling these ritual-murder charges were the Host-desecration libels, which were given birth to in the twelfth century with the enunciation of the Doctrine of Transubstantiation. This doctrine holds that in the drinking of the wine and in the eating of the wafer, or Host, the wine becomes the blood and the wafer the body of Christ. The rumor now became widespread that the Jews re-enacted the crucifixion of Jesus by stealing the wafer and piercing it with a sharp instrument to make it bleed. . . .

The first burnings of the Talmud took place in 1244 in Paris and Rome. It was burned four more times in fourteenth-century France, and then there were no more burnings for two hundred years. The two best years for Talmud burning were 1553 and 1554, when it went to the stake twelve times in various Italian cities. It was burned twice more, in Rome in 1558 and 1559, and then the fashion ended. In Eastern Europe, the Talmud was burned but once, in 1757.

The interesting aspect about Talmud burning is not that the Talmud was sent to the stake, for in the Middle Ages translations of the New Testament in languages other than Latin were consigned to the flames more frequently than the Talmud. The interesting aspect is that the Old Testament in Hebrew was never sent to the stake. Though Torah scrolls often were trampled underfoot by screaming mobs looting synagogues, or burned with the synagogue itself, such acts were never sanctioned by the Church, and the Torah was never officially condemned. Though Judaism was reviled as a blasphemy, though Jews were killed for being unbelievers, the Torah itself was looked upon with respect, for it was the Law of God.

It is of interest to note here that these anti-Jewish ritual-murder accusations, Host-desecration libels, and Talmud burnings all were first conceived by converted Jews. . . .

The "religious disputation" was also the innovation of apostate Jews. Many of these converted Jews were well versed in the Talmud and, to show off their learning to their new Christian brothers or, perhaps, to curry favor with the Church, they whispered in the ears of the powerful that if in a public disputation, it were shown how wrong the Jews were, then the entire Jewish community might convert.

These religious disputations, called "tournaments of God and faith," were a combination of intellectual chess and Russian roulette. If the Jewish scholars could not disprove the charges of the Christian scholars arrayed against them, then an entire Jewish community stood the threat of a forced march to the baptismal font. If, on the other hand, they mocked the Christian scholars with superior Jewish scholarship, they ran the danger of being put to death.

87. Jewish Respect for Learning

Max I. Dimont

A common feature of ghetto and *shtetl* life was the quest for *yichus*, an untranslatable word most closely akin to "prestige" and "status." Possessing *yichus* was much like charm in a woman—if she has it, it makes no difference what else she lacks, and if she does not have it, it makes no difference what else she has. *Yichus* was an amalgam of family background, tradition, learning, and occupation, which usually was inherited, but which could be possessed through the acquisition of knowledge. Good conduct was essential to keep *yichus* in the family. Whoever possessed it had to set for himself high standards in deportment, learning, charity. He could not be a drunkard or a cheat. The word of a man of *yichus* was law, and he would rather go to the torture rack than break it. He early learned to look a gentile defamer straight in the eye with such dignity that it made the detractor ill at ease. Whereas it was forgiven the *prost*, the common man, to cringe in deference to a gentile, the *yichus* man would lose status if he ever did so.

The *prost* could aspire to *yichus* through learning. The most important item in the budget of a Jewish household, no matter how poor, was for education. Even more than the father, it was the mother who yearned for an education for all her sons. She would cheat on her meager household

From *Jews, God and History* by Max I. Dimont (New York: Simon & Schuster, 1962), pp. 252-53. Copyright ©1962 by Max Dimont. Reprinted by permission of Simon & Schuster, Inc.

money and put away a few *pfennige* or *kopecks* each week so "maybe the younger brother could get an education, too." The Christians admired this quality in the Jews. As a pupil of Peter Abelard expressed it:

> If the Christians educate their sons, they do so not for God, but for gain in order that the one brother, if he be a clerk, may help his father and mother and his other brothers...A Jew, however poor, if he had ten sons he would put them all to letters, not for gain, as the Christians do, but to the understanding of God's Law, and not only his sons, but his daughters.

Jewish education was at its height in twelfth-century Western Europe. For example, the ordinary Jewish curriculum included Bible, Hebrew, poetry, Talmud, the relation of philosophy and revelation, the logic of Aristotle, the elements of Euclid, arithmetic, the mathematical works of Archimedes and others, optics, astronomy, music, mechanics, medicine, natural science, and metaphyics....

But Mama's *pfennige* and *kopecks* no longer brought the quality education they used to buy. By the fourteenth century, Jewish education began to deteriorate, and by the fifteenth century Christian education surpassed it in quality. By the seventeenth century, the curriculum had dwindled to reading, writing, Bible, and Talmud. To obtain a higher education, the Jews had to send their children to gentile universities.

88. The 'Aru<u>k</u>' and Library of R. Nathan ben Jehiel

H. J. Zimmels

The greatest Italian Jewish scholar of our period was without doubt R. Nathan ben Jehiel (born ca. 1035), the author of that classic lexicographical work, the *'Aru<u>k</u>*. R. Nathan belonged to the family *Min ha-'Anawim* (in Italian, Piatelli or Delli Mansi) which legendarily traced its origin back to the Judean nobility brought to Italy by Titus. His father was head of the academy of Rome and it was most probably he who introduced Nathan to the study of the Law which he later continued outside his father's house. As a youth he went to Sicily where he studied in the school of R. Mazliah al-Bazaq, who had shortly before returned from R. Hai's academy in Baghdad. It was through this master that R. Nathan became acquainted with

From "Scholars and Scholarship in Byzantium and Italy" by H. J. Zimmels in *The World History of the Jewish People*, Cecil Roth, ed. Vol. II, *The Dark Ages* (New Brunswick: Rutgers University Press, 1966), pp. 182-84. Reprinted by permission.

the Gaonic method of interpreting the Talmud. From Sicily R. Nathan went to Narbonne to study with R. Moses ha-Darshan. It is not quite certain whether he also attended some other schools, though it is not unlikely. Soon after his return home his father died, about 1070, and R. Nathan was entrusted with the presidency of the local academy, together with his two brothers. It was during that time that he compiled his famous dictionary, the *'Aruk*. This work is more than a glossary explaining the individual words of the Talmud: it is also in effect a Talmudic encyclopaedia. The author quotes difficult or unusual words taken from the Talmud and Midrash and explains not only these terms (resorting for the purpose to Hebrew, Aramaic, Latin, Greek, Italian, Arabic and even Persian) but also the passages in which they occur. He also quotes various comments of the Gaonim and the Rabbis who lived before him or who were his contemporaries, thereby giving us an idea of the works of Jewish authors available in Italy in the 11th century. The picture is impressive. In his library were to be found not only the Bible and the Babylonian and Palestinian Talmuds, but also the *halakic* Midrashim (*Mekilta, Sifra* and *Sifrei*), the Tosefta, the Targum on the Bible, *Avot de-Rabbi Nathan, Seder 'Olam, Midrash Rabba* on Genesis and on Leviticus, *Eka Rabbati*, the Midrash on Psalms, Proverbs, Canticles and Ecclesiastes, *Pesiqta de-Rabbi Kahana, Yelammedenu, Pirqei Rabbi Eliezer*, a *Chronicle of Moses, She'eltot* or R. Ahai, *Halakot Gedolot*, R. Zemah's *'Aruk*, a great collection of Responsa of the Gaonim, the Talmudic commentaries of Hai Gaon, R. Hananel, R. Nissim, and Rabbenu Gershom, *Seder Eliyahu Rabba* and *Zuta, Josippon, Ben Sira*, and various books on medicine and mathematics. Some sources preserved in the *'Aruk* are in fact extant nowhere else, while sometimes the author's versions are more correct than the current texts. The *'Aruk* also throws valuable sidelights on customs and cultural institutions. Thus when explaining the word "theater" (s.v. *tei'ater*) he says that "in lingua grammatica (i.e. in classical Greek) one denotes by this name a place in which people sit on raised seats, watching the play performed below either by men or wild beasts. Up to the present day people call the Colosseum 'theater,' for people used to sit there, in tiers one above the other, in order not to impede the view." The Babylonian custom of celebrating Purim by burning Haman in effigy is described in detail (s.v. *shewwar*): "Four or five days before Purim the young men make an effigy of Haman which is hung on the roof. On Purim they make a bonfire into which they throw the effigy as they stand singing around it. They hold a ring above the fire, waving it from side to side, and, hanging on it, jump through the fire." When explaining the expression *hamneq* (denoting a two-pronged fork) R. Nathan says (s.v. *hamneq*): "It is a metal implement used by the Persians when eating meat or other food as they do not touch their mouths with their hands." Belief in demons, amulets and spells is evident in the author's remark that "neither their causes nor their sources are known" (s.v. *gaf* 15). When explaining the word *lappid* ("torch") he observes (s.v. *ldp*). "There exists a custom in Arab countries of leading the bride at night from her father's house to the house of her husband and of carrying ten poles in front of her; on each of them is a brass vessel containing a piece of cloth with oil and tar which is kindled and shines before her." Elsewhere he mentions mosaic work (s.v. *razaf*): "From the root *rzf* the word *rizpa* ('pavement') is derived, denoting the juxtaposition of tablets of colored marble or wood."

89. Talmudic Studies Involve Many Disciplines

Max I. Dimont

Three main streams of Jewish thought flow through the Talmud, the first two through the head, the third through the heart. Intertwined through its thirty-five volumes are the complicated brain twisters of jurisprudence known as *Halacha*, or "law"; the philosophical dissertations on ethics, morals, conduct, and piety known as *Aggada*, or "narration"; and the beautiful, tender passages on Bible stories, wise sayings, and tales known as *Midrash*, or "sermons."

Because law and jurisprudence, ethics and morality, deal with many phases of human life, it is not surprising to find that the Talmud also touches upon the sciences, such as medicine, hygiene, astronomy, economics, government. The varied contents of the Talmud opened new vistas for the Jews, expanding their intellectual horizons, permitting them to discard the old and acquire the new. The study of the Talmud not only made the Jews jurists, it also made them physicians, mathematicians, astronomers, grammarians, philosophers, poets, and businessmen.

From *Jews, God and History* by Max I. Dimont (New York: Simon & Schuster, 1962), pp. 168-69. Copyright © 1962 by Max Dimont. Reprinted by permission of Simon & Schuster, Inc.

90. Rabbenu Gershom: Teacher at the Yeshiva at Mainz

I. A. Agus

The communities on the Rhine reached their highest point of cultural development in the 11th century. Already at the beginning of that century, the community of Mainz was a great center of Talmudic scholarship, attracting students from Germany, France, Provence, Italy and Spain. Among its outstanding teachers, the one who made the deepest impression on later generations was Rabbenu Gershom ben Judah (ca. 950-1028), probably a native of Metz, to whose *Yeshiva* at Mainz students flocked from all parts of Europe. After years of study these students, upon returning home, became prominent members of the communities that were then undergoing a period of expansion. These students continued to look to their teacher for guidance, often seeking his advice on matters of law and ritual. Thus Rabbenu Gershom became the religious guide and appellate judge for a large part of European Jewry.

Rabbenu Gershom, however, was not a giant in a generation of pigmies. In the community of Mainz he certainly was not the greatest and most authoritative personality to the exclusion of all others. . . .

. . . The Rabbinic learning of the Jews of Germany and France of the 10th century consisted mainly of an orally transmitted commentary on every term, phrase, and logical complex of the Babylonian Talmud. This oral commentary slowly solidified into a rigid phraseology, so that every teacher used more or less the same phrases in explaining a text of the Talmud. A young student of Lucca, Mainz, or Paris, learned from his teacher to read the text of the Talmud phrase by phrase and to interpolate between each phrase a few exact words—words that has once been carefully and painstakingly chosen, and then traditionally transmitted— that accurately elucidated that phrase in its particular context. At the end of a small portion of the text, a rigidly memorized sentence or two served as the explanation of that portion. The young students would faithfully repeat the text together with the interpolated oral explanations until the exact wording of the whole was well fixed in memory. Some students wrote down brief portions of these explanations on the margin of their text, while others relied completely on memory. Occasionally a student would add a brief explanation he had heard from his teacher, often appending the latter's name. Thus there came into being, among Italian, French and German Jews, a commentary on the Talmud that was the result of the teachings of many generations of scholars.

Abridged from "Rabbinic Scholarship in Northern Europe" by I. A. Agus in *The World History of the Jewish People*, Cecil Roth, ed. Vol. II, *The Dark Ages* (New Brunswick: Rutgers University Press, 1966), pp. 193-96. Reprinted by permission.

This commentary was loosely transmitted from generation to generation, every great teacher leaving his mark on it and enriching its content.
Rubbenu Gershom was a popular teacher at the *Yeshiva* of Mainz for
many years. His erudition and scholarship left its mark on this traditional
commentary, since a number of his observations became incorporated in
the traditional version, usually with the prefatory remarks: "Our teacher
told us," or "Our teacher explained.". . .

There is no doubt, nevertheless, that at the beginning of the 11th century Rabbenu Gershom was one of the great lights of European Jewry,
and that his influence on the Jews of his generation was profound. He was
a dynamic teacher, scrupulous in the study of Rabbinic traditions and their
application to actual life-situations. Many differences of opinion on Talmudic law and custom originated because of slight changes in the readings
of the text of the Talmud or of the Gaonic literature. Rabbenu Gershom,
therefore, made a painstaking study of the accurate texts available to him,
and wrote his own copy of the Talmud with scrupulous care. He constantly
trained his students to pay strict attention to the correct wording of each
Talmudic statement, to treat with great respect the traditionally accepted
readings, and to be very wary of what appeared to be brilliant emendations.
This preoccupation of his with variant readings and traditional versions
of the Talmudic text led him to a similar study of the Masoretic text of the
Bible, and to a thorough examination of the various lists and compilations
of Masoretic lore that were transmitted from former generations. . . .

91. Rhineland Yeshivas: Centers of Scholarship

I. A. Agus

Throughout the 11th century the communities of the Rhineland continued
their development as great centers of Rabbinic scholarship. The study of
Rabbinic lore at this time was, as we have seen, not confined to a particular
class of teachers and students. The most important members of these communities—those who carried on large-scale international trade and were
involved in the economic and political activities of the Emperor, the dukes,
the bishops and archbishops of Germany—considered such mundane activities as of secondary importance, devoting to them but a portion of their

From "Rashi and His School" by I. A. Agus in *The World History of the Jewish People*,
Cecil Roth, ed. Vol. II, *The Dark Ages* (New Brunswick: Rutgers University Press, 1966),
p. 210. Reprinted by permission.

time, while their primary preoccupation was with Rabbinic culture. Thus at this time a *Yeshiva* was not merely a "young men's college," but was rather an academic center, a gathering place for heads of families who spent a large portion of their time in the study, analysis and discussion of Talmudic literature. The synagogues (for a *Yeshiva* was usually housed in a synagogue, and practically every synagogue contained a *Yeshiva*) of Mainz, Worms and Cologne, as well as those of Paris, Arles, and Narbonne, were daily crowded with scholars both young and old. In these synagogues hundreds studied Talmudic literature, analyzed its legal principles and its logical categories, and brought to bear, upon the discussion of every page of the Talmud, the cumulative erudition of the entire group. The head of a great *Yeshiva* would spend but part of his time with his students. He would devote most of his energies to the group discussions of the mature scholars.

92. Rashi's Method of Study: Detailed Note-Taking

I. A. Agus

It was indeed Rashi's personal circumstances that determined in large measure the exact pattern of Rabbinic studies in Germany and France in the following centuries. Rashi was a zealous student of Rabbinic lore. He was deeply interested in every detail of the subject matter of the Bible and the Talmud. Every word, phrase, idiom and nuance of meaning of these two classical texts, aroused his curiosity and evoked in him a passionate desire for complete comprehension. Coupled with this thirst for knowledge was also a strong desire to transmit that knowledge to others. His ambition was to absorb all the traditionally transmitted knowledge of the Rhineland communities, and eventually to form a circle of students to whom he would, in turn, transmit that knowledge.

Two circumstances in Rashi's life, however, made this ambition impossible of attainment. a) He became an orphan at an early age and had no father to provide for him while at school. He therefore pursued his studies under the pressure of financial cares and worries. Twenty-five years later he still brooded over the fact that he had missed the opportunity of discussing with his teachers many an important detail. "For while I studied

From "Rashi and His School" by I. A. Agus in *The World History of the Jewish People*, Cecil Roth, ed. Vol. II, *The Dark Ages* (New Brunswick: Rutgers University Press, 1966), pp. 220-22. Reprinted by permission.

under my great teachers I was short of food and clothing and was burdened by a wife and children—my days were spent in adversity." b) The income of his family was not derived from business or banking—which can be shifted from place to place—but from an immovable vineyard.

The following, then, were the results of these circumstances in Rashi's life. a) He knew that the time allowed him to spend in the great centers of learning was short, and that it could quickly be terminated. He was therefore under great compulsion to accumulate knowledge as quickly as possible. Thus in the letter quoted above he states: "I never had the opportunity to discuss with my teachers these subtle niceties and these intricate details [of the problem]; for on account of my poor circumstances I was in a great hurry, and thus studied only the broad outlines and underlying principles of most subjects." Consequently Rashi could not rely wholly on the then traditional method of study—to commit to memory meticulously all the elaborate explanations of the teacher—but had to resort to note-taking. Although some of his fellow-students also took notes of the teacher's lectures, there was a radical difference between Rashi's notes and those of his friends. For the latter's notes were brief and sketchy, a mere aid to memory, while those of Rashi had to be complete and fully understandable even to a person who did not hear the original, oral explanations. The time expended by the average student in committing to memory the daily lectures, was spent by Rashi in gaining additional information. This method of study was quite costly, since the parchment required for elaborate note-taking was very expensive. It was this tremendous pressure, however— the desire to take full and accurate notes on the enormously rich material of Rabbinic lore on the one hand, and the high cost of parchment on the other—that forced Rashi to develop the masterful brevity and conciseness of style that enabled him to compress elaborate explanations in a few simple words. It was indeed this highly compressed though lucid style that earned for Rashi the admiration and gratitude of future generations of Talmudic scholars.

b) Moreover, the hasty study of "broad outlines and underlying principles" had an additional purpose. Thus while studying in Worms and Mainz Rashi had no time for many "subtle niceties and intricate details." He therefore planned eventually to master his subject and arrive at a full comprehension of these niceties and details through the process of logical reconstruction. For, argued Rashi, a knowledge of fundamental principles will enable one to derive all corollaries and inferences by a purely logical process. This again marked a radical departure from the traditional method of learning Rabbinic lore. Until this period students learned all possible details of that lore from the mouth of the teacher. The exact application of each law or ritual, the textual source of that law or ritual, all the possible difficulties presented by a text, and the proper solutions of such difficulties, were all explained by the teacher. A student rarely had the need for solving intricate problems on his own initiative. The teacher was always ready with the proper answer—an answer traditionally transmitted for many generations.

Rashi, on the other hand, knew that he would have to rely a great deal on logical inference. As a student, therefore, he already laid stress on the logical relationship of broad general principles to their inherent particulars and details. Afterwards, in his lonely years in Troyes, he had ample opportunity further to develop this method and to apply it to a wide range of subjects. Thus when the centers of learning in the Rhine communities were destroyed by the ravages of the First Crusade, the method developed by Rashi (of reconstructing details by logical deduction and inference) became the very foundation of the Rabbinic studies of German and French scholars. Logical consistency, conciliation of contradictory statements, discoveries by means of inference and deduction became the typical characteristic of the scholarship of Ashkenazi Jewry.

c) Rashi's voluminous note-taking eventually caused him to find in the written word a highly satisfying outlet for self-expression. On returning from the Rhine communities he felt isolated and alone, away from the stimulating atmosphere of a great school. The Jews of Troyes were businessmen and traveling merchants. Their leisure hours did not correspond to those of the few who were still engaged in agriculture. Rashi continued his studies whenever he could find a moment of leisure; but during these moments he was mostly alone with his books. Several times he restudied the text of the Bible and of the Talmud, constantly referring to his notes. Every time he gained deeper insight and profounder comprehension of many fine details and nuances of meaning. He had, however, few discerning friends with whom to share his intellectual triumphs. The passionate craving of the natural teacher for guiding and molding the minds of others, had to find its outlet in writing. Thus Rashi, the master teacher, denied the audience of a large group of enthusiastic pupils, was forced to direct all his pedagogical instincts and compulsions to the unseen students, to the readers of the written word. Although in later life a considerable number of students were attracted to his circle, the pattern developed in his youth, of addressing himself to an unseen audience, was rooted in his nature. Thus when the holocaust wrought by the First Crusade destroyed the centers of learning of Ashkenazi Jewry, leaving in its wake a number of students without teachers, the matchless work of the great teacher-without-students soon found the many students-without-teachers, and the whole pattern of Rabbinic learning of Germany and France underwent a radical change.

93. Rashi: The Teacher and the Writer

Max I. Dimont

...Rashi's yeshiva attracted Jewish scholars from all over the world. These scholars found lodgings with the Christians. Contrary to the popular prevailing notion that a gulf of hostility separated Jews and Christians from each other during the Middle Ages, Rashi and the Jews of Troyes had active social dealings with their Christian neighbors. From his college days, Rashi retained a great love for the songs of the Christians. He was greatly interested in the hymns of the Church, taught the local priests Hebrew melodies, and translated French lullabies into Hebrew.

Throughout their history, Jews have always believed that at the right time, the right man would appear. Rashi was the right man for the times. Life in eleventh-century Europe no longer related to many precepts in the Talmud. The people did not understand Aramaic, did not understand the phraseology, and did not understand its application to modern life. The *Responsa* was dying. There was a need for a universal Talmud which could be understood without interpreters. It was this need that Rashi served. His great contribution to Jewish life was his reinterpretation of all relevant passages into the vernacular of the day, in such clear, lucid language, with such warmth and humanity, with such rare skill and scholarship, that his commentaries became revered as scripture and loved as literature. Rashi wrote Hebrew as though it were French, with wit and elegance. Whenever he lacked the precise Hebrew word, he used a French word instead, spelling it with Hebrew letters. As over three thousand of the French words he used have disappeared from the language, Rashi's writings have become important source books on medieval French.

94. Moses Maimonides: Medieval Judaism's Greatest Thinker

Abram Leon Sachar

"From Moses till Moses there arose none like unto Moses," was the verdict of posterity upon Maimonides, the most influential Jewish thinker in the Middle Ages. As an expounder of Judaism, as a philosopher, as a

From *Jews, God and History* by Max I. Dimont (New York: Simon & Schuster, 1962), p. 177. Copyright ©1962 by Max Dimont. Reprinted by permission of Simon & Schuster, Inc.

Excerpts from *A History of the Jews*, revised edition, by Abram Leon Sachar. Copyright, 1930, 1940, and renewed 1958, 1968 by Alfred A. Knopf, Inc. Reprinted by permission of the publisher.

lover of learning, as a gentle, human character, few have surpassed him in Jewish history.

He was born in Córdoba in 1135, probably near the little street or alley which today bears his name, Calle Maimónides. The Almoravide rulers, still firmly rooted in the country, patronized all branches of learning, and the precocious youngster was soon deeply immersed in the arts and sciences and in all branches of Jewish scholarship. His father dreamed of a brilliant career for him in the congenial atmosphere of Córdoba. Soon after Maimonides had reached this thirteenth year, however, the onrushing Almohades stormed the city, and the little family joined thousands of other exiles who fled to Africa and to all parts of the Peninsula. Maimonides spent the most formative years of his life wandering about in various Spanish centres. Perhaps the adventures were a very useful part of his education, for he learned to know life and men and was saved from the narrow pedantry of a scholarly recluse. Moreover, his wanderings did not seem to affect his industry. Before he was twenty-three he had prepared a treatise on the calendar and was at work on a critical commentary in Arabic, on the Mishnah. Already so early he displayed his clear, orderly mind, which cut through confusion and obscurity like a keen drill.

After innumerable hardships the little family arrived in Fez. Here the Almohade scourge had driven thousands of Jews into a nominal submission to Islam. Many of them, shaken by a decade of bigotry, had cut themselves altogether adrift from Judaism. Maimonides and his father, as secret Jews, strove to steady those who wavered and wished to assimilate completely. The authorities, justly suspicious of their activities, tormented them until they took up the staff again. More wandering, more trials, more adventure, until at last in Egypt the family found rest and security and ample facilities for scholarship. . . . Maimonides turned to his practice of medicine, and though he was later highly successful, the early years were filled with struggle. Ill health stretched him on a bed of sickness and quarrels with the Karaites disturbed his peace of mind. Fortunately Maimonides was blessed with an indomitable will which conquered all difficulties. He was able to work under the most adverse conditions. "I wrote notes on many an *halakah*," he said later, "on journeys by land, or while tossed on the stormy waves at sea." In the very year in which he completed the *Siraj*, upon which he had been engaged through all his travels, old Cairo was destroyed by fire.

The *Siraj*, a masterly commentary on the Mishnah, the first of a magnificent trilogy, showed no effects of its troubled authorship. It is a model of clarity and keen thinking. Maimonides had the rare gift of bringing the most abstruse conceptions close to the mind of the common man. In the *Siraj* he summed up the essence of the Mishnah, illustrating his points from a wide and varied learning, often filling old themes with original meanings. Modern authorities hold that it is still indispensable for the study of the Mishnah. At the close of his work Maimonides entered upon a discussion of the principles of Judaism and formulated them in the Thirteen Articles, which became, to most Jews, the authoritative creed of the Jewish faith.

Fortune began to show Maimonides favours. Soon after the *Siraj* was completed, Saladin, the most genial character in Moslem history, became master of Egypt and inaugurated an enlightened reign, which lasted nearly twenty-five years. His vizier, Alfadhel, to whom he left the administration of the country, was also a chivalrous spirit and a patron of learning, "sovereign of the pen, who threaded discourse with pearls of style." He sought out the friendship of Maimonides, and the intimacy ripened until, in 1185, the Jewish philosopher was added to the royal staff as a court physician. Here he was so cordially welcomed that when an attractive offer reached him from Richard Coeur de Lion to accept a similar post in the English court, he refused.

Meantime Maimonides had completed his second great work, the *Mishneh-Torah*, a codification, in fourteen books, of all Biblical and rabbinical law. It had required more than ten years of steady labour; but it was a stupendous achievement to bring together the vast material even in ten years. "The Talmud," says Graetz, "resembles a Daedalian maze, in which one can scarcely find his way even with Ariadne's thread, but Maimuni designed a well-contrived ground-plan, with wings, halls, apartments, chambers, and closets, through which a stranger might easily pass without a guide, and thereby obtain a survey of all that is contained in the Talmud. Only a mind accustomed to think clearly and systematically, and filled with the genius of order, could have planned and built a structure like this."* Maimonides covered the whole range of Jewish learning and impregnated it with the Aristotelian spirit. He virtually created a new Talmud, eliminating, however, its confusion and its non-essentials.

The *Mishneh-Torah* gained immediate recognition and was discussed and commented upon by students everywhere. The Jewish world, impressed by Maimonides's immense learning, turned to him in every difficulty. Communities appealed to him for advice on policy, individuals wrote to him to solve legal problems, and all alike heaped praises and honours upon him. Maimonides became the intellectual arbiter of the Jewish world, an Erasmus of the twelfth century.

In each of his treatises Maimonides had been deeply interested in philosophical problems, but their analyses had been merely incidental. Now, in the full vigour of his early fifties, he determined to construct a philosophical interpretation of Judaism. *The Guide for the Perplexed,* which was

---

*Graetz: *History of the Jews.* III, 466.

completed in 1187 or 1190, became the most important of his works. It was written for men who wished to place their faith upon a rational basis, for those who sought to reconcile revelation with the truths of science. Maimonides worked upon the premise which Saadiah had developed, that the law was perfect and complete and would be found rational in all its parts if one only searched long enough. He proceeded to prove the assumption by rationally interpreting every Biblical precept.

The courageous philosopher had none of the modern scientific equipment with which to approach the inner problems of the Bible; his thoughts on God and the universe were later antiquated. But the intellectual honesty which he applied to his problems remained an influence long after his content was superseded. In his own generation he led men open-eyed and questioning into every avenue of faith. He rescued many of his people from degrading superstitions by interpreting away all of the anthropomorphisms of the Bible, often giving them exquisitely beautiful ethical meanings. He explained rationally the miracles, the practice of sacrifice, and the nature of prophecy. The theme ran through all his work, like a golden thread, that faith and reasons lead equally to the truth, that God must be worshipped with understanding, that religion is not only an emotional phenomenon, but an answer as well to the deepest searchings of the mind.

The remaining years of Maimonides's life were filled with ceaseless activity. He continued to write, to dispute, to advise, to perform his duties as court physician. But though he was spared for another fourteen or seventeen years, his task was completed when the *Guide* was published. He died in 1204, the idol of his people; the whole world mourned as his remains were borne to Tiberius for burial. There is a legend that a host of bedouins attacked the funeral train; when they were unable to move the coffin, they joined reverently in the procession!

After his death and even during his lifetime Maimonides was fiercely attacked by conservative forces that distrusted his philosophical views and regarded his interpretations of the law as heretical. They were also fearful that his *Mishneh-Torah*, as a concise code of Jewish law, would supersede the Talmud itself. His disciples defended him vigorously and a controversy raged about his writings for more than a century. The *Guide* was even excommunicated and burnt. But as time passed, Maimonides rose to a foremost place in the estimation of all his people, and his influence became enduring....

European thought too was indebted to the Jewish philosopher. His *Guide* contained trenchant and independent criticism of Aristotle's principles. His masterly analysis of the dual role of revelation and reason was taken over by Albertus Magnus (d. 1280), Thomas Aquinas, and other scholastics. It was from the works of Maimonides that the mediaeval Church received its authoritative knowledge of the synagogue.

95. Rabbi Berechiah's Fables: A Sample

Rabbi Berechiah ben Natronai ha-Nakdan

LION, BEASTS, CATTLE

Many are the lovers of the rich man when his splendor shines;
But when he is humbled and his power curtailed, they change.

Once there was a lion, old and sick, whose loins were diseased, so that his spirit panted in travail; his fate was uncertain, whether he would live or die. To behold the lion's discomfiture there came all cattle and beasts, even from the desolate ends of the earth: some for love to visit the sick, some to see his anguish, some to succeed to his rule, some to know who would reign after him. So grievous was his malady that none could discern whether he were yet alive or already dead. The ox came and gored him, to try whether his strength were ended and empty; the heifer trampled him with her hoofs; the fox nipped the lappets of his ears with his teeth: the ewe brushed his moustaches with her tail, and said: "When will he die and his name perish?" And the cock pecked at his eyes, and broke his teeth with gravel. Then the lion's spirit returned, and he preceived that his enemies were gloating over him, and he lamented: "Alas for the day when my trusted counselors despise me, when my power and glory have turned to my bane, when my erstwhile slaves lord it over me and they who loved me aforetime are become my enemies."

The parable is of a man filled with riches and honor whose neighbors serve him all. But when the day of calamity comes upon him, when he is bowed down and his power humbled, then they stand afar from his plague and separate from him and strip him of his righteousness, and despise him they had chosen.

From *Fables of a Jewish Aesop* by Moses Hadas (New York: Columbia University Press, 1967), pp. 7-8. Reprinted by permission.

Summary

DURING the medieval period most of western Europe was united with a common Christian heritage, providing a set of symbols, a liturgical ritual, eccesiastical functionaries, common religious and moral beliefs, and religious institutions which shaped the education of all classes of people—be they peasants, craftsmen, merchants, or nobility. It is impossible to fully estimate the pervasive influence of the Christian experience upon the lives of people living during the Middle Ages. (Indeed, even the Jews and Moslems were not left untouched by the engulfing Christianity surrounding and sometimes threatening them and their culture.) However, the very fact that recipe books often admonished the cook to allow water to seethe for three *pater nosters* suggests that not only the calendar, but also the daily timetable, of the people was deeply influenced by Christianity. To be touched by the Christian experience does not mean that all of its theological and ritualistic complexities were understood fully by everyone; there is good reason to believe that many rural parish priests were incapable of reading theological treatises and controversies with any degree of understanding, to say nothing of explaining these to their parishoners, and some of the information Chaucer provides on the charlatanry of the summoner and pardoner indicates that church officials were not above hoodwinking the more credulous segments of the population with their falsified relics and indulgences. But the abuse of religious authority as well as the misunderstanding of theology does nothing to undercut the argument that the education of all people in the Middle Ages was deeply influenced by the Church. Emile Mâle* has argued that the heaven-pointing spires of gothic cathedrals, as well as the religious didacticism of the stained glass windows, triforium carvings over the doors entering the nave of the Church, and cross-shaped plan of the cathedrals all served to educate the worshippers who came within as well as those who walked along the street in front of the church.

But the medieval population was not only educated by its contact with the physical structure of the church and her priests. Pilgrimages, such as the one from the Tabard Inn to Canterbury, were not merely occasions for the display of religious piety — as Chaucer makes abundantly clear — but were also a means for learning about different communities and the customs and life-styles of a variety of people. Travel has been thought to be educative by many (as perhaps the bishops forbidding monkish wanderings were well aware) and pilgrims, crusaders, wandering scholars, merchants, and specialized craftsmen, particularly the stonemasons hired to work on the cathedrals, all took advantage of this experience.

Fairs and markets offered the rural peasant the opportunity to open his eyes to a world of goods and amusements seldom encountered on the manor estate. Pageants and feast day celebrations, as well as the visitation of important dignataries — secular or ecclesiastical — were another educative influence. The miracle, morality, and mystery plays which originated with the simple "Quem Queritis?" within the Church and gradually became more elaborate as they moved to the square in front of the church, complete with "mansion

---

*Emile Mâle, *The Gothic Image; Religious Art in France of the Thirteenth Century*. Translated by Dora Nussey. Published in paperback edition by Harper & Row, 1958, from the third French edition originally published in 1913 by E. P. Dutton & Co.

houses" to represent heaven and hell, ultimately in England became mounted on travelling wagons which went through the cities to perform segments of a cycle of plays. Such plays were often produced by gilds who competed amongst themselves for the most elaborate of "sets" by which to convey part of the meaning of their story. As these plays contained themes related to episodes in the Bible, such as Abraham and Isaac, or the life of Christ, or lives of the various saints, as well as allegories in which goodness and evil were personified (and, often, also the seven deadly sins), they served to provide religious and moral instruction—as well as amusement—for adults and children.

Games and sports, whether chess, or hoop-rolling, or hawking, or jousting, or round-singing, or dancing, or ice-skating on the Thames, or blindman's bluff, all served to provide not only diversion, but also opportunities to acquire skills, and, thus, were educative.

Aside from the pervasive influence of the Church, the single most important educational experience for medieval people was occupational training. Inasmuch as people were defined by their work (as the present existence of surnames such as Smith, Cooper, Cartwright, Fuller, and Joiner make abundantly clear), the training received in order to perform those tasks was considerable. For the most part, a child's choice of occupation was fairly limited; he was expected to maintain the same social status, and, in some cases, the same occupation as his father. Religious vocation offered the chance for some children to follow in paths quite different from those their parents had trod, but the choice of such a vocation was not always made by the child. Similarly, as carpenters apprenticed their sons to merchants or pewterers, the occupational choice was made for the child, not by him. This volume has attempted to display some of the occupational "choices" as well as the institutional and social provisions for acquiring the requisite skill, information, and theory to perform those occupations that medieval people needed to learn.

Bibliography

Abelson, Paul. *The Seven Liberal Arts: A Study in Mediaeval Culture.* New York: Russell & Russell, 1965. (Reprint of a 1906 edition published by Teachers College, Columbia University, New York.)

Agus, I. A. "Rabbinic Scholarship in Northern Europe" and "Rashi and His School" in *The World History of the Jewish People.* Cecil Roth, ed. Vol. II, *The Dark Ages.* New Brunswick, N.J.: Rutgers University Press, 1966.

Altman, Alexander, ed. *Jewish Medieval and Renaissance Studies.* Cambridge, Mass.: Harvard University Press, 1967.

Arber, Edward, ed. *The Revelation to the Monk of Evesham.* London: English Reprints, 1869.

Ariès, Philippe. *Centuries of Childhood.* Translated by Robert Baldick. Paris: Librairie Plon, 1960; London, Johathan Cape Ltd., 1962; New York: Random House, 1962*.

Augustine, Saint. *On Christian Doctrine.* Translated by D. W. Robertson, Jr. Indianapolis: Bobbs-Merrill Co., 1958.

Bagley, J. J. *Life in Medieval England.* New York: G. P. Putnam's Sons, 1960.

Baldwin, Marshall. *The Mediaeval Church.* Ithaca, N. Y.: Cornell University Press, 1953 (1964*).

Banks, Mrs. Mary MacLeod, ed. *An Alphabet of Tales.* London: Kegan Paul, Trench, Trübner & Co., 1905.

Barraclough, Geoffrey. *Social Life in Early England.* London: Routledge & Kegan Paul, 1960.

*Reprint series and paperback editions.

Beckwith, John. *Early Medieval Art*. New York: Frederick A. Praeger, 1964 (1965*).

Belfour, A. O., ed. *Twelfth Century Humilies in Ms. Bodley 343*. Early English Text Society (1909), 1962 (reprinted) Oxford University Press.

Bennett, H. S. *Life on the English Manor*. Cambridge: Cambridge University Press, 1937 (1962*).

Bishop, Morris. *The Horizon Book of the Middle Ages*. New York: American Heritage Publishing Co., 1968.

Boissonnade, P. *Life and Work in Medieval Europe*. Translated by Eileen Power. London: Kegan Paul, Trench, Trübner & Co., 1927; New York: Harper & Row, 1964*.

Bolgar, R. R. *The Classical Heritage and Its Beneficiaries*. Cambridge: Cambridge University Press, 1954.

Bowie, Theodore, ed. *The Sketchbook of Villard de Honnecourt*. Bloomington, Ind.: Indiana University Press, 1959.

Butler, Dom Cuthbert. *Western Mysticism*. London: Constable & Co., 1922; New York: Harper & Row, 1966*.

Cam, Helen. *England Before Elizabeth*. London: Hutchinson & Co., 1950; New York: Harper & Row, 1960*.

Cambrensis, Giraldus. *The Itinerary Through Wales and the Description of Wales*, with an Introduction by W. Llewelyn Williams. Everyman's Library, Ernest Rhys, ed. New York: E. P. Dutton & Co., 1908.

_____. *The Historical Works of Giraldus Cambrensis*. Thomas Wright, ed. London: H. G. Bohn, 1863; New York: AMS Press, 1968.

Cantor, Norman F., and Michael S. Werthman, eds. *Medieval Society: 400-1450*. New York: Thomas Y. Crowell Co., 1967.

Caron, M., and S. Hutin. *The Alchemists*. Translated by Helen R. Lane. New York: Grove Press, 1961.

Cary, George. *The Medieval Alexander*. Edited by D. J. A. Ross. New York: Cambridge University Press, 1956 (1967).

Cassidy, Frank P. *Molders of the Medieval Mind: The Influence of the Fathers of the Church on the Medieval Schoolmen*. New York: B. Herder Book Co., 1944; Port Washington, N. Y.: Kennikat Press, 1966.

Castle, E. B. *Educating the Good Man*. London: George Allen & Unwin, 1958; New York: Collier Books, 1962*.

Cawley, A. C., ed. *Everyman and Medieval Miracle Plays*. 2nd edition. New York: E. P. Dutton & Co., 1959.

Chaucer, Geoffrey. *The Canterbury Tales*. Translated into Modern English by Nevill Coghill. Baltimore: Penguin Books, 1962.

Chauviré, Roger. *A Short History of Ireland*. Old Greenwich, Conn.: The Devin-Adair Company, 1956; New York: Mentor Books, New American Library of World Literature, 1965*.

Cheyney, Edward P. *Readings in English History Drawn from the Original Sources*. Boston: Ginn & Co., 1908.

Chute, Marchette. *Geoffrey Chaucer of England*. New York: E. P. Dutton & Co., 1958.

Clark, Andrew, ed. and intro. *The Old English Register of Godstow Nunnery, Near Oxford*. London: Kegan Paul, Trench, Trübner & Co.; Henry Frowde, Oxford University Press, 1911.

*Reprint series and paperback editions.

Compayré, Gabriel. *Abelard and the Origins and Early History of Universities.* New York: Charles Scribner's Sons, 1893.

Corbett, James A. *The De instructione puerorum of William of Tournai, O.P.* Notre Dame, Ind.: The Mediaeval Institute, University of Notre Dame, 1955.

Coulton, George Gordon, trans. *Life in the Middle Ages.* London: Constable & Co., 1910; Cambridge: Cambridge University Press, 1967.

_____. *The Medieval Scene.* Cambridge: Cambridge University Press, 1930 (1961*).

Cozens, M. L. *A Handbook of Heresies.* New York: Sheed & Ward, 1928 (1959*).

Crombie, A. C. *Medieval and Early Modern Science*, Vol. I, Vol. II. Garden City, N. Y.: Doubleday & Co., 1959. (Originally published in 1953 by Harvard University Press as *Augustine to Galileo: the History of Science A.D. 400-1650.*)

D'Arcy, Martin C., et al. *St. Augustine* (a collection of essays). Cleveland: World Publishing Co., 1957 (1964*). (First published in 1930 by Sheed & Ward as *A Monument to St. Augustine.*)

Davidson, Charles. *Studies in the English Mystery Plays.* New York: Haskell House, 1965.

Davis, William Stearns. *Life on a Mediaeval Barony.* New York & London: Harper & Brothers Publishers, 1922.

Dawson, Christopher. *Medieval Essays.* New York: Sheed & Ward, 1954; Garden City, N. Y.: Doubleday & Co., 1959*.

Dickinson, J. C. *Monastic Life in Medieval England.* London: Adam & Charles Black, 1961.

Dimont, Max I. *Jews, God and History.* New York: Simon & Schuster, 1962.

Dodge, Bayard. *Muslim Education in Medieval.Times.* Washington, D. C.: Middle East Institute, 1962.

Donohue, John W., S. J. *St. Thomas Aquinas and Education.* New York: Random House, 1968.

Douglas, David C., and George G. Greenaway, eds. *English Historical Documents, 1042-1189.* Vol. II. New York: Oxford University Press, 1953.

Downs, Norton, ed. *Medieval Pageant.* Princeton: D. Van Nostrand Co., 1964.

Eby, Frederick, and Charles Flinn Arrowood. *The History and Philosophy of Education Ancient and Medieval.* New York: Prentice-Hall, 1940.

Ernle, Rowland Edmund Prothero. *English Farming Past and Present.* 3rd edition. New York: Longmans, Green & Co., 1922.

Epstein, Morris. *Tales of Sendebar.* Philadelphia: Jewish Publication Society of America. 1967.

Evans, Joan. *Monastic Life at Cluny.* London: Oxford University Press, 1931; Hamden, Conn.: Archon Books, 1968.

Evans, Joan, ed. *The Flowering of the Middle Ages.* New York: McGraw-Hill Book Co., 1966.

Fremantle, Anne. *The Age of Belief.* Boston: Houghton Mifflin Co., 1957.

Furnivall, Frederick J., ed. *The Babees Book.* London: N. Trübner & Co., 1868.

_____. *Early English Meals and Manners.* Oxford: Oxford University Press, 1868.

Gabriel, Astrik Ladislas. *The Educational Ideas of Vincent of Beauvais.* Notre Dame, Ind.: The University of Notre Dame Press, 1962.

Ganshof, F. L. *Feudalism.* Translated by Philip Grierson. New York: Harper & Row, 1961 (1964*).

Gaskoin, C. J. B. *Alcuin: His Life and His Work.* New York: Russell & Russell, 1904.

*Reprint series and paperback editions.

Gilson, Etienne. *Heloise and Abelard.* Translated by L. K. Shook. Paris: Librarie Philosophique J. Vrin, 1948; Ann Arbor: University of Michigan Press, 1963*.

Goodrich, Norma Lorre. *Medieval Myths.* New York: New American Library of World Literature. 1961*.

Gransden, Antonia, ed. and trans. *The Chronicale of Bury St. Edmunds.* London: Thomas Nelson & Sons, 1964.

Graves, Frank Pierrepont. *A History of Education during the Middle Ages and the Transition to Modern Times.* New York: Macmillan Co., 1919.

Gulley, Anthony D. *The Educational Philsosphy of Saint Thomas Aquinas.* New York: Pageant Press, 1964.

Haarhoff, T. J. *Schools of Gaul.* 2nd edition. Johannesburg: Witwatersrand University Press, 1958. (First edition published by Oxford University Press in 1920.)

Hadas, Moses. *Fables of a Jewish Aesop.* New York: Columbia University Press, 1967.

Haskins, Charles Homer. *The Rise of Universities.* Ithaca, N. Y.: Cornell University Press, 1923 (1965*).

_____. *Studies in Mediaeval Culture.* New York: Frederick Ungar Publishing Co., 1958.

Hay, Denys. *The Medieval Centuries.* New York: Harper & Row, 1953 (1965*).

Herlihy, David. ed. *Medieval Culture and Society.* New York: Harper & Row, 1968.

Holmes, Urban Tigner, Jr. *Daily Living in the Twelfth Century.* Madison: University of Wisconsin Press, 1952 (1964*).

Homans, George Caspar. *English Villagers of the Thirteenth Century.* New York: Russell & Russell, 1960. (Originally published in 1941 by Harvard University Press.)

Hone, Nathaniel. *The Manor and Manorial Records.* London: Methuen & Co., 1906.

Hoyt, Robert S., ed. *Life and Thought in the Early Middle Ages.* Minneapolis: University of Minnesota Press, 1967.

Huizinga, J. *The Waning of the Middle Ages.* Translated by F. Hopman. Garden City, N. Y.: Doubleday & Co., 1924 (1954*).

Hunt, Noreen. *Cluny Under Saint Hugh: 1049-1109.* London: Edward Arnold (Publishers), 1967.

Hussey, J. M. *The Byzantine World.* London: Hutchinson & Co., 1957; New York: Harper & Row, 1961*.

Hyman, Albert. *The Brethren of the Common Life.* Grand Rapids, Mich.: Wm. B. Eerdmans Publishing Co., 1950.

Ker, W. P. *The Dark Ages.* Edinburgh: Thomas Nelson & Sons, 1904; New York: New American Library of World Literature, 1958.

Kibre, Pearl. *The Nations in the Medieval Universities.* Cambridge, Mass.: Mediaeval Academy of America, 1948.

Kitzinger, Ernst. *Early Medieval Art.* Bloomington: Indiana University Press, 1940 (1964*).

Knowles, Dom David. *The Evolution of Medieval Thought.* New York: Random House, 1962 (1964*).

_____. *Saints and Scholars.* Cambridge: Cambridge University Press, 1962.

_____. *The Monastic Order in England.* 2nd edition. Cambridge: Cambridge University Press, 1963.

*Reprint series and paperback editions.

Kramer, Stella. *The English Craft Gilds*. New York: Columbia University Press, 1927.

Lacroix, Paul. *Manners, Customs and Dress, During the Middle Ages*. London: Bickers & Son, n.d.

Lamond, Elizabeth, trans. *Walter of Henley's Husbandry*. London: Longmans, Green & Co., 1890.

Leach, A. F. *The Schools of Medieval England*. New York: Macmillan Co., 1915.

Leclercq, Jean, O.S.B. *The Love of Learning and the Desire for God*. New York: Fordham University Press, 1961.

Lewinsohn, Richard. *A History of Sexual Customs*. Translated by Alexander Mayce. Greenwich, Conn.: Fawcett Publications, 1956 (1964*).

Luchaire, Achille. *Social France at the Time of Philip Augustus*. Translated by Edward Benjamin Krehbiel. New York: Henry Holt & Co., 1912; New York: Harper & Row, 1967*.

Lydgate, John. *Reson and Sensuallyte*. (Edited from Bodleian MS. Fairfax 16 and British Museum additional MS. 29729 by Ernest Sieper.) London, New York: published for the Early English Text Society by the Oxford University Press, 1965. (First published in 1901.)

MacKinney, Loren C. *Bishop Fulbert and Education at the School of Chartres*. Notre Dame, Ind.: The Mediaeval Institute, University of Norte Dame, 1957.

Mâle, Emile. *The Gothic Image*. Translated by Dora Nussey. New York: E. P. Dutton & Co., 1913; New York: Harper & Row, 1958*.

Meech, Sanford B., ed., intro., and glossary; Allen, H. E., preparatory note. *The Book of Margery Kempe*. London: Oxford University Press, 1940 (1961*).

Morrall, John. *Political Thought in Medieval Times*. London: Hutchinson & Co., 1958; New York: Harper & Row, 1961*.

Muller, Herbert. *The Uses of the Past*. London: Oxford University Press, 1952; New York: New American Library of World Literature, 1960*.

Mundy, John H., and Peter Riesenberg. *The Medieval Town*. Princeton: Van Nostrand, 1958.

Mundy, John, et al. *Essays in Medieval Life and Thought*. New York: Columbia University Press, 1955.

Nagler, A. M. *A Source Book in Theatrical History*. New York: Dover Publications, 1952 (1959*).

Nakosteen, Mehdi. *History of Islamic Origins of Western Education, A. D. 800-1350 with an Introduction to Medieval Muslim Education*. Boulder, Col.: University of Colorado Press, 1964.

O'Leary, De Lacy, D. D. *Arabic Thought and Its Place in History*. London: Routledge & Kegan Paul, 1922 (1963*).

Ott, H., and J. M. Fletcher. *The Mediaeval Statutes of the Faculty of Arts of the University of Freiburg im Breisgau*. Notre Dame, Ind.: The Mediaeval Institute, University of Notre Dame, 1964.

Painter, Sidney. *French Chivalry*. Baltimore: Johns Hopkins Press, 1940; Ithaca, N. Y.: Cornell University Press, 1957, (1965*).

Pegis, Anton, ed. *Introduction to Saint Thomas Aquinas*. New York: The Modern Library (Random House), 1945, (1948*).

Pirenne, Henri. *Medieval Cities*. Translated by Frank D. Halsey. Cambridge, Mass.: Princeton University Press, 1925; Garden City, N. Y.: Doubleday & Co., 1956*.

*Reprint series and paperback editions.

Poole, Reginald Lane. *Illustrations of the History of Medieval Thought and Learning*. 2nd ed. New York: Johnson Reprint Corporation, 1920. (Minerva GmbH, Frankfurt am Main, 1963.)

Power, Eileen. *Medieval People*. London: Methuen & Co., 10th edition, 1963. New York: Barnes & Noble, 1968*.

Power, Eileen, trans. *The Goodman of Paris*. New York: Harcourt, Brace & Co., 1928.

Quennell, Marjorie & C. H. B. *A History of Everyday Things in England, Part I, 1066-1499*. 3rd edition. London: B. T. Batsford, Ltd. 1948.

Rait, Robert. *Life in the Medieval University*. Cambridge: Cambridge University Press, 1931.

Rashdall, Hastings. *The Universities of Europe in the Middle Ages*, Vols. I, II, III. Edited by F. M. Powicke and A. B. Emden. London: Oxford University Press, 1936. (First published in 1895.)

Rickert, Edith. *Chaucer's World*. Edited by Clair C. Olson and Martin M. Crow. New York: Columbia University Press, 1948, (1962*).

Ross, James Bruce, and Mary Martin McLaughlin, eds. *The Portable Medieval Reader*. New York: Viking Press, 1949 (1966*).

Ross, Woodburn, O., ed. from British Museum MS. *Middle English Sermons*. London: Oxford University Press, 1960.

Roth, Cecil, ed. *The World History of the Jewish People: The Dark Ages*. Vol. II, New Brunswick: Rutgers University Press, 1966.

Sachar, Abram Leon. *A History of the Jews*. New York: Alfred A. Knopf, 1930 (1940*).

Salzman, L. F. *English Industries of the Middle Ages*. Oxford: Clarendon Press, 1923.

_____. *English Life in the Middle Ages*. London: Oxford University Press, 1929.

Sharpe, William D. *Isidore of Seville: The Medical Writings*. Philadelphia: American Philosophical Society, 1964.

Southern, R. W. *The Making of the Middle Ages*. New Haven: Yale University Press, 1953, (1967*).

Steele, Robert, ed. *Medieval Lore*. London: Elliot Stock, 1893.

Steele, Robert, ed. and intro. *The Earliest Arithmetics in English*. London: Oxford University Press, 1922.

Stephenson, Carl. *Mediaeval Institutions: Selected Essays*, edited by Bryce D. Lyon, Ithaca, N. Y.: Cornell University Press, 1954 (1967*).

Taylor, Henry Osborn. *The Classical Heritage of the Middle Ages*. London: Macmillan & Co., 1901; New York: Harper & Row, 1963*.

_____. *The Mediaeval Mind*, Vol. I. and II. 4th edition. Cambridge, Mass.: Harvard University Press, 1951.

Taylor, Jerome, trans. *The "Didascalicon" of Hugh of St. Victor, A Medieval Guide to the Arts*. New York: Columbia University Press, 1961.

_____. "The Origin and Early Life of Hugh of St. Victor: An Evaluation of the Tradition" in *Texts and Studies in the History of Mediaeval Education*, No. V, A. L. Gabriel and J. N. Garvin, eds. Notre Dame, Ind.: The Mediaeval Institute, University of Notre Dame, 1957.

Temko, Allan. *Notre Dame of Paris*. New York: Viking Press, 1952; New York: Time, Inc., 1962*

*Reprint series and paperback editions.

Thorndike, Lynn. *University Records and Life in the Middle Ages.* New York: Columbia University Press, 1944.

Thrupp, Sylvia L. *The Merchant Class of Medieval London.* Ann Arbor: University of Michigan Press, 1948 (1962*).

Tomkeieff, O. G. *Life in Norman England.* London: B. T. Batsford, Ltd., 1966: New York: Capricorn Books, 1967*.

Treece, Henry. *The Crusades.* New York: Random House, 1962; New York: American Library of World Literature, 1964*.

Unwin, George. *The Gilds and Companies of London.* New York: Barnes & Noble, 1964.

Van der Meer, F. *Augustine the Bishop.* Translated by Brian Battershaw and G. R. Lamb. New York: Sheed & Ward, 1961; New York: Harper & Row, 1965*.

Vinogradoff, Paul, ed. *Oxford Studies in Social and Legal History.* Vol. IX. Oxford: Clarendon Press, 1927.

Waddell, Helen. *The Wandering Scholars.* London: Constable & Co., 1927: Garden City, N. Y.: Doubleday & Co., 1961*.

White, Lynn, Jr. *Medieval Technology and Social Change.* New York: Oxford University Press, 1962 (1966*).

Williams, Arnold. *The Drama of Medieval England.* East Lansing, Mich.: Michigan State University Press, 1961.

Zimmels, H. J. "Scholars and Scholarship in Byzantium and Italy" in *The World History of the Jewish People.* Cecil Roth, ed. Vol. II, *The Dark Ages.* New Brunswick, N. J.: Rutgers University Press, 1966.

*Reprint series and paperback editions.

Index